THE WAY IT WAS

Mobil

GREAT SPORTS EVENTS FROM THE PAST

THE WAY IT WAS

Edited by George Vecsey   Introduction by Curt Gowdy

McGraw-Hill Book Company

New York   St. Louis   San Francisco   Düsseldorf
London   Mexico   Sydney   Toronto

Dedication: To Leonard Shecter
Sportswriter and Friend

Based on the television series,
The Way It Was,
which is made possible by a grant from
Mobil Oil Corporation.

The Way It Was was conceived
by Herbert Schmertz.

123456789KPKP7987654

Library of Congress Cataloging in Publication Data

Vecsey, George.
     The way it was.

     1. Sports—History—Addresses, essays, lectures.
I. Title.
GV576.V42   796'.09   74-8985
ISBN 0-07-067391-8

Contents

———————————

Introduction by Curt Gowdy

I do not know where you were on December 7, 1941. I was in my room on the campus of Wyoming University studying for an exam. The radio on my shelf over the bed abruptly stopped the music, and an excited voice blared out the news that Pearl Harbor had just been bombed. I was five months away from graduation and a Second Lieutenant's commission in the U.S. Air Force. I knew that post-graduation plans were suddenly altered, to say the least.

Where were you on July 20, 1969, when astronauts Armstrong and Adrian landed on the moon? I'll never forget where I was—sitting in Bud Wilkinson's apartment in Washington, D.C., watching the tube in total fascination along with millions of others around the world. It was fitting that Bud and I were together on that historic date, because we had become close friends when I was broadcasting the Oklahoma University football games and Wilkinson was building a dynasty as the Sooners' young coach.

These were two big days in the lives of all Americans. This book is about other momentous moments, less serious but as well-remembered, moments in sports that provided unforgettable drama and delight. I can vividly recall, for example, driving from Boston to New York on that fall day of 1951 when Bobby Thomson hit the home run heard around the world, as the Giants defeated the Dodgers in the third game of their playoff to decide the National League pennant. I nearly drove off the highway in excitement as broadcaster Russ Hodges hysterically screamed: "There's a long drive to left. The Giants win the pennant! The Giants win the pennant! The Giants win the pennant!"

I remember watching with rapture in my basement playroom in Wellesley Hills, Massachusetts, on a day in October, 1956, as Don Larsen systematically reeled off the first perfect game in World Series history. I can still feel the tension and drama, as I rode with the right hander on every pitch—then the final strike on Dale Mitchell and catcher Yogi Berra racing to the mound and vaulting on Larsen's back.

I will never forget that short shot from the side with three seconds to play taken by Frank Selvy of the Los Angeles Lakers against the Boston Celtics in the Boston Garden in 1962. If Selvy hit, the Celtics' championship reign would be over. I was seated in the front row about ten feet on the forecourt side of the Lakers. When the shot left Selvy's right hand, I thought he had it. It was true but struck the side of the rim. Bill Russell leaped up to grab the rebound as the final buzzer sounded.

I was in the front room of my home in Cheyenne, Wyoming, glued to the radio as my Dad and I listened to the start of the Joe Louis-Billy Conn heavyweight championship fight. I can still hear a young announcer named Don Dunphy calling the play-by-play. He was new to us, but you could tell he was a boxing announcer for the future. He was right with it. Conn jabbing and dancing. Louis shuffling after him. As round after round went by, I couldn't believe that the "Brown Bomber" was being beaten. Then suddenly it was over. Louis had knocked him out. What a fight! What an unforgettable night back there in a home town where radio gave us the only means of big league sports participation.

There is no doubt that sports is a part of American history. The great sports events of the past are firmly anchored in the country's memory. Those big games, those almost perfect matchups, all have a place in our minds. They live on as they should, preserved because they aroused interest and excitement in a nation that has always cherished its sports.

I have been fortunate enough to handle the play-by-play on just about every big sporting event during the last twenty-five years—the World Series, the Super Bowl, the Olympics, bowl games, NCAA basketball championships and regular season football, baseball and basketball. And I have hosted for eleven years a hunting, fishing and out-door adventure show called "The American Sportsman." I thought I had done it all. But not quite.

Not too many months ago, I was approached by television sports producer Gerry Gross to host a series called "The Way It Was." I was told the series was to be made for public television, which appealed to me, and that Herb Schmertz, who heads Public Affairs for Mobil Oil, was enthusiastic about the idea and wanted Mobil to give the series as a grant to the Public Television Network.

"It's going to be a nostalgic sports series," Gross explained. "We'll tape here in Hollywood. We'll do twelve of the great classics in the history of American sports. We're working on obtaining the original films of the events, getting in touch with every sports film library. We're going to bring back the stars of the games, too, and the announcer who called the event."

"Which ones are you planning to do?" I asked Gerry.

"The Bobby Thomson home run, for starters," Gross answered. "We've already got Durocher, Mays and Thomson lined up from the 1951 Giants. Branca, of course, from the Dodgers. He threw the pitch. Duke Snider and Clem Labine, too."

"That's quite an order," I said. "Getting six men like that to come from all over America for one night."

"That's nothing," Gross added. "We'll tape another show that night too. Bevens' near no-hitter against the Dodgers in 1947. He's agreed to be here. Also Joe DiMaggio and Tommy Henrich. We have to have Cookie Lavagetto, who broke up the no-hitter in the ninth, and Gionfriddo, who made the famous catch off DiMag."

Twelve of the biggest names in baseball's past gathered that winter evening in the studios of KCET, the public television station in Los Angeles. The logistics of getting those twelve men there was amazing, but even more so was their enthusiasm for the project and almost total recall of every pitch and play of the two premier events. Six more times we gathered through the next few months, putting the shows together. My biggest kick was working and visit-with these sports stars, most of them now legends, and comparing them as they are now and as they were in their athletic prime on the original films of the events.

I can recall the night we taped the Louis-Conn fight. It was difficult to real-ize as we watched the film of the fight that thirty-three years had passed. Conn still had his appealing Irish looks. Louis was no longer the sleek de-stroyer, but on that particular evening, he was looser and more articulate than Conn. Quite a switch. Both remembered perfectly the buildup to the match, the round-by-round strategy. The TV cameras recorded their facial reactions as they watched the film action. You just knew they were both back there in 1941, going at it again, and perhaps sadly wondering where all the years had gone.

During those taping sessions, I was impressed with the way the boxers maintained the closest of relationships. Conn and Louis are still buddies. So are Rocky Graziano and Sugar Ray Robinson. I can still see those two leav-ing the studio arm in arm, though they nearly beat the hell out of each other years ago.

And how about the night we relived the famous Army-Navy classic of 1946? There, sitting at one table, was the heart of one of the greatest college back-fields—Davis, Blanchard and Tucker. Sitting with them were their Navy oppo-nents, who nearly pulled the upset of any year, only to be thwarted by the final gun with the goal line a few yards away.

Perhaps I enjoyed even more the appearance on our series of the an-nouncers who made these classics come alive to millions of Americans. Most of our events were selected from the 1940s and 1950s. In those days of radio sports, the broadcaster was the only link between the happening and the public. If the announcer was great, so was the event. Millions of fans grew up listening to their voices and becoming familiar with their distinctive styles.

It was the sports announcer who put in his listener's mind the image that would remain there for years to come. Red Barber's famous "Oh, doctor!" when Gionfriddo robbed DiMaggio of the home run in the 1947 Series. That tremendous voice of Mel Allen's sweeping you through inning after inning as Larsen went for the perfect game. Don Dunphy, boxing's greatest announcer. Bob Neal describing the thrilling Rams-Browns championship game of 1950. The late Dizzy Dean recalling Slaughter's mad dash from first to score the winning run in the final game of the 1946 World Series. Chick Hearn describ-ing Selvy missing the short one-hander.

These and many other dramatic moments come to life again in this book. The choice was not easy, believe me. There were plenty of arguments and much table pounding before the final decisions were made. I think you will agree, though, as you turn the pages, the events that finally made it are well worth remembering.

Thomas B. Allen

THE UNLUCKY THIRTEENTH

The winner and new champion—Joe Louis after he beat Jimmy Braddock in 1937

Joe Louis/Billy Conn Heavyweight Championship Fight June 18, 1941

By Leonard Koppett

ost sports need a frame of reference. A visitor from Mars, walking in cold to a baseball stadium, would probably not appreciate the nuances of the pitcher shifting his pattern from one hitter to another. It takes a knowledge of the personnel to appreciate most sports.

Even in boxing, where, basically, two men hit each other, it helps to know that so-and-so is on his way up, while so-and-so is trying for one more big payday. That gives the sport its dimension. But there are greater dimensions, too—the year, the place, the world condition.

To set such a scene, there could be no better writer-historian than Leonard Koppett. Koppett has taken a fistfight between two men, Joe Louis and Billy Conn—two products of their time—and shown the backdrop of a world marching off to a war that would change things for everybody.

Leonard Koppett is a man of many worlds—a mathematician and musician who chose to write about athletics. He covered basketball and all other sports for the *New York Post* before joining the *New York Times* more than a decade ago. He is famous for his analysis of the deeper themes of sports—the statistical trends, the historical contexts, the human motivations. He is the intellectual's sportswriter, who can also tell a humorous tale of man's victories and defeats.

Currently based in Palo Alto, California, as the *Times'* sports man on the West Coast, Koppett is the author of several provocative books on sports. He is also an excellent speaker who once held a twitchy high-school class spellbound for two full periods describing the experience of being Russian (which he is). He never mentioned sports once, either.   G.V.

The rousing fistfight Joe Louis and Billy Conn staged for the Heavyweight Championship of the World on June 18, 1941, would have been a beautiful fight even if it had taken place on a street corner between non-entities for private purposes.

But its context, as much as its content, made it memorable. It was the next-to-last major event of the Age of Innocence in American sports.

The scenario would have been dramatic enough at any time: brash young challenger, twenty-five pounds lighter than the undefeated and perhaps invincible champion, winning the title for twelve rounds before getting overeager and being knocked out just two seconds before the thirteenth round ended.

However, June of 1941 was a very special time, in much larger frameworks than spectator sports. If it can be said that the twentieth century was cut in half by World War II, with the fabric of life following it fundamentally different from what went before, then the end of June of 1941 can be focused upon as the razor's edge. That was when Hitler, having won in the West, turned the German armies against Russia and dispelled any remaining doubt that somehow the United States would be able to stay out of active warfare, or that anything less than sheer military victory, by whichever side, would determine the future of the world.

For much of the American population, and especially the less sophisticated segment habitually attracted to sports, this realization didn't hit home until December and Pearl Harbor. But June was ominous enough for everyone to sense storms brewing, and the pre–World War II attitude towards a sport event—that nothing in the world could possibly be as significant or as emotionally compelling as the legends and happenings on the ball field or in the ring—flowered for the last time. Unlike World War I, the second war was real to Americans, un-romanticized; and once it was over, the day-to-day con-sciousness of a world with atomic bombs, cold-war enemies, and internal civil strife could never be entirely ignored, even by the sports fan.

But in June of 1941, the viewpoints were still those that had been building for half a century, and the sports scene had only three subjects of transcendental interest: major league baseball, championship fights, and special horse races. Everything else, even college football and the Olympics, commanded a lower order of attention; and the medium through which attention functioned was the word, written or spoken. Television, newly invented, was not yet publicly available, but radio was ubiquitous and the number of big-city newspapers and general-circulation magazines was perhaps five times what we have now.

How an event was written about, therefore, had much greater impact on the anticipation aroused, and the judgments finally embedded in millions of memories, than it does today.

So the Louis–Conn fight, that night in the Polo Grounds in New York, was perceived in the old context, that it was the most important thing happening on earth. A few months later, the same atmosphere would sur-round a World Series between the Yankees and the Dodgers. After that, though, such purity of response would never again be possible.

Other things in 1941 were also different than after the war. Race prejudice was not only pervasive but essen-tially acceptable; a certain number of enlightened liber-als might object to it, but the mass of "nice" people sim-ply didn't question it. Equally acceptable was ethnic rivalry in its crudest form: dialect comedians abounded, discrimination against Jews and Italians was openly ac-knowledged if not boasted about (anti-Semitism was getting a bad name only because of Hitler), and the word "immigrant" still had demeaning connotations hard to define in retrospect.

Louis was black—a "Negro" was the polite reference then—and he was accepted by the white world as "a credit to his race," without the slightest awareness in the white world of how innately insulting such a compliment was. But he was accepted, by and large, as a great and worthy champion in ways previous black athletes had not been.

Conn was as Irish as a character in a Hollywood movie, and the Irish in movies were always pugnacious.

Today, such a match-up would undoubtedly arouse subliminal sympathies that would be expertly manipulat-ed by marketers with degrees in psychology. Then, there wasn't anything subliminal about it.

Favored in pre-fight odds, Louis had no trouble with Conn in early rounds

The Unlucky Thirteenth

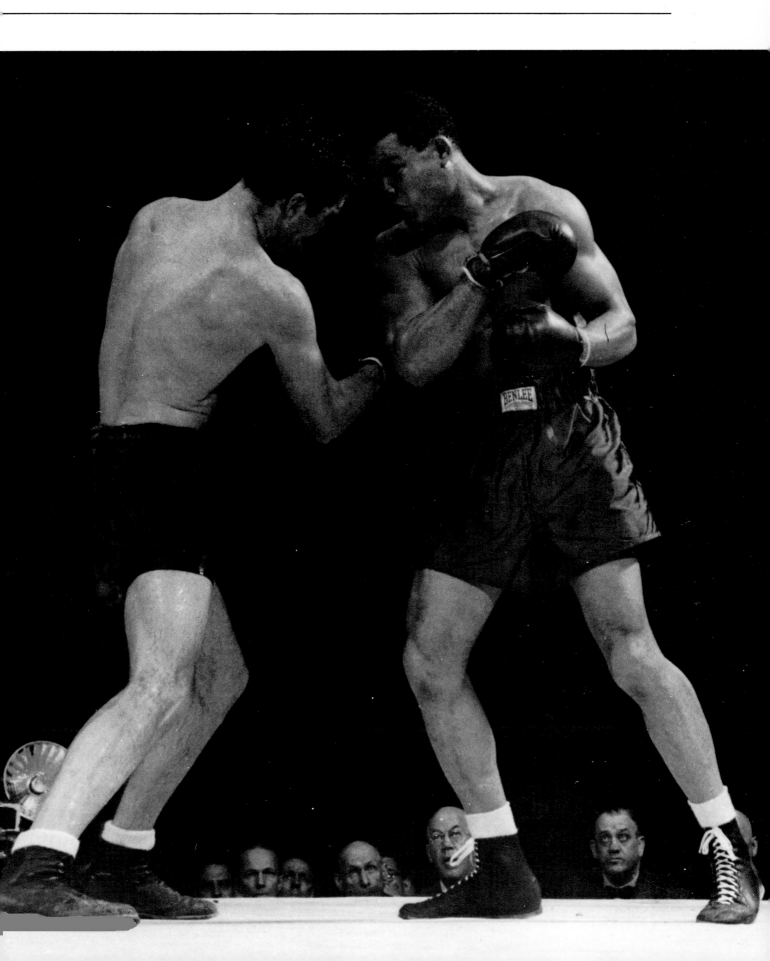

"He's a real good hitter." BILLY CONN

Louis had been champion for four years. He was twenty-seven years old, and had lost only one fight. In 1936 he had been knocked out by Max Schmeling, a former world champion. The next year, Louis won the title by knocking out Jim Braddock, and the year after that he got revenge on Schmeling with a furious first-round knockout. (That quick victory over a "Nazi" undoubtedly increased Louis's "acceptability," since this was already the year of Munich).

By the middle of 1940, Louis had defended his title eleven times, and there didn't seem to be a worthwhile challenger in sight. His professional record showed 46 victories, 39 of them knockouts, and arguments about his prowess in comparison to Jack Dempsey, the knockout king of the 1920s, were endless. His stature was such that any appearance, even if no one thought the opponent had a chance, would guarantee a profitable gate.

Since there was no television to reach millions simultaneously and make instant millionaires, the only way to cash in was to keep fighting so that tickets could be sold to live audiences.

Thus Louis embarked on the most remarkable sequence in the history of boxing, the bluntly named "Bum of the Month" campaign.

In December, in Boston, he knocked out Al McCoy in the sixth round.

In January, in New York, he knocked out Clarence (Red) Burman in the fifth.

In February, in Philadelphia, he knocked out Gus Dorazio in the second.

In March, in Detroit, he knocked out Abe Simon, but not until the thirteenth.

In April, in St. Louis, he knocked out Tony Musto, in the ninth.

And in May, in Washington, he knocked out Buddy Baer, in the seventh.

Other champions had, and have since, gone more than a year without stepping into the ring with the title at stake. After all, an accident could always happen—a lucky punch, a slip, even a bee sting might strip a man of the most valuable single commodity in sports, no matter what the prefight odds said. But Louis had just laid his title on the line in six consecutive months, without avoiding anyone remotely qualified.

Conn started slowly, but after the sixth
round he began to attack and pile up points

And what was the response to this performance? Admiration? No. Louis must be slipping, people said, because how come Simon lasted so long, and Musto and Baer? Perhaps nothing reveals so clearly how firmly Louis had established his ability than the fact that people could be honestly surprised when he didn't flatten an opponent in the first few rounds.

All of which helped create a circumstance in which Conn could be a believable challenger. Billy wasn't even a true heavyweight, fighting at 174 pounds. His last fight had been back in November, against Lee Savold, and his career record included seven defeats (and 57 victories). Speed and boxing skill—and, of course, aggressiveness—were his assets, and four out of every five opponents he had faced had finished the fight on their feet.

Since he didn't seem strong enough to hurt Louis even with a lucky punch or big enough to take any extended pounding, on sheer physical statistics he seemed a suitable candidate for the Bum of the Month list.

But he was never considered that, not from the day the buildup began, right after the Louis–Baer fight of May 23. Again, subliminal feelings that were not very subliminal probably came into play. Any white man Louis fought was automatically (and publicly) proclaimed "a white hope"; but hulking giants like Abe Simon and Buddy Baer just couldn't generate a romantic identification simply on the basis of race. A Billy Conn—young, good-looking, glib, flashing a handsome smile, bursting with good cheer, the size of an ordinary man—could.

It was taken seriously, then, from the start, even by those who felt confidence in Louis. Was the champion really slowing up, was he sated with success? Could he really handle someone so much quicker and cleverer than anyone he had fought before? These were the cornerstone questions in the intensively planned and planted prefight ballyhoo campaign, but they had enough validity to make people wonder, even those who knew how classically orchestrated prefight ballyhoos always were.

And this one was no exception. The day Conn left his native Pittsburgh by midnight train to go into training at Pompton Lakes, New Jersey, he was not the big story. Lou Gehrig, once the symbol of indestructibility as a baseball player, had just died of an illness at thirty-eight. But the Conn contingent did what it could.

Johnny Ray, his manager, had asked the New York State Boxing Commission for special consideration.

"I'd have got him even if he hadn't changed his style

Conn was a notoriously slow starter, he pointed out, needing a long warm-up to be at all effective in the early rounds. Could he remain in the dressing room during the national anthem, introductions, and other prefight ceremonies, getting himself properly juiced up?

Gen. John J. Phelan, chairman of the New York Commission, rejected the request: "Conn must come in as usual," he ruled. "If he wants to be hot, then his handlers had better bundle him up in plenty of clothes, towels and bathrobes." It wasn't much in the face of 1,000-word Gehrig obituaries, but it was something.

Four days later, Ray tried another approach. He announced that arrangements had been made for Conn to have one of those newfangled electric heating blankets plugged in at his corner. (Westinghouse was big in Pittsburgh, right? Right.)

Immediately, various stories dubbed Conn "The Kilowatt Kid" and "The Amperage Assassin." What if, one writer wondered, he finds himself in an A.C. ring with a D.C. blanket?

On Saturday, June 7, the sports world had its serious business: Calumet Farm's Whirlaway won the Belmont Stakes and became the fifth triple-crown winner, having previously won the Kentucky Derby and the Preakness; Craig Wood won the U.S. Open Golf championship; and Bob Feller, that sensational young pitcher who had a 12-2 record with the Cleveland Indians, filled out his draft papers.

What Conn got was a rhapsodic lead on a story by Regis Welch in the *Pittsburgh Gazette,* a paragraph that summed up accurately enough how the fight was being viewed: "How long can a moth stay away from the inviting—yet consuming—flame; how often must a fellow with a flyswatter hit an elephant in order to disturb, hurt or destroy him; how long can a fellow—without a tin hat—stand in the midst of exploding shrapnel without getting hurt; how long can a whiplash stave off an enraged tiger?"

Such questions, perhaps, triggered the next phase of the word war. By Monday, Conn himself was ready to be explicit about the main theme:

"Louis is a big, slow-moving Negro. Nobody knows this better than Joe himself. He's a dangerous fighter, because he can punch and because he's been taught well. But he's a mechanical fighter, doing only what he's been told. He can't think under pressure in the ring, and

he knows it. He showed this every time he met a man who wasn't a rule-book fighter."

Ray added: "Louis is as slow on his feet as he is in his brains. Louis knows this and when he thinks about Conn, it's like a kid thinkin' about matchin' his wits with one of those magic guys."

"You mean a magician," said Jack Miley, the publicity man assigned to Conn's camp.

"Okay, a magician."

In short, the party line was that Louis was "psychologically" whipped before he started, and the racial insult, while calculated to annoy, seemed naturally permissible.

Jack Cuddy, the boxing expert of the United Press, reflected how lightly all such things were taken.

"They're tossing this word 'psychologically' around like a medicine ball," he wrote. "The adverb is getting cauliflower ears from rough treatment by the handsome Irish challenger; by his Jewish manager, Johnny Ray; by his Italian trainer, Freddy Fierro; and even by the German chef, Willie Handeler. And Jack Miley, the publicity man, is outraged.

"'Imagine a bunch of dese and dose guys goin' Tunney on me,' he said. 'What they mean is that Louis is licked mentally before he gets into the ring.'"

(The reference to Gene Tunney as the exemplar of intellectualism among heavyweight champions was widespread in those days. The reigning intellectual of

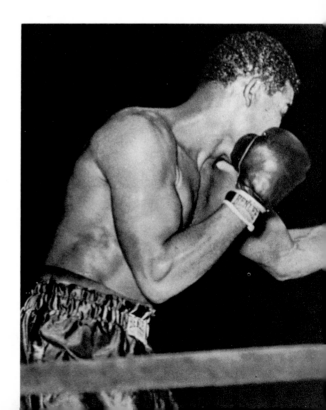

all sportswriters was John Kieran, already more famous as a panelist on the "Information Please" radio quiz show than as the original and only sports columnist of the *New York Times,* and Kieran often wrote of his friend Tunney. It was Kieran who, in a column dissecting the ballyhoo process a couple of days before the fight, wrote of an exchange of public insults by Dempsey and Tunney in building up their second fight. Tunney's final salvo ended: "P.S. I wrote this myself.")

The obligatory reply from Louis came the next day: "That Conn talks too much."

Three more days passed before Louis elaborated: "Maybe I ain't the smartest feller in the world," he said, "but who is Conn to go calling me dumb? I never heard of him getting no college degrees. He talks too much and I'm going to push some of his gab right down his throat."

So much for subtlety.

During the week preceding the fight, the world news couldn't really be ignored. A Gallup poll showed that 62 percent of the populace believed that the safety of the United States depended on British control of the seas, and that the United States should fight if there seemed to be any danger that Britain would lose. British bombers hit the Ruhr Valley for six straight nights. A German submarine torpedoed an American ship. The CIO purged leaders of wildcat strikes that were interfering with war production (for the British). German and

Italian consulates in the United States were closed. The Free French were driving on Damascus, but Vichy France announced drastic anti-Jewish laws.

And on June 12, not prominently displayed, a headline: HITLER HOLDS MILLION MEN READY TO STRIKE AT RUSSIA. On June 16, more prominently: NAZI–RED TENSION RISES, BUT MAY BE SMOKESCREEN. FINLAND CALLS RESERVISTS. RUSSIAN BALTIC FLEET ALERTED.

The same day, on the sports page, Louis said: "If Conn comes out fighting, he jes' ain't gonna be there long."

Wednesday, June 18, was the day of the fight. The morning sports pages carried the following key items:

- The weather forecast was for possible showers during the late evening. (With the fight scheduled for 10:00 P.M. it was agreed that it might start earlier if the clouds really threatened.)
- Louis was a 4–1 favorite, 11–5 to win by a knockout.
- Joe DiMaggio had just hit safely in his thirtieth consecutive game, a Yankee record, (He would go on for 56 games.) Ted Williams was hitting .424. (He would wind up at .406). The Dodgers, managed by Leo Durocher, were making a serious drive for their first pennant in twenty-one years.
- And Conn had girl trouble. It seemed that Conn and his girl friend, Mary Louise Smith, had applied for a marriage license a month before. Her father, a former major

Heavy action: the champion and the challenger exchange left-hand smashes to the jaw

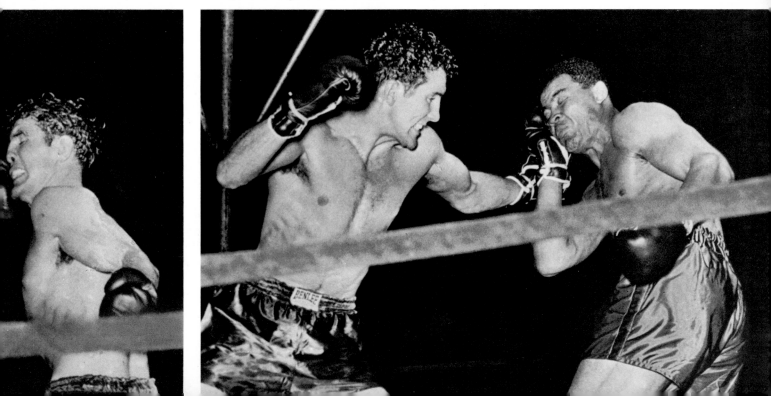

"If I stayed away, I would have won it." BILLY CONN

league baseball player named Jimmy, had strong objections. The marriage had been deferred. Now, on the eve of the weigh-in, the 152-pound father threatened to punch the heavyweight challenger to pieces if he came around his daughter again.

Nevertheless, Conn showed up for the weigh-in on time. Louis didn't. Conn weighed in at 174 and didn't wait around for Louis. He even asked to be excused from making any comment about his romance. Obviously, he was getting stoked up for the fight.

Louis showed up ten minutes late and weighed in at 199 1/2. His party had taken the wrong road driving in from Greenwood Lake, New York. So the two fighters never did confront each other until they reached the ring.

s it turned out, it didn't rain.

The Polo Grounds, an oval-shaped, two-deck structure worse suited for its native baseball use than for a fight, could hold more than 55,000 people. The most expensive ticket was $25.00, the cheapest $2.50. Louis would get 40 percent of the net receipts, Conn 20 percent, and the promoter (Mike Jacobs) the rest. The paid attendance was 54,487 and the gate $451,776. Special trains came from Pittsburgh. There were 700 accredited reporters at ringside. The referee, announced only at fight time, was Eddie Joseph.

Electric blanket or no, Conn did start slowly, as usual. Louis won the first two rounds in everyone's opinion, both men moving cautiously. The next two rounds, with Conn moving faster, staying out of reach, and scoring points with brief flurries, went to Conn.

The next two, the referee, the judges (Morty Munro and Eddie Healey), and most observers agreed, belonged to Louis. But there was no indication, after six rounds, that Louis was about to knock anybody out, and Conn seemed to be growing in confidence. From the seventh round on, he began to carry the fight to the champion, hitting as well as dodging. Louis did begin to appear slow and confused, and occasionally hurt. When Louis rallied a bit in the tenth, Conn came on stronger than ever in the eleventh and twelfth.

At that point, Referee Joseph had Conn leading, 7–5,

in rounds; Munroe had it 7–4, with one even. Healey had it 6–6. Most experts at ringside had it even more heavily in Conn's favor.

There were three rounds—nine minutes of fighting—to go.

Conn knew he was ahead, and that if he could just stay out of reach for the rest of the fight, winning at least another round by the same moves that had won the last two, he would be Champion of the World. Louis knew he was behind, and that if he didn't find an opening for a knockout punch, he wouldn't be champion any longer.

But on his stool, waiting for the thirteenth, Conn told his seconds: "I'm going to knock that bum out." And he went out to try.

For two minutes, Conn had the upper hand, and Louis seemed in trouble. Suddenly, a short right-hand punch slowed Conn down, as nothing else had before. In the next few seconds, everything changed.

Louis had found his opening. He poured punches through it, almost too fast to count. Conn sagged. He fell. He didn't even quiver until the count of 8. The count of 10 was over at 2:58—two seconds before the bell.

Louis was still champion. And Conn had proved, as melodramatically as possible, the old equation about valor and discretion. The "sooner or later, he'll hit him once" theory proved true. And the dumb one under pressure turned out to be Conn.

"I guess maybe I had too much guts—and not enough common sense," Conn said in his dressing room afterward. First he had cried openly, and Ray had asked people to let him.

"Don't bother him; if he wants to cry, let him have a good one," said the manager.

Then Conn said a strange thing: "I shouldn't have got up at 4. I should have taken a 9-count that first time I was knocked down."

Evidently he thought he had been knocked down twice, and that he had stood up too soon once. None of that had happened. It was a measure of how thoroughly he had been knocked out.

Louis, of course, wasn't confused at all. "I figured it would end just as it did," he said. "I felt sure that sooner or later he would be very wide with one of those lefts and that I would nail him with a right. That's just what happened.

"I hurt my right wrist in the seventh and then got into

trouble in the twelfth when he caught me on the ear and on the nose. But then, in the thirteenth, he did it and I shot over the right. That one punch got him, although it took another seven or eight to finish him off.

"He was a pretty tough boy up to then, you know. He punches as fast or faster than anybody I fought before. While you may not think he punches hard—let him hit you two or three and you start covering up."

And a little later: "I couldn't get started against his speed. I knew I was losing the fight when the thirteenth started. My handlers let me know it even if I didn't know it myself. He hurt me pretty much in the twelfth, and I was hoping he'd lose his head pretty quick, because I knew I was losing the title."

He said he'd like to fight Conn again.

"Every time I looked up, Joe Louis was standing there," Conn was saying across the hall, in the other dressing room. "I fought a good man and he beat me."

But he wanted to fight Louis again. And everybody wanted to see him fight Louis again. Eventually he did— but not in September, as he had been promised. Mike Jacobs decided the next Louis fight should be against Lou Nova, and it didn't take place until November, while Louis's wrist healed.

After November came December, and Pearl Harbor, and both fighters went into service. They fought again in 1946, both five years older and slower, selling almost $2 million worth of tickets—but it was just another fight. Louis knocked him out in the eighth round.

The special moment could not, of course, ever be recaptured. Tommy Loughran, himself a great boxer, summed up the Billy Conn of 1941: "He's one of the grandest boxers I have ever seen; it's too bad he likes to fight so much."

And Regis Welch summed up the event: "Conn hit a home run—but was caught trying to stretch it into a five-bagger."

On the same Page One that carried Welch's story, in the paper of June 19, another headline read: YIELD OR FACE INVASION, NAZI THREAT TO RUSSIA; NAZI DECISION TO ATTACK DUE IN 48 HOURS.

The decision did come, in forty-eight hours, and everything moved to the other side of the dividing line.

Beginning of the end: battered Conn holds rope as he goes down. Overleaf: Conn looked as if he might get up, but the count reached 10 and the fight was over

As the fight began, Conn and Louis were both wary, kept their distance

Nimble Conn evades a Louis punch, following his strategy of keeping away from champ

"Billy was the best light heavyweight I've ever seen.

"I wanted to get him in the corner, cut his speed down, but he stayed in the center of the ring.

"I wasn't hurt at all in the twelfth round, I wasn't in danger.

"He gave me my toughest fight of all my fights."

JOE LOUIS

Ballpark Break

The fight took place in New York, but it was a bigger event in Pittsburgh than anywhere else, because hometown rooting interest for Conn knew no limits.

One remarkable facet of that interest was its effect on baseball, the other major topic to which Pittsburgh sports fans paid attention.

The night of the fight, the Pittsburgh Pirates were scheduled to play the New York Giants (whose home field, the Polo Grounds, was the site of the fight). Arrangements were made to have the radio broadcast of the fight piped over the public address system at Forbes Field, and it was agreed that the baseball game would be interrupted for as long as it took to complete the fight.

This well-advertised promotion brought out 24,738 customers—about twice as many as the baseball game itself could be expected to draw. (Even though night games were still a new and relatively rare event in those days, the average attendance for a major-league baseball game was about 7,500, with the average night game drawing not quite double that figure.)

Game time was 9:15 P.M. In 1941, ball park lights weren't as powerful as they are now, and Pittsburgh was on daylight saving time in the westernmost part of its time zone, so it was felt that twilight had to be out of the way before lighting conditions were good enough.

The game started with Johnny Wittig pitching for the Giants and Max Butcher for Pittsburgh. At ten o'clock, three-and-a-half innings had been played, and Pittsburgh was ahead, 2-1. The game stopped, most of the players went to the clubhouse to listen there, and the crowd turned its attention to the loudspeakers.

During the early rounds of the fight, when it seemed that Louis was winning and might end it soon, Cliff Melton went out to the bull pen to warm up for the Giants, since Manager Bill Terry had decided to replace Wittig. But when Conn rallied, Melton came in again and sat down.

The interruption lasted fifty-six minutes, and the game resumed with Melton pitching against Butcher. Presently the Giants tied the score, 2-2, and a new problem loomed: the curfew. No inning was allowed to start later than 12:50 A.M. The eleventh began, with the score 2-2, at 12:49. Neither team scored and the game ended in a 2-2 tie—a thoroughly frustrating evening for Pittsburgh fans of both sports.

Conn moves in and jolts Louis with a looping left to the jaw

The One He Won

Conn and Mary Louise Smith were supposed to slip away right after the fight to get married, but Poppa Smith still objected and Billy needed more time to bring him around.

It took only about a month, and the marriage was a lasting one. In 1974, Billy and Mary Louise celebrated their thirty-third anniversary, and they had lived in the same house in Pittsburgh's Squirrel Hill section all that time. Their children were grown (three sons and a daughter), and the youngest, Mike, was in his last year of college.

"It goes quickly," says Conn, looking back over the years, his voice still radiating that personal charm.

*Trying to knock Louis out in the thirteenth,
Conn leaves himself open for Louis attack*

*Louis hurt Conn badly with hard left that
was the beginning of the end for challenger*

Friends

*During those thirty-nine minutes in the ring together,
Louis and Conn developed enormous respect for each
other. They were thrown together frequently in later years—
in the build-up and aftermath to their second fight, and
then in many social situations and sporting events that
made their own seem ever more glamorous in retrospect.
And they became fast friends. The ugly remarks were forgotten, or at least accepted for what they were: a part of
their time—half cynical promotion and half a warrior's
way to stir up adrenalin-producing hatred for combat.*

*As recently as the spring of 1974 in Pittsburgh, they
shared the dais at a Dapper Dan dinner, Pittsburgh's biggest sports charity. Films of the 1941 fight were shown.
For twelve rounds, both men and the rest of the audience
sat in silent fascination and watched the shadows dance.
Then, just before the thirteenth round began, Louis (now*

Conn's legs are rubbery after Louis hits
him with knockout punch, a jolting right

Battered Conn is revived after fight is over.
Overleaf: *The challenger and the champion*

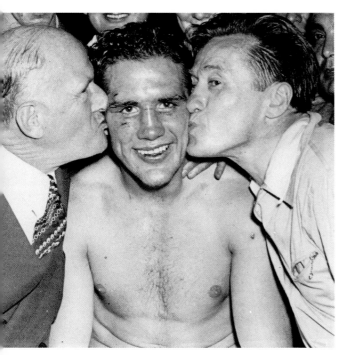

Defeated challenger is consoled by promoter Mike Jacobs
(left), manager Johnny Ray (right). Friends gather at
birthday celebration (left) for Joe Louis in Las Vegas
in 1971: (from left) Sugar Ray Robinson, Max Schmeling,
Joe Louis, Billy Conn, Gregory Peck and Chuck Connors

"I hit him with a good left in
the twelfth round. I figured
I could knock him out.

"First rounds don't count. It's
the last round."

BILLY CONN

sixty years old) stood up suddenly and uncharacteristi-
cally sang out, "Bye-bye, Billy!"

It got a big laugh from everyone, including Conn, and of
course Billy had to reply.

"Why didn't you loan me the title for six months or so?"
Conn said. "You wouldn't have missed it."

"I did lend it to you, for twelve rounds," Louis answered,
"and you didn't know what to do with it."

The slugger and his bat—Ted Williams swings a large model at Fenway Park promotion in 194

St. Louis Cardinals/ Boston Red Sox World Series October, 1946

By George Vecsey

In 1946 the baseball players returned from the service—and an astounding eighteen million fans turned out to watch them. Two of the greatest hitters in baseball history, Stan Musial of the St. Louis Cardinals and Ted Williams of the Boston Red Sox, powered their teams into the World Series.

First the Red Sox won, and then the Cardinals, and so on for six games. Then, as the teams struggled into the eighth inning of the seventh game, a nation starved for peacetime heroes followed on the radio as Enos (Country) Slaughter began a mad dash around the bases.

Baseball has its roots in sudden, dramatic motions erupting from the ritual of the game—the sliding of Ty Cobb, the fastballs of Walter Johnson, the home runs of Babe Ruth. In the Depression, while Bonnie and Clyde were robbing banks in the Dust Bowl, jobless fans paid twenty-five cents for a bleacher seat to watch Pepper Martin crash around the dusty base paths. In 1946 it was time for a reaffirmation.

As Country Slaughter tore his way toward home, he was like a steam engine racing its way across the country, telling the people: "Look—look—the men are back—the war is over—baseball has survived!"

George Vecsey listened to the 1946 Series with his father, also named George, who was a sportswriter. The younger Vecsey later became a baseball reporter for *Newsday.* In 1970 he became Appalachian correspondent for the *New York Times,* based in Kentucky. He is the author of *One Sunset a Week—The Story of a Coal Miner.*

G. V.

hen Enos Slaughter came back from the army in 1946, he was eager to resume the social amenities. The first time his St. Louis Cardinals met the Brooklyn Dodgers, he sidled up to Eddie Stanky and said:

"So you're the little SOB who's been acting so big while the men were away."

Stanky agreed that, yes, it was indeed he.

"Well, look out for me," Slaughter concluded.

It was a sporting gesture on Slaughter's part. After three years in the service he was eager to make up for lost time. And true to his word, he never stopped running, right up through the last inning of a memorable World Series, the first peacetime Series in five years.

Baseball's quality had dropped during World War II. When told to keep going by Franklin Delano Roosevelt, baseball served the country by putting any twenty-five men in flannels and calling them a major-league team.

The Cardinals won three straight pennants in 1942–43–44 as their vast reserves went off to war. By 1944, the American League had been watered down so badly that the St. Louis Brownies actually won their first and only pennant.

In 1945, the Detroit Tigers had beaten the Chicago Cubs in a comic-opera Series, featuring those two never-to-be-forgotten shortstops, Roy Hughes of the Cubs and James "Skeeter" Webb of the Tigers. Then the baseball players came home.

"Oh, man, we were fearless," recalls Joe Garagiola, the television celebrity, who was then a twenty-year-old catcher. "Anything you did, you felt you were ahead of the game. Not that you'd been in the trenches necessarily. But you were so glad to be back. . . .

"You'd hear rumors. 'Wait till you see so-and-so. He's in great shape.' Harry Walker told us some war stories. Then he warned us about this guy Ewell Blackwell, with his sidearm fastball. Man, we didn't care. Let us at him."

The St. Louis Cardinals had a tradition of fearlessness, going back to the teams of Rogers Hornsby and Pepper Martin, who won five pennants from 1926 to 1934, fighting their way around the base paths. The Gashouse Gang

Happy Days Are Here Again

of the 1930s had carried workmen's tools on the road, disrupting hotel lobbies with their pranks, and they carried guitars and harmonicas and washboards, playing favorites like "Turkey in the Straw" on the long train rides.

When that gang had grown old, Branch Rickey had stocked hundreds of depression youths in his "farm system"—hungry boys like Stan Musial from smogbound Donora, Pennsylvania, with his weird peek-a-boo batting stance, and Albert (Red) Schoendienst, a freckle-faced river boy from southern Illinois, one eye weakened from an accident in the Civilian Conservation Corps.

"Terry Moore was our captain," recalls Harry Walker, a young outfielder in 1946, now an official with the Cardinals. "Terry was more of a leader than any man I've ever seen—I named my only son after him.

"Terry would chew you out in a nice way. He'd say: 'Don't fraternize with the other team. What are you gonna do if you've got to break up the double play and it's your buddy out there?' Heck, Terry wouldn't let me talk to my own brother [Dixie, of the Brooklyn Dodgers]."

The Cardinals had a new manager in 1946, an excitable former pitcher named Eddie Dyer, who relied on the older players to maintain control. Joe Garagiola claims that the infield of Musial, Schoendienst, Marty Marion, and Whitey Kurowski would not shout twenty words a season. But they knew how to calm down a faltering pitcher—or a shaky twenty-year-old catcher.

Like the old Gashouse Gang, the 1946 Cardinals played music on the long train rides (St. Louis was still the western outpost in both leagues). The trainer, Doc Weaver, played the mandolin while Musial beat coat hangers on a chair. Kurowski liked country music. Musial and Murray Dickson were amateur magicians.

"And the whole club was good at wholesaling," Joe Garagiola recalls. "Hey, we could all turn an autographed baseball into a sport coat in New York. Enos Slaughter was a master at that."

Slaughter was the closest link to the old Gashouse Gang, having escaped from the Carolina mills with the nickname of "Country" and a reputation for aggression. Scolded one time for not hustling in the minors, the tobacco-chewing outfielder vowed he would never stop running again. With the Cardinals in 1941, he ran into a concrete wall, breaking his arm—but trying to stay in the game. Five weeks later, he insisted on returning to

The 1946 Cardinals in spring training (left), *with manager Eddie Dyer in foreground. At Fenway Park. Ted Williams and 1946 Red Sox teammates. Big bat was symbolic of Boston's strong-hitting team.*

action. Swinging violently, he tore open the skin where the bone had fractured, turning his uniform as crimson as the Cardinal insignia.

When Slaughter returned from the service, he was in the midst of a costly second divorce—and tougher than ever. His warning to Eddie Stanky could have been dis-

tributed around the National League—and to the Boston Red Sox as well.

The Sox had their own winning tradition, but further in the past. From 1903 to 1918, they had won five World Series, paced in several by a slugging pitcher named Babe Ruth. But the Sox' owner, Harry Frazee, a theatrical

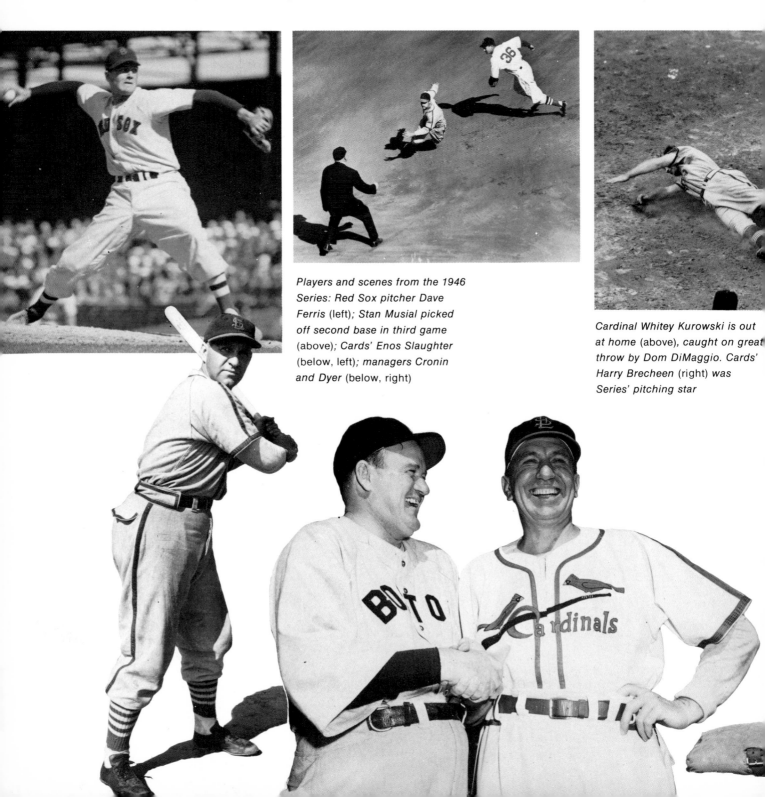

Players and scenes from the 1946 Series: Red Sox pitcher Dave Ferris (left); Stan Musial picked off second base in third game (above); Cards' Enos Slaughter (below, left); managers Cronin and Dyer (below, right)

Cardinal Whitey Kurowski is out at home (above), caught on great throw by Dom DiMaggio. Cards' Harry Brecheen (right) was Series' pitching star

producer, sold Ruth to the lowly New York Yankees to finance his shows.

As Ruth became baseball's greatest hero, the Red Sox hit the bottom. But in 1933, the club was sold to Thomas Yawkey—wealthy, independent, and a fan. Yawkey spent money—$250,000 for Joe Cronin, the slugging short-stop-manager who had led the Washington Senators to a pennant in 1934. Cronin became a favorite with Boston's Irish-Catholic fans, but, as the Sox made a habit of finishing behind the Yankees, the fans turned on Cronin.

Soon, Yawkey's millions began producing fine players, including Theodore Samuel Williams, a slender, moody

*Joe Garagiola is out at third (above)
trying to stretch double. Cardinal
Red Schoendienst (below, left),
Boston's Ted Williams and Dom DiMaggio with Dom's brother, Joe (below)*

outfielder from San Diego. In 1941, Williams batted .406 —the last time any hitter has gone over .400. Yawkey also bought Dominic DiMaggio, bespectacled little brother of the Yankee star, Joe. In the infield there were quiet Bobby Doerr, sufferer of migraine headaches, and John Michael Paveskovich (Pesky), who had once shined Doerr's shoes as a clubhouse boy in Portland, Oregon.

The Sox had another tradition—the swarm of sportswriters sent by dozens of New England newspapers, many of them competing for "scoops" about trades or gossip about personalities. And the biggest celebrity was T.S. Williams. Writers like "Colonel" Dave Egan of the *Daily Record* set the tone, speculating when "The Kid" would tip his cap to the fans, or visit his mother, or enlist in the services. And the Boston fans, with their powerful mixture of Yankee wit, urban brashness, and collegiate intelligence, usually addressed these questions at the flaming red ears of Mr. Williams.

For example: after Pearl Harbor, Williams requested a deferral because he was supporting his mother, a Salvation Army worker. But the Boston press pressured Williams into enlisting as a combat pilot while other stars were still in the major leagues or playing service ball.

n 1946, Yawkey was ready to spend more money to surpass the Yankees. He traded for Rudy York, a lumbering slugger—"part Cherokee, part first baseman," somebody said. For a change, the Sox had some pitching, including an asthmatic Dave Ferriss, who had won 21 games in wartime 1945.

"Oh, we had ballplayers all over the place," recalls Johnny Pesky, now a Boston broadcaster. "We were allowed to keep thirty because of the vets coming back. Cronin was a good manager, aggressive. He'd pick his best nine and play 'em."

Cronin knew how to relax Williams by chatting about hitting strategy. And Rudy York once bawled out Williams in the dugout for not hustling: "I've never stopped trying and I expect you to do the same." Williams, who respected older sluggers, apologized.

With Williams back in prewar form, the Sox ran off early streaks of fifteen and twelve victories, taking a huge lead. One double-header Williams drove in eleven runs before Cleveland's shortstop-manager, Lou Boudreau, shifted most of his fielders to the right side, leaving only the left fielder in shallow left field.

The obvious goal was to dare Williams to give up his power to right field and change his batting stance. But Williams staunchly tried to smash hits through—and over—the "Boudreau Shift" when it was picked up by other teams.

Cronin advised Williams to keep the opponents honest by stroking an occasional hit to left field. Ty Cobb, the great batting star of the early 1900s, made similar suggestions. One day Williams slapped a hit down the left-field line and chortled, "Who is this Ty Cobb?" But the next time up, he again challenged the shift. The controversy went further than baseball strategy—it became a match of Williams's ego against the "wisdom" of press and fans.

The Sox slumped late in the season, carrying champagne from town to town, waiting to celebrate the pennant. On September 13, Williams poked an inside-the-park homer to left field for the 1-0 victory that clinched the title.

That night, Williams was at a friend's house, tying fishing lures as his teammates drank champagne. He has maintained he was not aware of the party, but "Colonel" Egan wrote: "Williams is utterly lacking in anything that even bears remote resemblance to team spirit." Williams then went into a slump as the Red Sox killed time before the World Series.

The Cardinals did not have that luxury. Picked to romp to a pennant, they slumped as Red Barrett, a 23-game winner in 1945, turned into a postwar pumpkin, and Johnny Beazley, 21-game winner in 1942, came back from service ball with a sore arm.

Then a Mexican named Jorge Pascual, wearing sleek clothing and a big pistol, tossing around $100 bills as if they were pesos, came to woo players for the Mexican League. On one trip, the Cardinals came to the Polo Grounds in New York and found three lockers empty. Gone were Chuck Klein, Fred Martin, and pitcher Max Lanier, who had won his first six decisions.

One night in the Fairgrounds Hotel in St. Louis, another Pascual brother dropped $50,000 on the table and offered Stan Musial $200,000 for a five-year contract.

Musial, the best hitter in the league, was making $18,500 a year. But he turned the offer down.

The Cardinals also had competition from the Dodgers, now run by Branch Rickey. Under hunch-playing manager Leo Durocher, the Dodgers took a 6½-game lead, paced by Pete Reiser, Pee Wee Reese, and the thirty-six-year-old "Peepul's Cherce," Dixie Walker.

But the Cardinals caught the Dodgers in late August, and when both teams lost on the final day, they finished in a tie—forcing the first playoff in major-league history.

On October 1, with only 26,000 fans showing up in St. Louis, Howie Pollet ignored his aching back and beat the Dodgers, 4-2. Then the two teams jumped on separate trains and headed east. On October 3, Harry (The Cat) Brecheen struck out tall Howie Schultz with the bases loaded for an 8-4 victory that invoked the familiar Brooklyn refrain: "Wait 'til next year."

But waiting was not good for the Red Sox. While the National League settled its playoff, the Sox tried to keep in shape with exhibitions. In the first game, Williams took a curveball on the right elbow. The elbow was not broken, but it was badly swollen.

While Williams recuperated, "Colonel" Egan broke a "scoop" that the Sox were going to trade him to Detroit for Hal Newhouser. A few days later, Egan had Williams going to the Yankees for Joe DiMaggio. A posse of reporters hounded Williams as the Red Sox headed to St. Louis to open the Series at last.

The nation prepared to listen to the radio broadcasts of the duel between baseball's two greatest left-handed hitters. And the "Betting Commissioner" of St. Louis established the Red Sox as 7-20 favorites, meaning you had to put up $20 to win $7.

Owner Yawkey gave the Red Sox brand-new uniforms. The Cardinals' owner, Sam Breadon, had their old uniforms dry-cleaned.

When Williams arrived at Sportsman's Park, he took aim at the pavilion in right field he had often reached against the Brownies. In practice, he slammed several drives over the "short porch" and pronounced: "I'm ready."

Eddie Dyer unveiled his version of the Williams shift when the Series opened on a warm afternoon on October 6. Dyer stationed his aching shortstop, Marty Marion, near his normal position, and he placed the left fielder in left-center. But everybody else was on the right side. Williams came up in the top of the second inning and, as

usual, tried to beat the shift with power. On his first swing, his drive to right field hooked foul by a foot.

Joe Garagiola, squatting behind the plate, heard Williams come back to home sputtering: "Hit it on the blankety-blank trademark"—meaning he didn't get "good wood" on the ball. Then Williams slashed a grounder that would have been a single to right field against a normal defense. But Red Schoendienst, the second baseman, was only twenty-five feet from the foul line, and he easily threw Williams out.

The score was tied, 1-1, with two out in the eighth, when Kurowski singled past third. Then Dominic DiMaggio, wearing sunglasses over his regular glasses, misplayed Garagiola's soft fly as Kurowski raced for home. Wily old Pinky Higgins, at third base, did an intricate little rhumba in the baseline, slowing Kurowski down as Garagiola was out at third. But the umpires ruled Kurowski's run counted because of the interference.

he happy Cardinal fans were quickly let down by the heat-baked infield, known as "Hogan's Brickyard." With one out, Higgins's grounder skipped past Marion for a freak single. Then singles by Rip Russell and Tom McBride tied the score.

Earl Johnson, who had spent 190 days at the Battle of the Bulge earning the Bronze and Silver Stars, pitched for the Red Sox in the ninth. In the tenth inning, the cast-off, Rudy York, blasted a homer deep into the left-field stands. Pesky made an error in the bottom of the tenth, but Johnson escaped with a 3-2 victory.

Hogan's Brickyard evened things up in the second game, as two run-scoring shots took strange bounces for the Cardinals. Del Rice, replacing Garagiola, hit two singles, and Brecheen also drove in a run. The Sox, shut out only eight times in 154 games during the season, couldn't do much with Brecheen's screwball. Williams was hitless as Brecheen scattered four singles for a 3-0 victory that tied the Series. Then the teams headed east, with the Cardinal train reaching speeds of 110 miles per hour.

Boston had not seen a World Series since 1918, and the fans poured in from all over New England—many of them the same cigar-smoking, side-of-the-mouth critics who had burned Ted Williams' ears. Few Cardinals had ever seen Fenway Park, with its looming left-field wall, since the National League's Boston Braves played in a different stadium. Eddie Dyer took one look at the wind blowing in from deep right field and decided to pitch Williams inside, to dare him to buck the wind.

Williams took early batting practice to try slapping the ball to the short left-field wall. But he never got to swing on his first trip. With two out and a runner on second, Dyer had Williams intentionally walked, to let right-handed Murray Dickson pitch to York. The big man promptly slugged a curveball into the left-field screen for a three-run homer. Dave Ferriss didn't need much more. He scattered six hits for a 4-0 victory, his fourteenth straight victory in Fenway Park, giving the Sox a 2-1 lead in the Series.

But the biggest cheer of the day came in the third inning, when Williams pushed a bunt down the third-baseline and romped to first base, laughing at his effort. In the papers the next day, the headline was "WILLIAMS BUNTS."

The fourth game was what ballplayers call "a laugher." The Sox made four errors, and the Cardinals tied a record with 20 base hits, as the visitors tied the Series with a 12-3 romp. Bobby Doerr came down with a migraine headache and left the game early, along with many of the fans. Garagiola, Kurowski, and Slaughter all tied the Series record by making four hits apiece. In the ninth inning, the home-plate umpire, Charley Berry, informed Slaughter he had a chance to break the record. But Slaughter popped up on a fat pitch.

"If Berry kept his big mouth shut, I'd probably have hit it out of the park," groused Slaughter, who already had one homer.

Doerr stayed home for the fifth game, but his replacement, Don Gutteridge, slapped two hits, as did another substitute, Leon Culberson. Williams drove in his first run of the Series as Joe Dobson won a relaxed 6-3 decision that put the Sox ahead three games to two.

To make things worse for the Cardinals, Slaughter was hit by a pitch on the right elbow. Although he jogged to first base without rubbing it ("I wouldn't give 'em the satisfaction," he said), he eventually had to leave the

Cardinal infield shifted to right side against Williams, but the Boston slugger refused to try to hit to left

game. On the train ride west, Dr. Robert F. Hyland, the team physician, packed the elbow in ice. When they got to St. Louis, Hyland determined that no bones were broken but warned Slaughter not to jeopardize his career by playing.

"Doc, I thought you were smart," Slaughter said. "Man, how in the world do you think I'm gonna miss this one? If I'm breathing, I'm all right to play."

Slaughter fulfilled that promise on October 13, trotting out to right field, cheered by the fans in the pavilion. Needing two straight victories at home to win the Series, the Cardinals went with Brecheen, who was tired and suffering from a cold. The Cat got in trouble early, giving up singles to Pesky and DiMaggio, then walking Williams. But now York, who had two big homers earlier, hit into a fast double play.

Then the Cardinals scored three times off Mickey Harris on a single by Rice, a double by Schoendienst, a run-scoring fly by Moore, an infield single by Musial, and run-scoring singles by Korowski and Slaughter, who was swinging basically one-handed.

The score was 4-1 going into the ninth when Williams slashed a single over the bunched-up infield, raising his Series average to .238. But York hit into another double play, sending the Cardinals to the clubhouse and their familiar victory polka, "Drink the Barrel Dry," to celebrate being tied at three games apiece. Now there was just one game left.

"We've won every tough one we've had to win all year," Dyer exclaimed, over and over again.

The teams took a day off to prepare for the payoff game, as Cronin nominated Ferriss, winner of 46 games in two years. Dyer had received fifty telegrams urging him to try Brecheen again in the seventh game. But the Cat was not equal to another start. Dyer told Brecheen, "I wish you were twins," as he nominated slender Murray Dickson to start. During the final workout, Williams predicted he would hit a homer. Meanwhile, the Betting Commissioner said the odds were 7-10 on the Red Sox, exactly half what they had been six games before.

The final game began badly for the Cardinals, when Wally Moses and Pesky singled and DiMaggio drove in a run with a sacrifice fly. Williams, swinging mightily to fulfill his prediction, blasted a drive to deep center field, left uncovered by the shift. But Terry Moore, the captain, playing with a damaged knee, made a running catch. York then popped up to end the threat.

The Cards tied the game in the second on a double by Kurowski, a purposeful grounder to the right side by Garagiola, and a line-drive out to left by Walker. It was still tied in the fifth when Walker singled up the middle and moved to second on Marion's sacrifice. Then Dickson, a good hitter, slapped a double over third base for a run. And Schoendienst hit the next pitch for a single to make it 3-1.

The lead seemed enough for Dickson, who got 18 of 19 men out from the second through the seventh innings, helped by great catches by Walker (on Williams) and Moore (on Higgins). But in the eighth, Rip Russell pinch hit a single, and George Metkovich, another pinch hitter, doubled him to third.

It was now time to let out The Cat. The fans cheered up as Brecheen struck out Moses on three pitches and got Pesky to pop up. But DiMaggio slashed a double off the right-field wall for two runs, tying the score. (DiMaggio pulled a muscle in his leg and had to leave the game.)

That brought up Williams in one of the most crucial spots of his—or any—career. There were two outs, a runner on second with the go-ahead run in the eighth inning of the seventh game of a World Series. Dyer had the alternative of walking Williams, setting up the force play, and letting Brecheen's screwball work against the right-handed York. But Dyer let Brecheen pitch to Williams, who tipped a foul off the bare hand of Garagiola. When Rice replaced Garagiola behind the plate, the drama seemed abated. Williams popped up to end the inning.

In the bottom of the eighth, Cronin brought in Bob Klinger, who had not yet pitched in the Series. The thirty-six-year-old right-hander had compiled a fair record in twenty-eight appearances after being dropped by Pittsburgh in May. Why Cronin did not throw in his first-line pitchers—since there was a whole winter to rest up—was already being debated as Klinger began to pitch to Slaughter. His right arm still weakened, Slaughter rammed the second pitch for a single to center.

Kurowski tried to bunt him over but popped to Klinger, thirty feet from home. Slaughter—taking a big lead—scurried back to first. Rice then flied out to Williams, too shallow to permit Slaughter to advance. That brought up Harry Walker, the fidgety "Harry the Hat," who looked at two balls and a strike. Then Dyer flashed the sign for the hit-and-run.

What happened next has been debated for more than a

quarter of a century. There are many different versions, but the basic facts are these:

Walker drilled a hit to left-center, where Culberson—replacing DiMaggio—came up with the ball.

Slaughter, running with the pitch, raced easily toward third.

Culberson threw the ball to Pesky, the relay man on the edge of the outfield grass.

Pesky turned toward the infield.

Slaughter raced past third-base coach Mike Gonzalez.

Pesky threw home, but the ball went ten feet up the line as Slaughter slid home for the tie-breaking run. The fans erupted as their heroes scored in the manner of the old Gashouse Gang.

Meanwhile, writers, players, and fans began to reconstruct that sudden, searing moment—asking whether Pesky had frozen with the ball or whether Slaughter had simply outrun the conventional defensive play.

But, of course, Brecheen still had to get three outs before the Cardinals could celebrate. Rudy York, a clutch hitter to the end, hit a single. Doerr then singled to left, as the pinch runner stopped at second. Dyer raced out to speak with Brecheen. The Cardinals had a glut of pitchers in the bullpen. But Dyer was going to win or lose with The Cat.

Dangerous old Higgins bunted too hard to Kurowski, who forced Doerr at second base. Now there were runners on first and third with one out. Roy Partee then fouled to Musial in front of the Boston dugout. And Tom McBride grounded to Schoendienst, who let the ball roll up his arm before flipping to Marion at second base, to end the season.

The fans erupted onto the field to celebrate the fourth straight time the Cardinals had won the seventh game of a World Series. They nearly crushed Brecheen, the first pitcher in twenty-six years to win three times in one Series.

The noise of the fans penetrated the Boston clubhouse, where Joe Cronin was saying: "We played our best and it just wasn't good enough. . . . The layoff [after the season] hurt us, despite our efforts to control it. . . . But there's no alibi. Three great catches beat us today—Moore twice and Walker."

Cronin did not blame Pesky for Slaughter's mad dash. The Red Sox, after all, had not qualified for the Series on their fielding.

Pesky, who had made four errors in the seven games, said quietly: "I should have been alert, I blame myself. Charge it up to me."

Ted Williams sat and stared at the floor between his feet. He had made five singles in twenty-five at-bats, driving in one run, in his first World Series. When Williams came out of the shower, his face was wet with more than water. When he got to Union Station for the long ride home, Williams bolted himself inside his private compartment. There he began to weep—a six-foot, four-inch man, shaking with tears falling. Then he looked up. The train was still in the station. The blinds of his compartment were not drawn. He was being observed by over 1,000 fans.

Back in the Cardinal clubhouse, Joe Garagiola lay on a training table, blood smeared over his dusty flannels. He watched the grown men, the former sergeants and the jeepdrivers, drinking more beer and champagne than they sloshed on each other. And he waved his bandaged finger in the air and proclaimed:

"I'm out for the season! I'm out for the season!"

In one corner of the clubhouse, the hot, blinding lights of the newsreel photographers made Enos Slaughter sweat. The wave of interviewers asked Slaughter whether the coach had signaled him to run.

"I just kept running," Slaughter said. "I knew I just had to score."

The interviewers seemed stunned by Slaughter's audacity. But Slaughter wasn't all that impressed. After all, he'd been warning people to look out for him ever since spring training.

Red Schoendienst plays leapfrog over Johnny Pesky to complete a double play. Overleaf: *Slaughter scores winning run from first base on Harry Walker's single*

In the first game, with score 1–1, Pinky Higgins
is called for interfering with Whitey Kurowski

Joe Cronin congratulates Eddie Dyer

"Rudy York did something to
our ballclub. It seemed
like he brought in a lot of
enthusiasm, and he was
heads-up all the way."

BOBBY DOERR

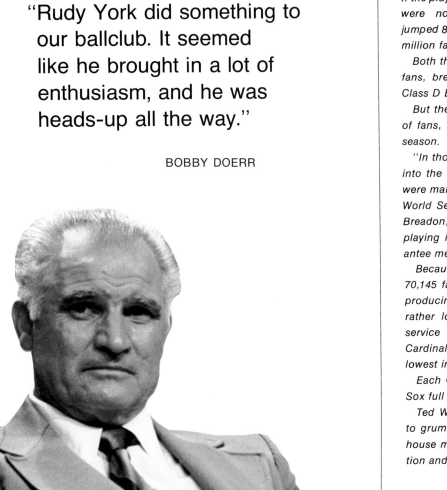

The Payoff

*If the players were glad to be back in 1946, the club owners
were not exactly disappointed. Baseball attendance
jumped 80 percent over its previous high, drawing eighteen
million fans for the sixteen major-league clubs.*

*Both the Cardinals and the Red Sox drew over a million
fans, breaking their own attendance records. Even the
Class D Evangeline League drew 757,000 fans.*

*But the players did not directly profit from the bonanza
of fans, since their contracts were drawn up before the
season.*

*"In those days, you didn't make any money until you got
into the World Series," recalls Harry Walker. "Heck, guys
were making eighteen to twenty thousand at the most. The
World Series was our big raise. In 1943, our owner, Sam
Breadon, told me I made an extra six thousand last year by
playing in the World Series. I told him, 'Would you guarantee me the money if we don't get in the Series?'"*

*Because small Sportsman's Park could pack in only
70,145 fans and Fenway Park only 72,133 in the revenue-
producing first four games, the Series money pool was
rather low. And because the rosters were swollen with
service verterans—the Red Sox had thirty players, the
Cardinals had twenty-nine—the players' shares were the
lowest in twenty-eight years.*

*Each Cardinal full share was only $4,742.34. Each Red
Sox full share was only $2,140.89.*

*Ted Williams didn't hold on to his check long enough
to grumble about its size—endorsing it over to the clubhouse man, Johnny Orlando, for his many acts of protec-
tion and friendship.*

Rudy York watches at the plate as his game-winning home run sails into the seats

The Cards won the second game, 3–0, as Del Rice hit two singles in Cards' attack

The Beginning

While the 1946 World Series was going on, the papers carried reports about the "Little World Series" between the winners of the American Association (Louisville) and the International League (Montreal).

The star of the Montreal Royals was Jackie Robinson, the first black man to play in "organized" baseball in the twentieth century. Signed by Branch Rickey of the Brooklyn Dodgers, Robinson led the top minor league with a batting average of .349. Then he helped the Royals win the "Little World Series."

That season, two black pitchers also made brief appearances in Montreal, while the Dodgers sent Don Newcombe and Roy Campanella to their Nashua, New Hampshire, farm team.

In 1947, several Southern-born Cardinals threatened to strike rather than play against Jackie Robinson. But the reaction was limited to vile language, as Robinson spurred the Dodgers to the 1947 pennant.

Slow to stock up on black players, the Cardinals did not win another pennant until 1964. By that time, the Brooklyn-Los Angeles Dodgers had won eight.

Owned by Tom Yawkey, a South Carolina millionaire, the Red Sox were the last major-league team to field a black player—in 1959. After 1946, they did not win another pennant until 1967.

"I did such great hitting at Ebbets Field and the fans were close to the stands . . . and every time I'd get a few hits, the fans would say, 'Here comes that man again,' and pretty soon it was 'Stan the Man.'"

STAN MUSIAL

Robinson is welcomed into Cardinal dugout in 1948, as hostility to blacks faded

Boston took third game easily, with Ted Williams contributing a bunt single

Cards won fourth game, 12–3, as Slaughter popped (above) up trying to break Series' record of more than four hits in one game

"I think the one thing that made a big difference was Harry Brecheen. I don't think guys who had never faced him realized what his screwball was like."

HARRY WALKER

War Stories

Joe Garagiola felt pretty proud of himself. Here he was, eighteen years old, catching opening day in a fast AA league. He was only a step or two from his boyhood dream of playing for his hometown St. Louis Cardinals.

When he got back to his hotel that evening, Garagiola found a letter of congratulations—not for catching opening day but for reaching eighteen, draft age. Before he knew it, he was playing for the Manila Dodgers, one of the many great service teams of World War II.

"Kirby Higbe was our manager," Garagiola recalls. "He had only one rule. Nobody could hit a triple with him on first base."

By the luck of the draw, Garagiola got to improve his hitting against major-league competition in Manila. Other young ballplayers had to fight before they could play again.

Harry (The Hat) Walker survived spinal meningitis to end up in mechanized reconnaissance in Germany—advancing thirty miles ahead of the infantry, chasing the retreating German army, meeting up with the Russians in 1945.

"Then we had 15,000 GIs just sitting around," recalls Walker. "The general ordered me to form a baseball league. We played in a huge stadium Hitler built in Nuremberg. All the guys wanted to play ball all day long. They didn't understand it was no toy for me—it was my livelihood.

"I was glad when we were sent home. But I still

Cards defensive star, centerfielder Terry
Moore just missed catching York's drive, but
Cards won anyway, 4-1, to tie Series 3-all

Harry (The Cat) Brecheen won sixth game
for Cards, his second victory in the Series

"You can't blame it on the ballfield. I blame it on the fleetfootedness of the outfielders, Moore, Walker and Slaughter. When I think of the catches that Moore made, climbing up the wall out there . . . why it makes you wince."

JOE CRONIN

regard the army as one of the proudest times in my life. I was able to pay back a debt for what other Americans had done for me in the past."

When the Cardinals reassembled in 1946, they discovered they had a million army buddies in every town.

"I got phone calls from everybody but General Eisenhower," Garagiola recalls. "They'd ask for tickets. They'd invite me home for dinner. Heck, I had a great time. But if I had to refuse, they'd say: 'Hey, Joe, gettin' a swelled head?'"

One of the Cardinal pitchers, Johnny Grodzicki, had been a great fastball pitcher in the minor leagues before the war. But his leg was injured while he was a paratrooper. In 1946 he made three token appearances, but his career was over.

"Some of the guys told war stories," Harry Walker recalls. "But Johnny never talked about the war. He kept everything inside."

The Mad Dash: Slaughter starts out from first base as Harry Walker hits single

In final game, Joe Cronin chose his top pitcher, Dave Ferris. Enos Slaughter (right) shows fans his elbow is okay before start of the sixth game

"As I rounded second, I saw this ball going into left center and I said, 'I can score.'"

ENOS SLAUGHTER

The Mad Dash

As soon as the 1946 Series ended, Johnny Pesky headed for his native Northwest, trying to forget about the mad dash of Enos Slaughter.

One day Pesky was watching a football game at Washington State in which the quarterback kept fumbling the ball. A fan spotted Pesky in the stands and shouted:

"Give Pesky the ball. He'll hold it."

There was no hiding from the controversy of the winning run, scored by Slaughter as Pesky handled the ball behind shortstop.

At first Pesky had said: "I'm the goat. I never expected he'd try to score. I couldn't hear anybody hollering at me above the noise of the crowd. I gave Slaughter at least six strides with the delay.

"It took a great ballplayer to get away with a play like that. Slaughter was a great ballplayer, but it was all my fault."

More than a quarter of a century later, Pesky has some second thoughts about his role in that play. Now a broadcaster with the Sox (he also managed Boston), Pesky says:

"I've looked at those films a thousand times. They said I took a snooze, but I can't see where I hesitated. Slaughter was at second when the ball was hit. He was twenty feet from home when I turned. I can't blame anybody. Those things have happened to better ballplayers than me. I guess you have to live with it."

As Pesky starts to throw from the edge of the infield, Slaughter is halfway home

Winning pitcher Brecheen, who tied Series record with three victories, gets hug

Originally, some people thought that Mike Gonzalez, the experienced Cuban third-base coach, had tried to hold Slaughter up. When first asked, Gonzalez said, "My God, I thought he was crazy. Who knows—maybe he is. But who cares?"

After the first thousand questions, Gonzalez decided that he had, indeed, told Slaughter to "go-go-go."

Slaughter's version never changed, as he moved to the New York Yankees and later to a job as a college coach.

"As I turned second, I saw (Leon) Culberson bobble the ball," Slaughter said that day. "It wasn't much but he just didn't have it in his control, and I knew for sure I could get third. Then he sort of made a slow throw to Pesky and that gave me the first inkling of scoring. I knew John would not be expecting it, and I knew I had to slow up just enough to decoy him into relaxing as I headed for third.

"Then I knew I really had to turn it on. Man, I don't think I ever ran that fast. All I kept seeing was the World Series flag over our stadium and the World Series ring on my hand. I honestly don't know where the ball was. But as long as I didn't see it in the catcher's glove, I knew I was all right."

Harry Walker, who made the winning hit, says he never heard any screams of advice from other Boston infielders.

"If they saw Enos running, they should have yelled. Pesky had to turn toward second to see where I was. When he realized Enos was running, he had to throw across his chest. That's why the ball was ten feet up the line."

Others say that Bobby Doerr, the second baseman, did yell to alert Pesky, but was not heard above the crowd.

But Joe Garagiola says: "Gonzalez couldn't have stopped Enos with a gun. You could have put four handball walls out there and he'd have run through them. Pesky took the rap for it, but Johnny never did hesitate. Heck, Enos was running with the pitch. He must have made up his mind when he reached second. You could almost say it was a dumb play that worked. You know the difference between dumb and smart—the word 'safe.'"

"I turned around to pick up Slaughter and he's fifteen feet from home. I'd have needed a shotgun to get him out."

JOHNNY PESKY

THE LAST STAND OF THE TOUCHDOWN TWINS

The Middies' Trojan mule gave spectators a surprise—and so did Middie team

Army/Navy Football Game November 30, 1946

By Robert Mayer

here have all the heroes gone? Probably to the bank. Americans wear their heroes' images on their sweatshirts these days, scream for them from distant balconies at $8.50 a pop. Bob Dylan, Billie Jean King, Rick Barry. They take the money and they run, or sing, or go into seclusion.

Robert Mayer recalls a time, not that long ago, when the nation's greatest sporting heroes were two young men whose most tangible reward would be a commission in the United States Army. It was 1946, before sportswriters took a serious, sociological view of sports. And Glenn Davis and Doc Blanchard seemed to be the epitome of an America that had just won the biggest game of all—World War II.

For their finale, these two apparently gallant knights had to take on their unheralded rivals from the Naval Academy—in a game that ended far differently than expected.

Robert Mayer remembers growing up in the Bronx in that era, listening to the radio every Saturday afternoon in the fall. As the sun set over the Grand Concourse, Mayer told his astonished mother that he was rooting for his hero—Doak Walker of faraway Southern Methodist University. As in the serials at the local movie theater, Doak Walker rarely failed to run and pass and kick and tackle his team to victory over Rice or Texas Christian —bringing joy to the Mayer apartment.

Mayer later was a reporter and columnist for *Newsday*, receiving the 1968 National Headliner Award for the outstanding feature column in the country. He twice won Columbia University's Mike Berger Award for superior coverage of New York City. Mayer now resides in Santa Fe, New Mexico, where he writes fiction and essays. G. V.

There had been a war. The women had put on coveralls to work the assembly lines; the men had donned uniforms and marched off to make the world safe for democracy—again. And out of the headlines and the weekly newsreels had emerged a glittering roster of new American heroes: Eisenhower, MacArthur, Bradley, Radford, Patton, Clark, MacAuliffe.

They were graduates of the service academies, Annapolis and West Point, and in time of trial they had worn their training well. And as these generals and admirals led their nation toward victory, there were heroes at the service academies back home—in football, America's sporting equivalent of war.

In 1944, football had provided America with two heroes to offset the grimness of the Battle of the Bulge. A pair of dashing future officers named Glenn (Junior) Davis and Felix (Doc) Blanchard had led the Army team to an undefeated season. As sophomores, they were both named to the All-America team. When the "Touchdown Twins" repeated their triumphs a year later—unbeaten and double All-American, the most effective one-two punch in football history—their names resounded beyond the bounds of sport. Blanchard and Davis, "Mr. Inside and Mr. Outside." They went together like Stars and Stripes.

And then they were seniors, undefeated in nine more games, their record marred only by a scoreless tie with mighty Notre Dame. The last game of the 1946 season—the last game that Doc Blanchard and Glenn Davis would play together—would be against arch-rival Navy, which had lost seven games in a row.

Much of the nation was listening on the radio that crisp November 30, to hear Blanchard and Davis end their careers in style. A hundred thousand fans, including President Harry S. Truman—the largest football crowd of the season—were jammed into Philadelphia's Municipal Stadium. And few could believe what was happening. With less than two minutes to play, powerful Army was leading upstart Navy by a scant three points, 21-18, and Navy had the ball on the Army three-yard line, with four chances to score. Navy was fired up and moving the ball against an Army team that looked battered and about to be beaten. The stadium was in

bedlam, the crowd surging out of the stands and lining the sidelines for the final plays.

For Blanchard and Davis, playing sixty minutes each in the era of one-platoon football, their place in football legend was on the line. After almost three unbeaten seasons, it came down to this: a last goal-line stand against Navy. "We had worked for three years to become a great football team," Glenn Davis recalled recently. "We could see that if we lost the ball game, we would be just another team."

At a time when national heroes have passed from the American landscape, when the country's motto might well be "Where have you gone, Joe DiMaggio?" it is difficult to fathom the impact of Blanchard and Davis. But righteous innocence was the mood of the time, and athletes embodied goodness. Only the most sedate sportswriters were content that week to refer to the last game of Blanchard and Davis as "the end of an era." Others reached for more poetic heights, such as "stark, staring tragedy."

Blanchard and Davis. Stars and Stripes. Women who couldn't care less about sports knew about Army's dashing duo. Immigrants who had never seen a football game knew their names, even if they couldn't pronounce them correctly. The pair seemed to dominate the nation's newsreels and magazine covers, as clean-living models for American youth.

Millions of Americans seemed to know that Blanchard was a six-foot, 205-pound fullback, with wavy black hair, brown eyes, full lips, and a rosy complexion that grew redder with exertion. A native of South Carolina, he had a Dixie drawl and an impish charm, liked Westerns and Betty Hutton movies. Off the field he was the picture of relaxation. But when he pulled on his black football jersey with the golden number 35 gleaming on the chest, he became a bone-crushing rusher and tackler. To the late Arthur Daley, Blanchard was "pretty close to being an all-time All-American fullback. He punts sixty yards a clip, he kicks off into the end zone, he's without peer as a blocker, he's a deadly tackler, he's a sure-fingered pass-catcher, he splinters a line and then breaks loose in an open field with the speed and elusiveness of a halfback."

When Army's opponents bunched up the middle to stop Blanchard, they had to contend with Davis around the ends. A 168-pound halfback, Davis had won sixteen letters at Bonita High School in Southern California,

f the Touchdown Twins

starring in football, baseball, basketball, and track. He continued his all-around prowess at West Point. When the football season was over he played varsity basketball, and in the spring he was such a good center fielder that Branch Rickey of the Brooklyn Dodgers said his name on a baseball contract would be worth $75,000, which was a lot of money in those days.

"Glenn is as bashful as a girl on her first date, even though he is All-American," Army coach Earl (Red) Blaik said in 1945. Davis had brown hair, blue eyes, good features, and, it was said, the manners of a gentleman. But, as with Blanchard, the quiet charm disappeared on the football field. In a cover story on the "Touchdown Twins" in 1945, *Time* magazine wrote: "A jet-propelled gent named Glenn ('Junior') Davis . . . carries a special kind of speed that is all his own. After a brief show of hippiness, enough to get around the end, he simply leans forward and sprouts wings. Once outside, he makes would-be tacklers look ridiculous as they try to cope with his speed, his willowy change of pace and starchy stiff arm. . . . Totally unlike most high-pressure halfbacks, he

takes high delight in mowing down a rival tackler while running interference for somebody else."

The stature of Davis and Blanchard was larger than life in those days, before television came along and packaged athletes into commodity size. In the weekly newsreels, every play was spectacular. In the purple prose of pre-television sportswriters, athletes moved more easily beyond stardom into legend, where some still reside: Jim Thorpe of Carlisle, perhaps the best all-around athlete America has ever produced; Red Grange of Illinois, the last three-year All-American before Blanchard and Davis, the "Galloping Ghost" who once gained 303 yards and scored four touchdowns in a span of twelve minutes against Michigan; and Knute Rockne, a good player who became a legendary coach, fabled for his inspirational locker-room talks.

And the football heroes were college players. A professional career was not a goal, just a faintly tawdry coda to an All-American career. That has changed, of course: except in the South and in football-mad college towns, Sunday is football day now. A college star, no

Passing of Reaves Baysinger, sophomore quarterback, led Navy to a first-period score

longer quite the hero he was, has to contend with one overwhelming question: Am I big enough to make it in the pros? Joe Namath fired nifty passes for Alabama, but he entered the national psyche only when the New York Jets gave him $400,000 for signing. Money is where the football action is. Doubters need only ask their local bookie.

The national outlook has changed, too. For much of the population today, it is not clean living and modesty that add dimension to an athlete but rather social rebelliousness, or sporty living. Muhammad Ali, Joe Namath, and Billie Jean King command the adulation that once went to college football players.

Asked recently about the decline of the athlete as hero, Glenn Davis said: "The athlete today doesn't have the feeling of responsibility for his conduct, the feeling for how his life may have an influence on the young people. Not the way we did."

It was different in 1946 for the hundred thousand fans who were screaming themselves into a frenzy in Municipal Stadium, as both battered teams lined up at the three-yard line, Navy ball, first-and-goal—nine feet between Navy and perhaps the most glorious victory in Army-Navy history.

The neutrals in the crowd had long since shifted from Blanchard and Davis to root for Navy, and for its fourth-string sophomore quarterback, Reaves Baysinger, who had not started a game until injuries riddled the Navy backfield late in the season. Most of the 100,000 fans were yelling "Go, Navy, GO!"

But Navy needed no cheers to goad it against Army. The sight of the grey uniforms in the stands, the sight of the black football uniforms, was enough. At both academies, there is the feeling that there are two seasons each year. All the other games are one season. The Army-Navy game is the other season. Coaches have been fired for losing to the other side two years running. Entire football careers are judged on how a man performed in the Army-Navy game. It is safe to say that much of the Davis-Blanchard luster was in jeopardy as young Reaves Baysinger moved his club toward the goal line on the last day of November.

The bedlam of that moment had its origins fifty-six years earlier, in 1890, when the Navy football team first challenged the cadets of West Point. Army did not have a team, but it couldn't refuse a challenge from the Navy. A cadet named Dennis Michie rounded up the best athletes at the Point and taught them the game, which in

Taking handoff from Tucker, Blanchard stampeded 53 yards to score second Army touchdown

those days was more like a bruising version of soccer than what we now know as football.

On November 29, the Middie team sailed up the Hudson and marched across the plains to meet the waiting Army players. On the way they saw a goat feeding in a pasture. The Middies commandeered the goat to lead them into battle against Army. A goat has been the Navy mascot ever since.

The next day, a headline in the *New York Herald Tribune* reported the outcome of the first Army-Navy football game. It said: "Sailor Laddies Beat Soldier Boys." The *Trib* correspondent was so taken with the pretty girls the cadets and midshipmen had brought along to watch the game that he omitted one item: the score. (It was Navy 24, Army 0.) That was Army's only game of the season, and its first game ever.

Shamed by defeat, the Army men hurled back an immediate challenge: Next Year at Annapolis. And Army football began in earnest. The Cadets practiced hard in 1891 and defeated the Middies, 32-16. The series was even, and a sporting tradition had begun.

Seven years later, Dennis Michie, the cadet who had brought football to West Point, was killed while leading a charge up San Juan Hill in the Spanish-American War. His death in combat foreshadowed the fate of many an Army football player in years to come. When West Point eventually built a football stadium, it was named after Dennis Michie.

From that first, casual game, Army-Navy football grew steadily into one of the biggest rivalries in sports, the tradition multiplying with each passing year. There were only four interruptions in the series: from 1894 to 1898, by edict of the United States Government; in 1909, following the death of an Army player; in 1917 and 1918, because of World War I; and in 1928 and 1929, when the academies quarreled about eligibility requirements.

Among the high points of the rivalry were 1924, when center Ed Garbisch kicked four field goals in a 12-0 Army victory; 1926, when the teams helped dedicate Chicago's Soldier Field before a crowd of 110,000 and played to a 21-21 tie; and 1934, when Slade Cutter's 20-yard field goal on a muddy field gave Navy a 3-0 win, its first triumph over Army in thirteen years.

The man who kicked all three extra points for Navy in the 1926 tie was a midshipman named Tom Hamilton. The same Tom Hamilton was the coach of the Middies in 1946. "The Army-Navy game is the closest thing to

war in peacetime you can have," he would say later.

Going into the 1946 game, Army led in the series, 24 to 19, with three ties. The unbeaten Army teams had swept by strong Navy squads in 1944 and 1945, and an even easier game was expected in 1946.

The only blemish on the Army record was that 0-0 tie with Notre Dame, while Navy, unbeaten in 1945 until the loss to Army, had not been faring well. Weakened by postwar resignations from the academy and crippled by injuries to its five best backs, it had lost seven straight games after winning its opener. Going into the finale against Army, Navy was rated a 28-point underdog by the bookmakers. Sportswriters predicted all week that it would be no contest, that it would be a miracle if Navy could even make it close. It was a shame, they wrote, that Mr. Inside and Mr. Outside, the golden boys of the Hudson, should have to end their careers in so predictable a mismatch.

All week long, Hamilton had been saying that his boys would be out to win. Well, the experts noted, what else could he say? All week long, Army coach Red Blaik had been saying that he was afraid of Navy, that they were better than their record indicated. Which, the experts pointed out, was what Red Blaik said before every game. This was the team of Blanchard and Davis, undefeated for three years. Who was he kidding?

Navy had practiced hard for the game. Army had held only light workouts, Blaik not wanting to risk a last-minute injury. The corps of cadets and the brigade of midshipmen had been in similar moods. The West Pointers, confident of victory, hung a few "Beat Navy" bedsheets out their windows and went about their business. The Middies, in contrast, had been building to a frenzy all week. Military rules at Annapolis were relaxed to allow a pep-rally atmosphere: marching midshipmen shouted "Beat Army" on every tenth step. The Wednesday night before the game a huge bonfire rally was held, at which every Navy player vowed to go out to win. The climax came when straw effigies of Doc Blanchard and Glenn Davis were strung in the air and burned. The noise that followed, it was reported, was the loudest ever heard on the Severn River.

Navy even tried a new mascot. A goat called Billy X had been leading them into losing efforts all season. For the Army game, Navy imported a replacement, Billy XI, reputed to be the smelliest, orneriest goat in Texas. After a personal welcome from the head of the academy, he was installed alongside his predecessor. But Billy X soon kicked the daylights out of the young usurper, and the spirted old goat was given a second chance.

The game had been sold out before the season started, and by the time the President arrived with a retinue of generals and admirals, the stands were full. The Pennsylvania Railroad had run twenty-two trains that morning from New York to Philadelphia, and seventeen from Washington to Philly. (A special thirty-six-car train had been scheduled to bring the entire cadet corps down from West Point. But the nation was in the midst of a coal crisis, because of a strike by John L. Lewis' United Mine Workers, and the coal-burning train was canceled. The cadets were brought instead by fifty buses.)

A huge roar arose before the game when a band of Army cheerleaders strode onto the field pulling a large wooden mule—the Army mascot. But the cheers quickly rolled to the other side of the field when the mule turned out to be more Trojan than khaki. A trap door opened in the belly of the mule, and down a ramp came plucky Billy X as the cheerleaders whipped off their Army uniforms and revealed themselves to be Navy men.

Thus did Navy win the pregame antics. The game itself loomed as something else. As the teams took the field for the opening kickoff, their records looked like this:

	Army			Navy	
35	Villanova	0	7	Villanova	0
21	Oklahoma	7	14	Columbia	23
46	Cornell	21	6	Duke	21
20	Michigan	13	14	N. Carolina	21
48	Columbia	14	19	Pennsylvania	32
19	Duke	0	0	Notre Dame	28
19	W. Virginia	0	20	Georgia Tech	28
0	Notre Dame	0	7	Penn State	12
34	Penn State	7			

The odds seemed justified.

Now it was game time. The weather was crisp and clear as Davis and Blanchard, the Army co-captains, met at midfield with Navy captain Leon Bramlett. Navy won the toss and chose to receive. The Middies took the opening kickoff and quickly surprised Army by shifting from their standard T-formation into a single wing. "We were trying to unhinge the Army defensive line some, and to affect their starting right with the snap," Coach Hamilton explained later.

The ploy worked well. The Army line was either jumping offside or waiting too long as Navy alternated between the single wing and the T. Navy moved the ball to the Army 45 before the Cadets held and Baysinger had to punt.

After an exchange of fumbles, the Black Knights began to roll. On second down, Davis went in motion, and quarterback Arnold Tucker hit him with a pass at the Navy 30. From there Davis raced down the sideline until he was knocked out of bounds by Pete Williams on the Navy 14. Blanchard picked up a yard hitting the line. Then Tucker shoveled the ball to Davis, swinging in motion to his left. The speedy halfback crashed between two Navy men and went in to score. The touchdown was the fifty-first of Glenn Davis' college career. He didn't know it then, but it was to be his last. Jack Ray, a substitute guard, kicked the extra point. The score was 7-0, Army. The expected rout had begun.

But not quite. Taking the kickoff on its 19, Navy began methodically to move the ball upfield. Pete Williams and Myron Gerber slammed into the line for small chunks of yardage. Baysinger threw to his left end, Art Markel, for 11 yards, then hit the right end, Bramlett, for 32. The quarter ended with the ball on the Army two-yard line. Two plays later, Baysinger scored on a quarterback sneak. But Bob Van Summern's extra-point attempt was blocked by Army lineman Goble Bryant.

Army began on its 18-yard line after the kickoff. With Blanchard slamming up the middle and Davis sweeping the ends, the Cadets moved to their own 47. Then Tucker called a play designated as 39 Trap, handing off to Blanchard, who erupted through the seven-man line like a rhinoceros in cleats. He cut to the outside and in three quick steps was speeding toward the Navy goal. Several Navy men gave pursuit, but nobody caught Doc Blanchard from behind. Another extra point by Ray made the score 14-6.

Late in the second period, an interception gave Army the ball again, and they moved to the Navy 26. Blanchard was shifted from his fullback slot and sent out as a flanker to the left. The ball was snapped to Davis. Blanchard ran directly at the defensive right halfback, then stopped. Davis pumped a throw. The fake drew the halfback up, and Blanchard sped around him, into the clear. He caught the pass at full speed, for a touchdown: the thirty-eighth of his career, and the last. Ray kicked a

third extra point, and the score at halftime was just about what had been expected: Army 21, Navy 6.

The Army locker room was calm and confident. "Nobody seemed too serious," recalled Joe Steffy, the left guard. The only problem was quarterback Tucker, a first-rate player who had been overshadowed every year by Blanchard and Davis. Tucker's ankle had become swollen during the first half, and he had a shoulder separation. But with no experienced replacement available, Blaik decided to leave him in the game. He could still hand off to Blanchard and Davis. That was all that Army would need.

The Navy locker room was noisy and alive. "It took us awhile to settle down," recalled Bramlett. "I remember telling Captain Hamilton, 'My God, we can beat these guys. They're not hitting out there.'"

When the second half began, Army resumed its relentless attack into Navy territory. But with fourth-and-two on the Navy 31, Tucker surprisingly called for a punt. Davis booted the ball 11 yards out of bounds. Navy took over and began another long, slow march upfield. Baysinger threw short passes into the zone of the injured Tucker, until Blaik had to send in a healthy but inexperienced substitute on defense. He ran line plays past left end Barney Poole, a hard charger who was being suckered in. Navy drove to the Army 18. Then the Cadets stiffened and held for three downs. On fourth down, Navy switched into its single wing. Bill Hawkins started into the line on a buck, then lateraled out to Williams, who skipped 15 yards to the three-yard line. Two plays later, Hawkins went in for the score. Again Navy missed the extra point. The score was 21-12, Army.

The Cadets seemed tired as they took the kickoff and moved it up close to their own 35. On fourth down, with half a yard to go, Tucker was preparing to call for a punt. But the players urged him to let Blanchard go for it. Doc, they felt, could always gain one yard against anyone. Blanchard hit the middle of the seven-man line—and was stopped cold. Exhilarated, Navy took over on the Army 35 and went into action.

A pass to Bramlett picked up 14 yards. Hawkins went through the middle for 16. The quarter ended with the

Elusive Glenn Davis took lateral from Tucker (top),
slipped away from Navy tacklers (2nd, 3rd, 4th photos),
finally broke Baysinger's hold on his jersey (bottom),
and spurted across goal to score Army's first touchdown

"We thought we had them on their knees." TOM HAMILTON

ball on the Army five. At the start of the fourth quarter, Bill Earl took a shovel pass from Baysinger, then slipped a pass into the end zone, where Bramlett made a neat catch. With Coach Hamilton not eligible to do the kicking, as he had done two decades earlier, Navy missed another extra-point try. But the score was 21-18 with most of the fourth quarter left to play.

The ball changed hands several times after that. There were seven-and-a-half minutes to go when Navy took over on its own 33. The Middies churned out three first downs, moving to the Army 23. For three downs the weary Army line stiffened, yielding no gain. But on fourth down, fullback Lynn Chewning raced across the left side of Army's six-man line into the open before being stopped at the three.

Now Navy had first down and goal to go on the three, and the crowd began charging out of the stands and onto the sidelines. There was 1:23 left in the game.

On first down, Chewning hurled himself at the wilting Army line. But Goble Bryant and Hank Foldberg of Army fought through the blockers and stopped Chewning at the line of scrimmage. The clock was running as the Navy men untangled quickly and hurried into their huddle. Across the line, Glenn Davis, playing the full sixty minutes, moved among his teammates, pleading, "Let's not blow it now!"

Baysinger, the sophomore quarterback, still calling all the plays himself, gave the ball to Chewning for the third straight time. This time Big Barney Poole of Army brought him down, again for no gain. Third down, goal to go, on the three. And the clock still running.

On the sidelines, coach Tom Hamilton wanted to call a play that had worked well earlier in the game—a buck-lateral, a fake charge into the line, then a lateral to the outside. He tried to send Bill Hawkins in from the bench with the play. But then referee Bill Halloran stopped the clock and stepped off a five-yard penalty against Navy, for delay of the game. Now it was third-and-goal on the eight, an entirely different situation.

Baysinger shouted signals into the deafening noise, Hawkins started into the line, then flipped the ball out to Williams. But this time Barney Poole wasn't fooled. He stayed with the play and tackled Williams at the four-yard line, in a mass of spectators near the sideline.

The clock was running. Hamilton shouted for the referee to stop the clock. He couldn't see if Williams had

gone out of bounds, but he felt that running into the wall of spectators amounted to the same thing. In desperation, Hamilton waved to Bill Earl to go into the game. The substitution would cost another five-yard penalty—but it would stop the clock, which would give Navy one last play.

Earl dashed onto the field, frantically waving his arms. But the officials, looking at the ball, or the crowd, or the clock, didn't see him. The last seconds ticked away and the gun went off, ending the upset of the century that didn't quite happen. The final score was Army 21, Navy 18.

Both teams trudged sadly off the field—Navy too tired to protest, aching for the victory that had seemed so near; Army weary and downhearted at having three years of glory end like this. In the press box, one writer wrote:

"Navy men the world over will dream to their dying days of what might have been."

With the passage of time—perhaps hours, perhaps days—perspective took hold. The Army men realized that they had put on a mighty goal-line stand, had, in fact, won the game, had preserved their unbeaten record for the third straight year, would go down in the record books as one of the best of all college teams. And the Navy men realized that even in defeat they had covered themselves with glory against a powerful Army team that was supposed to plow them under.

Those who played in the game remember it well. Glenn Davis, now an executive in Los Angeles, and Doc Blanchard, a retired colonel in Texas, both do. For others, the memories died young. Reaves Baysinger, the fourth-string quarterback who did so well that day, died in 1972 of Hodgkins disease, at the age of 45. Charles Galloway, an Army guard, was killed in an air accident in Japan in 1953. Chuck Strahley, a Navy tackle, became a fighter pilot and was killed in the nation's next war, Korea. Bill Kellum, an end, is presumed to have died while a prisoner of war in Korea in 1951. Ug Fuson, a center and halfback, died of a heart attack in 1951 after wounds suffered in Korea; Ray Drury, a tackle, died in Korea in 1951. Coach Red Blaik reported years later that of the undefeated 1944–45–46 teams, seventeen men had died in combat.

John Trent, an end who was captain of a later Army team, died in battle in Korea in 1950. "I was with Trent when he got killed," tackle Joe Steffy said. "I remember he was the best man at my wedding on a nice day in April, and I buried him in the snow in November."

Coming on strong in fourth period, Navy made the score 21–18 with touchdown pass to end Leon Bramlett (below), *then came close to Army goal line in closing seconds.* Overleaf: *Fans tear down goal posts as Army and Navy player demonstrate the spirit of the game by shaking hands*

In first period, Navy struck for its first touchdown as Baysinger mixed runs and passes, finally took the ball over himself from the two-yard line on a quarterback sneak

With the score 7–7, Army came back for a touchdown on Doc Blanchard's long run

"We were physically tired . . . Emotionally we were down. Not that we didn't want to win. But we weren't really ready to go out and beat them physically like you should be in that kind of game."

DOC BLANCHARD

D & B

Felix A. (Doc) Blanchard, a doctor's son from Bishopville, South Carolina, was raised with a football in his crib, because his dad wanted him to be an athlete. Glenn (Junior) Davis was one of twins born the day after Christmas, 1924, to a bank manager and his wife in Claremont, California. They grew up to become the best-known teammates in football history.

In 1944, Davis, a sophomore, was second in the balloting for the Heisman Trophy, awarded to the best college player in the nation. In 1945, Blanchard won the trophy—and Davis again placed second. In 1946, Davis won the trophy. Both were chosen All-Americans for three consecutive seasons. Never before or since have two players from one team so

Blanchard scores the thirty-eighth touch-down of his career on a pass from Davis

Navy's Hawkins went in for a touchdown at the end of a 58-yard drive to make score 21–12

dominated the football scene. Steve Owen, a professional coach, said he could think of only one thing that could stop them: graduation. He was right.

Hollywood tried to cash in on their exploits in 1947, with a fictionalized version of their careers, called *Spirit of West Point,* in which Blanchard and Davis played themselves. It was no *Jules and Jim.* It wasn't even *Tom and Jerry.* "Blanchard and I didn't come up for the Academy Award that year," Davis recalls.

Davis, who was never injured in a game, tore up his knee while making the film. "In the movie I was to catch a punt in a practice game, fake a handoff in a crisscross punt return, and go sixty yards for a touchdown," he said. "My cleats caught, I twisted my knee, pulled some ligaments, and had to have some cartilage removed."

Shortly after graduation in June of 1947, Davis attempted to resign from his mandatory service hitch in order to play professional football, but his resignation was refused. He served the minimum three years before joining the Los Angeles Rams, but

Blanchard and Davis with coach Red Blaik

the bad knee forced him to quit after two seasons. While with the Rams, Davis wed an actress named Terry Moore. The marriage lasted four years. He later remarried.

For the past twenty years, Davis has been director of special events for the *Los Angeles Times,* promoting charity sports events. The proceeds are used to encourage youth activities.

Doc Blanchard made a career of the military. From 1962 to 1966 he was stationed at the Air Force Academy in Colorado Springs, first as freshman football coach and then as assistant athletic director. In 1968, he flew F105s in eighty-four combat missions over North Vietnam. He had no close calls, he said. He left the Air Force as a colonel in 1971 and now lives with his wife in Burnet, Texas. He is retired.

"I'm doing what I want to do," he said recently in his Carolina drawl. "Fishing, and messing around the house. It's great fun."

The house is in the country, and there are not many neighbors to remember who Doc Blanchard used to be. The white bass and the catfish couldn't care less, and that's just fine with Doc.

Navy took the ball on Army's 35-yard line after Blanchard failed to make two yards for a first down, and the Army bench was concerned

Bramlett catches a 16-yard pass from Bill Earl to bring Navy within three points, 21–18

"We had the feeling that we could do it from the very start. Nobody slept all night long . . . The entire hall was lined with telegrams from all over the world. It was really a very inspiring thing. Something I have never experienced before or after."

DICK SCOTT

Legend Power

More than most sports, college football carries with it a freight of myth and legend that enhances and deepens the game. Thus, a modern-day O.J. Simpson is not merely competing against Notre Dame or Stanford—he is competing against the memories of Jim Thorpe and Red Grange.

Many of the ghosts are statewide or regional. Alumni from different generations can sit in the stands at Ohio State University and debate the merits of Rose Bowl squads from the thirties and the seventies. The beauty of the argument is, who can really judge?

Only three college teams can truly be said to have national stature: Army and Navy, the old service academies, and Notre Dame University of South Bend, Indiana. That fine institution has millions

Municipal Stadium, 1946

*Navy ball carrier Lynn Chewning is wrestled
down as Navy moves to the Army three-yard line*

*Chewning is stopped at the three by Army line
as the final seconds are ticking off the clock*

of "subway alumni"—vicarious Irishmen—who root for Notre Dame wherever it may play.

Sometimes the legends suffer in the long run. Because of the long mandatory service hitch and high academic and personal standards, Army and Navy no longer can recruit the "blue-chip" football player. Noboby with his eye on a million-dollar professional football career is likely to choose four years of academy discipline and as many as five more years of service—perhaps in combat. Yet Army and Navy continue to play the toughest teams in the country, partially out of custom, partially because they can still fill a stadium. In 1973, Army lost all ten of its games (and uncomprehending Army officials fired their fine coach, Tom Cahill). Yet fans at Notre Dame or Penn State or California would not easily believe that a victory over a 1973 Army team was not the same as a victory over Glenn Davis and Doc Blanchard.

The primal football legend involves coach Knute Rockne and his star player, George Gipp, who died of strep throat at the age of twenty-five. Eight years later, Notre Dame was playing—who else?—Army in Yankee Stadium before a jammed house. In the emotional dressing room, Rockne allegedly called his players around him and said that Gipp, on his deathbed, had made two requests. He wanted to join the Roman Catholic Church. And, some day, "when the boys are up against it and the odds are piled high against Notre Dame," he wanted Rockne to ask the team "to win one for The Gipper."

Then Rockne paused, his voice heavy. "All right," he emoted. "This is that game." The players took the field with tears in their eyes, legend has it, and won the game, 12-6, for The Gipper (with Army on

The Gipper (left), *Knuke Rockne* (right, center)

the Notre Dame one-yard line at the final whistle).

The Rockne legend was preserved in a movie called *Knute Rockne, All-American*, in which Ronald Reagan (yes, *that* Ronald Reagan) played Gipp opposite Pat O'Brien's Rockne. Throughout the film, Reagan chewed gum, a subtle example of Hollywood symbolism. In real life, George Gipp did not chew gum. He drank.

But heroes were heroes in those days, with no flaws exposed. It was a rather humdrum Notre Dame victory in 1924 that inspired sportswriter Grantland Rice to begin his story: "Outlined against a blue gray October sky, The Four Horsemen rode again today." Thus was coined one of the best-known nicknames in sports. It took a later journalist, Red Smith, to muse: "From what angle could Granny have been watching?"

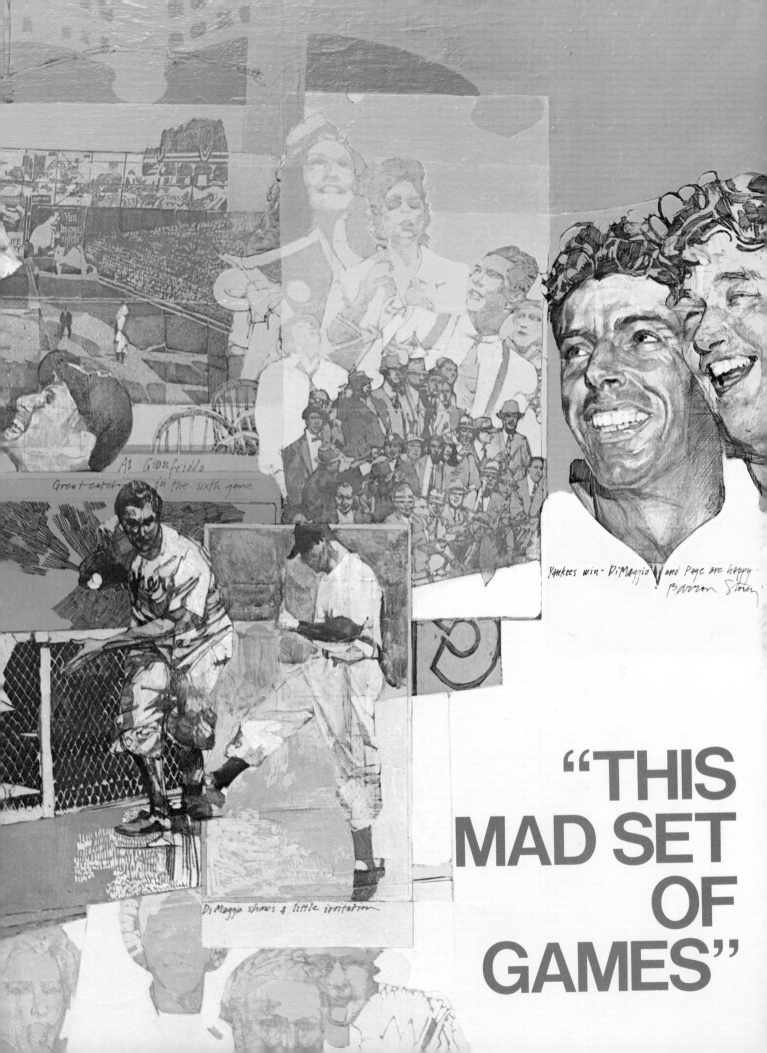

Al Gionfriddo
Great catch ... in the sixth game

Yankees win - DiMaggio and Page are happy.
Barron Storey

DiMaggio shows a little irritation

"THIS MAD SET OF GAMES"

Victory dance: the Dodgers leap with joy after Lavagetto's hit, while Bevens walks to dugout

New York Yankees/ Brooklyn Dodgers World Series October, 1947

By Jack Mann

The 1947 World Series brought Joe DiMaggio back and introduced Jackie Robinson as the first Negro ever to play in a series. Yet these great players performed supporting roles, while Cookie Lavagetto, Bill Bevens, and Al Gionfriddo dominated the headlines.

By all rights, it should have been a clash of dynasties, the perpetual Yankees back in gear again, the Dodgers coming of age in Brooklyn. Yet sometimes the 1947 Series seemed more like anarchy than dynasty. No Dodger pitcher managed to last five full innings; two games lasted longer than three hours. Art it wasn't. Exciting it was. And the Series is still remembered today, not because it was a flash point in history, the times a-changing or any of that business, but because it was like a Charlie Chaplin film—a little tragedy, a little comedy, some acrobatics, and lots of motion.

Jack Mann tells the story from the vantage point of a certain bar on 110th Street and Broadway. Mann did not invent this bar. He was there, in the third row of listeners crowding around a radio, of all things. And yes, he was cutting class from Columbia like the rest of them. The bartender, Mann remembers, also did some bookmaking on the side. Mann had supported himself for the entire 1946 school year on the 1946 Series. But nobody could safely bet on the 1947 Series.

After his three-deep undergraduate days, Mann moved on to *Newsday,* in Garden City, Long Island, where he established one of the country's best sports sections. Later he worked for *Sports Illustrated* and the *New York Herald Tribune,* and as a columnist for the *Washington Daily News.* The author of *The Year the Yankees Lost the Pennant,* Mann is currently a free-lance writer living in McLean, Virginia. G. V.

One fall afternoon in 1947, a batch of class-cutters from Columbia University, along with other idlers, packed themselves into a beer joint at Broadway and 110th Street to experience something they had never experienced before.

They knew they were about to hear another installment of the 1947 Dodger–Yankee World Series, and that was reason enough to cut class and stay out of the October sunshine. As it turned out, whatever else they were missing, it was worth it. Through the noise and the smoke they listened to Red Barber tell them that a Yankee pitcher named Bill Bevens was in the process of pitching a no-hitter—in the World Series.

It was entirely possible that more people in that bar knew what Bevens was doing than among the 33,443 witnesses in Ebbets Field, a few miles away in Brooklyn. Unless those spectators happened to notice the "0" in the Dodger "Hits" column on the scoreboard, they might have missed the point of what Bevens was up to between all the bases on balls he was handing out.

Bevens was a right-handed pitcher who had produced only a 7-13 won-lost record for a team that won 97 games that year. He threw hard, but he didn't seem to know where the ball was going. He walked only four batters in the first three innings, but it seemed like more. After four innings, the Dodgers had not hit a ball hard. In fact, they had only hit six balls fair.

Still, this fourth game of the Series didn't feel like a no-hitter, just as the games already played often didn't look like the two best teams in baseball fighting for a World Championship. That was the way the Series would go. Pitchers were unable to finish what they started, games dragged on, and before it was over, improbable heroes like Cookie Lavagetto, Al Gionfriddo, and Bill Bevens would obscure the Rizzutos and the Reeses. It was frantic, you could say that. One reporter called the Series "this mad set of games." Yet some critics were not satisfied with madness.

"Worst World Series we ever saw," carped Jimmy Powers, sports columnist of the *New York Daily News.* "It took exactly four minutes short of five dismal hours to play the first two alleged games," Powers wrote "Sorry for the radiochatter boys [who] can't say a game is lousy."

Those old enough to remember the influence of Powers' mass-circulated arbitrariness on a generation of New York sports fans can also remember the Dodger-Yankees World Series for the transpontine holy wars they were. They had played one in 1941; they would play five more before the Dodgers would move beyond reach of bridges and subways. But this Series was, as baseball players like to say, something else.

The 1947 Series actually featured the mighty Yankees, with the incomparable Joseph Paul DiMaggio, in a sort of comeback—qualifying for the World Series after three long years of war-induced abnormality. For the Yankees, who had won fourteen pennants from 1921 through 1943, it was a long dry run.

Besides DiMaggio, the Yankees had Rizzuto and Tommy (Old Reliable) Henrich and a rookie catcher-outfielder named Lawrence Peter Berra, who had been nicknamed "Yogi" in his youth. They also had strong arms like Vic Raschi and Allie Reynolds, who would endure into the fifties, and Frank (Spec) Shea, who would win his two decisions in this Series but would not endure. Also, they had Joe Page, a relief pitcher who kept late hours and was nicknamed "The Gay Reliever"—"gay" meaning "jolly" in those days, "reliever" being a pun on an advertisement for "falsies"—"gay deceivers."

The Dodgers, once the butt of all the bad jokes about the borough of Brooklyn, were suddenly respectable. They had won a pennant in 1941, sparked by young Pete Reiser before he hit too many outfield walls going full tilt. They had lost the National League playoff, the first ever, to the St. Louis Cardinals in 1946. And now, like Communist China exploding its first nuclear weapon, they were here—inevitably, the future. They had old standbys like the damaged Reiser, the unreconstructed Dixie Walker and Eddie Stanky, and the shortstop, Pee Wee Reese, called "The Solid Man" by Red Barber. And at first base they had Jack Roosevelt Robinson, Rookie of the Year as the first Negro in the so-called "major leagues," and the first Negro ever to play in the Series.

The Yankees' 5-3 victory in the opener seemed somehow dull once the Yankees exploded for all five runs in the fifth inning. A two-run double by hulking Johnny Lindell was the big blow in that rampage. Page saved Shea's victory over Ralph Branca. The game was briefly enlivened by Jackie Robinson, who stole a base to set up

This Mad Set of Games"

Brooklyn's first run, then discomfited rookie pitcher Spec Shea with his yes-I-will move off first until Shea simply dropped the ball, for a balk. If big-league pitchers had not yet attained a détente with baseball's first black man, the press was also less than comfortable with Robinson. "The swift Negro" of Tuesday's Game One became "the usually reliable Negro" on Wednesday, when he joined a general Dodger collapse by booting an easy ground ball.

The condescension record would be broken in Game Six, when Robinson, with the Dodgers a game down, took all the air out of Phil Rizzuto in a play at second base. "Rizzuto went down under a flying block by Robinson," Joe Trimble of the *New York Daily News* reported.

"It was the Negro's right to break up the DP and he played it clean and straight, but the crowd booed as he left Rizzuto crumpled in a heap. It seemed Phil must be suffering from the collision but, after getting his breath back, he was able to continue." Whew. But that was a good game. First the bad part.

The Dodgers were as embarrassed as a team can be in their 10-3 failure in the second game. Allie Reynolds coasted for a nine-hit effort while the Yankees banged fifteen hits off an assortment of Dodger pitchers. George (Snuffy) Stirnweiss had three hits and Lindell drove in two more runs.

But the main sufferer was the once-sensational Pistol Pete Reiser, whose humiliation was so stark that not

Almost in Stadium bullpen, Gionfriddo makes amazing catch of DiMaggio's home run drive

The men and the action: DiMaggio
is out at second (above)
as Stanky fires on to first

DiMaggio and George McQuinn,
top Yankee hitters, work on
bats before the start of the Series

Dodger president Branch Rickey
consoles manager Burt Shotton
after the Dodgers' defeat

even the Yankees could enjoy it. Some of the Yankees could remember the swift, sure young batting champion they had faced in 1941, and after Reiser's ordeal on Wednesday even the superaloof DiMaggio tried to explain the horrors that happened in center field that day. It was as if the Stadium were a colosseum and the smoke-filtered sun a tawny spotlight on Reiser's torments. Pete fell down chasing one triple, lost two others in confusion ("Gotta see the ball first, while it's in the shade," he muttered afterward, "*then* flip the glasses down. . . ."), let a pop fly fall in front of him for a double, and had a single filter through him. It was awful.

Although the third game was disgraceful, as the *Daily News's* brash, young Dick Young suggested, at least it was long—the longest Series game ever, a 185-minute, eight-pitcher, twelve-walk mishmash won by the Dodgers, 9–8, because innkeeper Hugh Casey put a stop to the nonsense for the last three innings. Somehow all seventeen runs were earned, the Dodgers getting six of them in the second inning, chasing the well-traveled Bobo Newsom in the process. DiMaggio drove in three runs, which wasn't quite enough.

Perhaps the most notable event was the first Series pinch home run, which should have been the second. In the seventh inning, off Ralph Branca, Yogi Berra hit a ball on top of the scoreboard. The outfielders always

had to stand around underneath to see if a ball would bounce back. This one stayed up there. Home run. The inning before, Yankee bonus boy Bobby Brown had clouted a Branca pitch against the foul-pole screen, fifteen feet above the wall, a home run everywhere ever afterward, but not in 1947. Screens on foul poles were novel, brought on by a riot that threatened in the Polo Grounds in 1939, when Harry Craft hit an either-or cheapie for the Reds. Thus Ebbets Field, with its *sui generis* tradition, had a ground rule that said such a ball was in play. Two-base hit.

Trivia mounted, but the Series dragged and Jimmy Powers's patience waned. "Tch-tch!" he chided in his Molly Bloom format, "more passed balls and hit batters! Where are the pros of yesteryear?" The Brooklyn pitchers' record of nobody's "going nine" in a seven-game Series would be tied by the 1960 Pirates. But no Dodger even "went five."

In the fourth game, Harry Taylor went none. The sore-elbowed rookie left after two singles and an error by Pee Wee Reese, the usually reliable Caucasian shortstop, loaded the bases, and a walk to DiMaggio forced in a run. Into such a predicament strode Hal Gregg, who had fireballed his way to a 5.88 earned run average during the season. But don't go away. From this rocky beginning would develop one of the most improbable games

Signing contract with Dodgers, Jackie Robinson became first black to play in major leagues

Pee Wee Reese slides safely into third on Robinson's single in the fifth game of the Series

'uto scores in seventh game as catcher
:e Edwards leaps for throw from Carl Furillo

in Series history, as the obscure Bill Bevens would keep getting Dodgers out, his success sandwiched among all the walks. And while Bevens careened toward his destiny, neither purist nor Philistine would care how many hours and minutes it took to end.

Gregg, who stood three victories away from the close of a never-was career, got out of that inning with no more damage. For six more innings Gregg was what the Pirates would think they were getting when Branch Rickey unloaded him the following spring. Striking out five and walking three—none where it hurt—he gave up only one run, when Billy Johnson led off the fourth with a triple off the center-field gate and Johnny Lindell followed with a double high off the scoreboard.

Meanwhile, strange things were happening to the Dodgers at the plate—when Bevens could locate it. In the fifth the Dodgers scored, on two walks, a bunt, and an infield out. That gave them a total of one run and no hits for five innings—as Red Barber so clearly explained when the Dodgers came up in the sixth.

Baseball tradition says that nobody in the ball park (except maybe the opposition) mentions a no-hitter while it is in progress, lest they jinx the pitcher. Sports announcers, being employees of the ball club or the sponsors, do what they are told. But Barber had made up his mind a long time before.

"I had a decision to make," he said. "Was I a reporter or a dealer in superstition?"

He, at least, was a reporter. While other announcers quaked in their boots, he described no-hitters. He had first done it in 1938 while working for the Cincinnati Reds as Johnny VanderMeer worked on his second no-hitter (and got it). He did it again in 1947 while working for the Dodgers, when Ewell Blackwell of Cincinnati went into the late innings (and gave up a hit). Nineteen years later, more gray than red but still as honest, and working for the New York Yankees, he would tell the people out there that only 413 fans had shown up for a nothing September game in Yankee Stadium. He would also be fired days later, partially for that.

So Barber's position was established: tell the truth. The three-deep gang in the bar at 110th Street and Broadway knew just what the score was as they listened to the radio commentary,* supplied by Barber and Mel Allen, the Voice of the Yankees. It was Allen who had dubbed Tommy Henrich "Old Reliable," and it was the thirty-four-year-old Henrich who would have the last chance to cram this mocked and vilified World Series

*In 1947, radio rights were worth $175,000. There was also limited television coverage, for which the clubs received $65,000. Twenty-five Series later, this amount would not quite buy enough commercial time to See Joe Namath Get Creamed.

into the file-and-forget category. Tommy the Clutch was waiting at the plate in the ninth inning, as Hugh Casey came in from the bullpen with the bases loaded and one out, the Dodgers still hitless and still losing, 2–1. The Series' star hitter (.333, with a .500 slugging average) faced the Dodgers' only effective pitcher as the Dodgers faced oblivion.

A big hit by Henrich would not precipitate a rush for the exits, but it would render Bevens' potential and sloppy no-hitter moot: nice, but not necessary. Even a non-hit—a fly, or a grounder to the second baseman—would deliver the "insurance" run that would deprive the Dodgers, in their last turn at bat, of tools like the sacrifice and the stolen base (Brooklyn had stolen six, and the unsophisticated Berra was catching again).

Those were the stakes, but there had to be a side bet. Henrich and Casey had to be thinking of another ninth inning of another one-run game, in the same setting, six years and one global war earlier. Casey had given Henrich a pitch down-and-in, and Tommy had missed it. And Mickey Owen had missed it, too. A lot of people said it must have been a spitter. A lot of people still say that when a very good pitcher makes a very good pitch to a very good hitter. Hugh Casey killed himself in 1951, after three years of failure, but Tommy Henrich was at home in Massillon, Ohio, to tell about that pitch of 1941:

"Greatest curve I ever saw, and Owen said likewise. I knew he wasn't supposed to have a good curve, and that was a three-and-two pitch. It just broke down through the strike zone. I've been asked a dozen times why I didn't hold up, because it was a lousy pitch. Well, all they saw was where it hit Owen's glove, down low."

Both men had been twenty-eight in that 1941 confrontation—baseball's prime age—and they'd never be better. But would they be smarter in 1947? Both of them? All the great ones, it is axiomatic, "have an idea up there [at bat]" or "out there [on the mound]." On October 4, 1947, it turned out, Old Reliable Tommy The Clutch Henrich had no idea up there. "One of the lousiest mental preparations I ever had. Usually I'd lecture myself, but I can't remember a blooming thing I was thinking. . . ."

To hear Henrich tell it, Casey also didn't have much of an idea out there: "Oh, I don't know what he threw,

but I know I'm not about to bounce that pitch back to him. Yeah, it was a strike, but it was nothin'. I'm gonna pull that pitch. Could'a hit it out of the ball park. But I was kinda stupified. . . ." The first pitch did bounce back to Casey, who started a 1–2–3 double play, and Bill Bevens' ninth inning was going to matter, after all.

By then the entire crowd was hip to the no-hitter, untidy as it was. There was a civic gasp as Bruce Edwards' drive backed Lindell against the left-field wall for the first out. After Carl Furillo walked, Spider Jorgensen fouled out to thirty-eight-year-old George McQuinn at first base. Dick Young of the *News* noted from the press box high over home plate that McQuinn "was white as a sheet as he made the catch."

It was managing time. Al Gionfriddo, a ten-second-flat sprinter in high school, thief of 51 bases in the Eastern League in 1944 and .175 spear carrier for the 1947 Dodgers, replaced Furillo and did little deep knee bends on the first-base bag. It is standard for a man on first with two out to try stealing second, if he can run at all. A hit scores him from second, the logic goes; it takes two hits to score him from first. The Dodgers, with no hits, could not figure on two.

The crowd would have been very much surprised to see Pete Reiser hitting for Casey if the crowd had known where he'd been. In the first inning of the third game, Pete had made his cheerless Series fairly complete by jamming his right ankle in an attempted steal (unsuccessful, of course). During batting practice the next day the swollen ankle would not support him, so he retreated to the clubhouse to soak it in hot water. He dressed and sat on the bench for three innings, then went to soak it again. It was Reiser's idea, against trainer Harold Wendler's judgment, to go back to the dugout in the seventh.

Burt Shotton was the Dodger manager; Leo Durocher had been suspended for a year for involvement with undesirables. Shotton called for Reiser to pinch-hit, possibly for reasons beyond the fact that Shotton had no other left-handed hitter available. Pete could not have run out any kind of ground ball, and the Yankees knew it. But perhaps they—and Shotton—had the feeling that this snake-bitten man at the plate, this aging athlete of twenty-eight, for all the bludgeonings of outfield walls, the drag of three dreary years of wartime service, bitter disappointment in his personal life, and the wretchedness of that day before yesterday, was the ethos of the new, liberated, dignified Brooklyn Dodgers.

The long walk to the locker room—Bevens and DiMaggio reflect Yankee feelings after no-hitter turned into a loss

The Dodgers were not funny any more, and it was their $100 "find," a fugitive from the St. Louis Cardinals' "Chain Gang," who first gave them class. Perhaps Shotton sensed that Reiser would have some extra dimension to him—and that the Yankees would not mess with him.

The count was two balls, one strike, when Ray Blades, the third-base coach, gave Gionfriddo the sign. He could have sent a singing telegram. Bevens, knocked after the game by mouthy Yankee president Larry MacPhail for "not holding him close enough," came in with a high fastball. If Gionfriddo had a good jump on the pitcher, he lost it when he spun his wheels at the start.

"I sort of slipped," he recalls, and was "a little late" when he belly whopped into second. Berra's throw was high and the play wasn't close, but the crowd seemed to catch its breath until umpire Babe Pinelli flapped his palms down.

What happened next was so delectably second-guessable that it drew an innuendo from John Drebinger on Page One of the *New York Times*. With the count three-and-one, Yankee manager Bucky Harris—also new that year—ordered Bevens to deliver a fourth ball to Reiser, who limped to first as the bearer of the potential winning run. That, to strict constructionists of The Book, was a no-no. "Most observers," Drebinger wrote, "seemed to

Yogi Berra, George McQuinn (with glove), Joe Page and George Stirnweiss lost this argument to umpire Babe Pinelli, but the Yankees won the game, the first in the Series, 5–3.

feel the usually astute Yankee skipper had pulled something of a strategic 'rock.'"

In Harris' explanation, Reiser's abilities made the situation "an exceptional case." Pete already *was* the winning run as he stood at the plate, "because he has power and could hit a home run. I knew that Stanky [the next batter] would be easier to pitch to, and that they were out of left-handed hitters. . . . I'd do it again, tomorrow. A single drives the tying run in and the winning run is on base anyway." The essence of Harris' thought was that a three-and-one count is a heavy advantage to give any hitter, especially a good left-handed hitter against a right-handed pitcher who, however good, had already thrown a day's allotment of pitches. MacPhail didn't knock that logic.

With the no-hitter still one out from ludicrous reality, Shotton called for Harry (Cookie) Lavagetto to bat for Stanky. Now three men in the drama were playing their next-to-last major-league games. Not Cookie nor Bevens nor Gionfriddo would make their teams the next spring or any team again.

The Dodgers' scouting report had told the right-handed Bevens to pitch the right-handed Lavagetto high and away. It seemed a good idea when Cookie swung at the first pitch and missed. Another fastball, high and away, and Lavagetto hit one that Henrich, playing the batter to pull, couldn't reach in right field. It rattled off the concrete, and Bevens, backing up home plate as a professional pitcher should, watched Gionfriddo run across home plate just ahead of pinch-runner Eddie Miksis, who came in on the seat of his pants, not because the play was close but because he was a kid. Then Bevens watched umpire Larry Goetz brush the dirt off home plate, as if there were going to be more baseball played that day instead of a wild celebration of the 3–2 Dodger victory.

Jolted by losing both a no-hitter and a World Series game on one swing of a rusty pinch-hitter's bat, Bevens somehow managed to pose for a picture with the silly-grinning Cookie ("I assume he'd have done it for me," Bevens reasoned). Bevens wanted to know one thing: would it have been "in" (the right-field seats) in Yankee Stadium? Yes, people had to tell him, it would have been. The right-field corner in quaint little Ebbets Field was 297 feet from home plate, twelve inches more distant than the forty-three-inch fence cleared by the home runs of Ruth (and Berra and Maris and Pepitone). In

right-center, where the Brooklyn scoreboard began at 352 feet, the Stadium was 344.

So Bevens had to accept that he would have been a loser in either borough. Manager Harris was second-guessed by the press and the fans that day, but the Yankee players were heard to mutter about the scouting reports, neatly mimeographed things prepared from the reports of their coaches, Charley Dressen and John (Red) Corriden, who had been shanghaied away from Brooklyn by Larry MacPhail, presumably bringing all the family secrets with them. "The sheets said to throw hard to Lavagetto," Bevens said later, "and away from him."

"Hard," Lavagetto said much later. "Hell, yes. But inside, tight. They were doing me a favor if they didn't jam me." Cookie was only thirty-two, but physical problems and the loss of four years in the service had aged him. The first property older players lose is their reflexes; a pull hitter, no longer "getting around" on a fast pitch, finds himself hitting the ball just as hard, but straight-away—long outs. Lavagetto's drive hit concrete in the opposite field, and all of Brooklyn toasted him.

Given a new respectability, the 1947 series produced a fifth game that was classic in its simplicity. Shea pitched nine full innings, of all things, and even drove in the first run himself, in the second inning. Rex Barney, twenty-two-year-old embodiment of the cliché fireballer who could throw the strawberry through the locomotive if he could hit the locomotive, lasted two outs into the fifth inning—longest of any Dodger starter—despite nine bases on balls. He fanned DiMaggio with the bases full and none out in the first, but it was an upstairs home run by DiMag that did him in, 2–1. Robinson drove in the Dodgers' only run with a single in the sixth. Second-guess: Arky Vaughan's pinch double in the seventh would have tied it if young Carl Furillo, who had hit .295 for the season, had bunted successfully. A dozen years later old Carl Furillo went into his sixth series, .300 lifetime, and still couldn't bunt.

Sunday, the day of Al Gionfriddo, was the longest game. The Yankee Stadium game began at 2:06 P.M. because of the New York blue law. It was into its third hour by the sixth inning, when Gionfriddo was sent in as a defensive replacement for Eddie Miksis in left field for the fourth-to-last inning of Gionfriddo's major-league life.

With two out and two on in the sixth, Joe Hatten,

Brooklyn's left-handed specialist at beating second-division teams, pitched to DiMaggio. Joe took that flawless swing and hit the longest ball the '47 Series would see. "I have seen many, many greater plays," Reese reflected later, "but I did not expect that one to be made." It was headed for the left-field bullpen, toward the 415-foot sign. Bobby Bragan, the extra catcher in the bullpen, was ready to catch the ball when Gionfriddo, a southpaw, leaped and back-handed it. "I do remember," said Reese, "wondering where the hell he had been playing for DiMaggio."

"Shotton said play him to pull," Gionfriddo recalled. "Keep him from getting an extra-base hit." It is sound practice to "guard the foul line" in late-inning crises, but common tactics did not necessarily apply to Yankee Stadium geography or to DiMaggio, who had hit as many as 46 home runs in a season and was his league's Most Valuable Player in 1947 for the third time.*

Gionfriddo's catch helped the Dodgers struggle through seven innings with an 8–5 lead. Seven of those runs were earned off Reynolds and his five successors, as Reese made three hits and drove in two runs. The Yankees got more hits, fifteen to twelve, chasing starter Vic Lombardi in the third inning. By the start of the eighth, it was 4:48 P.M. and getting darker as Commissioner Happy Chandler huddled with the umpires. If the score was tied at the end of nine, Chandler decreed, the World Series would be played under lights, like a carnival. Hugh Casey took care of that, coming into a two-on, none-out ninth inning and squelching the Yankees with only one run. Ralph Branca was the winner of the 8–6 decision, which tied the Series; Joe Page, the playboy relief pitcher, was the loser. The game took three hours and nineteen minutes to complete—breaking Wednesday's record.

In the finale of the Series (by then known in the tabloids as "this mad set of games" and "dizziest of all time") Shea started with one day of rest, while the Dodgers' paucity of pitching caught up with them in an ironic way. Shotton started Hal Gregg, because he hadn't pitched for two days and because the or-else was Harry

Taylor. Gregg retired the Yanks in order in the first. In the second, the Dodgers took a 2–0 lead as Bruce Edwards and Spider Jorgensen drove in runs to chase Shea. There were still men at second and third with one out when it became Gregg's turn to hit. He was a good hitter "for a pitcher," .265 for thirty-four at-bats during the year. But he was no Arky Vaughan, or even a one-legged Pete Reiser. If Shotton were alive* he would probably admit to being tempted, but if he hit for Gregg, who would pitch? It was too early for Casey, who had been in every game but the lopsided second one. So Gregg hit, right at Rizzuto, and soon it was too late for Casey.

The Yankees came back for a run in the second inning. Then it was the fourth inning and the Yankees put men at first and second with two out. Bucky Harris, the manager, had the option of hitting for Bevens, who had pitched well in relief of Shea. In the bullpen, Harris had Joe Page, who had been rudely whacked around by the Dodgers the day before and wanted very much to pitch. Only in 1947 and 1949, and never again, Joe Page on his good days operated as the best pitcher in the world.

Dr. Robert W. Brown, later a cardiologist and more recently president of the Texas Rangers baseball team, remembers it well. In 1947 being "the highest-paid bonus player in New York history," as MacPhail advertised him, was somewhat like being the tallest midget in town, but Bobby Brown did get $52,000, salary and all, spread over three years, which was useful to a twenty-two-year-old medical student. And that day Dr. Brown did get what he could call, on the eve of his fiftieth birthday, his thrill of a lifetime.

Bevens had entreated Harris to let him stay in the game, for redemption, but Bucky called on Brown, his "Golden Boy," who had walked, doubled, and singled in three pinch-hit spots. Brown was golden again, lashing Gregg's 3–1 pitch to left for a double, tying the score. ("I knew where my folks were sitting," Brown recalled recently. "Standing out there on second base, I could see my dad throw his hat in the air.")

Henrich drove in the tie-breaker one out later with a

---

*Even though Ted Williams of the Red Sox outdid DiMaggio in batting, .343–.315; home runs, 32–30; runs batted in, 114–97; runs scored, 125–97; games played, 156–141; doubles, 40–31; bases on balls, 162–64; and total bases, 335–279. Williams struck out more times, 47–32, but DiMaggio hit into more double plays, 14–10. Joe had him in triples, 10–9, and stolen bases, 3–0. That was The Way It Was.

*"Kindly Old Burt," as Dick Young of the *New York Daily News* later tagged him, died in 1962, at the age of seventy-seven. K.O. Burt (naturally) was dismissed as Dodger manager after three seasons, having won two pennants and lost a third in the tenth inning of the last day of the season.

single off Hank Behrman—the third time in the Series that "Old Reliable" had put the Yankees ahead for keeps. Allie Clark and Aaron Robinson drove in runs in the sixth and seventh innings, respectively, which was enough, that day, for Page. The once and future playboy allowed one Dodger to reach base: Miksis, on a single with one out in the ninth and the Yanks ahead, 5–2—the final score.

Page was a hero, and this strange World Series was finally over. The "mad set of games" had its fitting epilogue. Even as the Yankees celebrated in the clubhouse, the tempestuous club president, Larry MacPhail, circulated to announce he was quitting the New York Yankees.

An unpredictable and volatile man, MacPhail had been feuding with the other Yankee owners, Dan Topping and Del Webb. Later that day, barring the press as if he knew what he was going to do, he punched one minor Yankee official at the victory party and reaffirmed his departure—getting $1.6 million for his share, a profit of $700,000 for his three-year tenure. MacPhail's intrusion upon the celebration seemed just about the right way to end one of the weirdest of all World Series.

Acrobatic leap by Phil Rizzuto came in sixth game as he completed double play to get Robinson at second, Dixie Walker at first. Overleaf: The bomb that exploded a no-hitter—Lavagetto's double off the right field wall

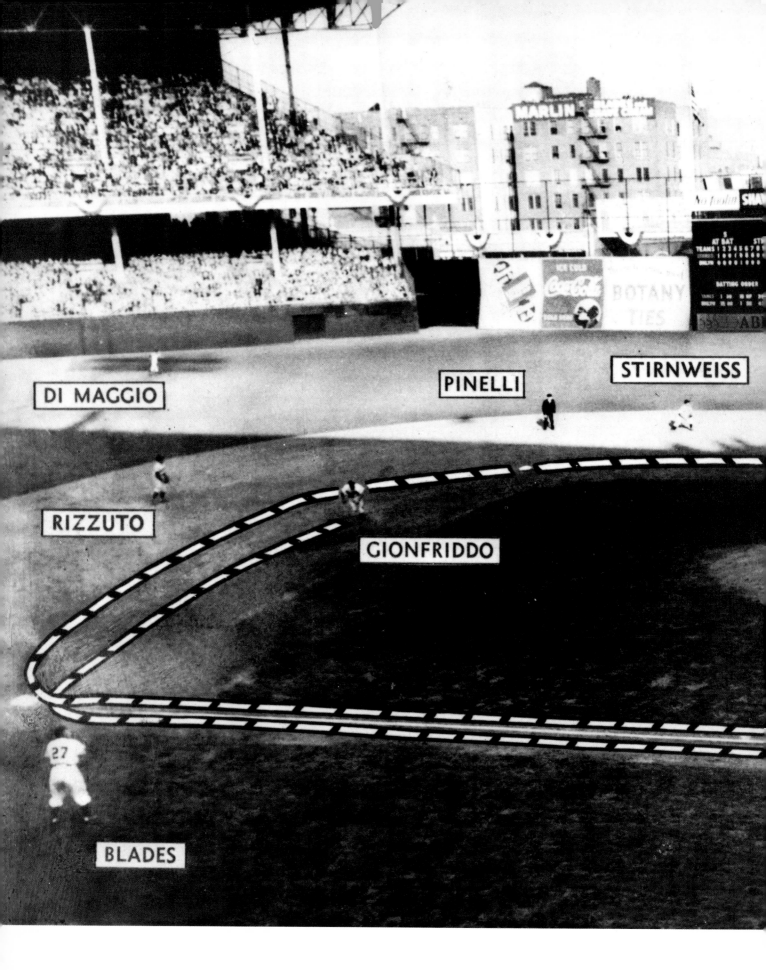

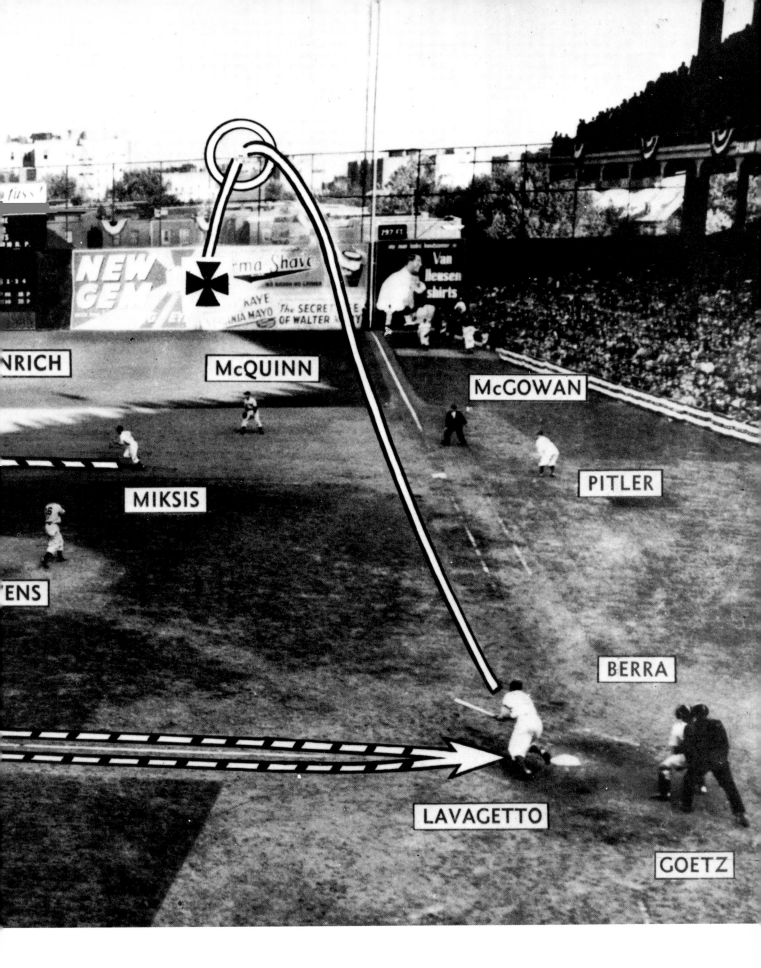

NRICH

McQUINN

McGOWAN

MIKSIS

PITLER

ENS

BERRA

LAVAGETTO

GOETZ

*Tommy Henrich slammed hit in first game
as Yankees' "Spec" Shea got 5–3 win*

*Joe DiMaggio clouted home run, drove in
three runs, but Dodgers won third game, 9–8*

A manager's hug

The "In and Out" Man

Cookie Lavagetto's storybook drive hit the concrete right-field wall just above a sign that said Danny Kaye and Virginia Mayo were starring in *The Secret Life of Walter Mitty.* You could look it up.

"As an expert major-league outfielder, " Tommy Henrich said an epoch later, "I knew it was creamed, *at least* to the wall. But fifteen feet high, or seven? That was the dilemma: if I get away from the wall to play the carom and it's only six feet high, I've given away a no-hitter. If I go to the wall and it's too high to catch it, I've given away the game."

Very professional Henrich had done his homework, having Joe Page fungo line drives off the tricky wall for fifteen minutes in pregame practice. In the previous inning he had "owned" the wall,

leaping to catch Gene Hermanski's menacing drive. Now he played the right-handed Lavagetto to pull, "because Joe [DiMaggio] said to c'mon over. I guess Dressen told him, and who knew better? Not the most scientific approach . . . 'Get away,' I said to myself. 'You can't catch it.' But I had committed myself. The carom hit the hell of my glove and dropped. Pretty good play, really, but that took one second: one extra base for Miksis, one ball game."

Cookie's wife, Mary, couldn't talk when she picked up the phone in Oakland a few minutes later. Some of her sobs may have been postnatal emotion: fifteen days earlier she had borne her first child, Harry Michael, Jr. But Mary Lavagetto also knew her man was in that World Series on a pass. She had known his despair the year before, when he went to spring training a month early, after four seasons

*Fans examine right field wall, trying to pinpoint
spot where Lavagetto's hit landed*

Yogi Berra came through with first pinch-
hit home run in Series history in third game

Bevens allowed one run but no hits until
he faced Lavagetto in ninth inning

in the Navy, and discovered at thirty-one that he
couldn't play baseball anymore. Bone chips "locked" the elbow of his throwing arm, and surgery
didn't help enough. "When I ran hard my right leg
doubled up, like a charley horse. The doc used ethyl
chloride and burned half my butt off, it felt like."
Keeping his symptoms to himself, and moved by
the acerb encouragements of manager Durocher,
Cookie winged it through 88 games in 1946. He hit
only .236, some of it helpful, he recalls: "A double
that went foul by inches" would have clinched the
pennant, saving the Dodgers from the embarrassing
debacle of the playoff loss to the Cardinals.

Even with each team allowed to carry three extra
returned servicemen, it was unlikely the pragmatic
Durocher would have found room for Lavagetto
again. But Commissioner Happy Chandler disap-
proved of some of Leo's friends and set him down
for the 1947 season. "Interim" manager Burt Shotton
had a fatherly talk with Lavagetto and Arky Vaughan,
another superannuated third baseman who hit left-
handed—better than some people in the Hall of
Fame. "He said we'd be in and out, but we could
help."

Lavagetto was in and out of forty-one games that
season, two as emergency first baseman when "the
Negro," as the press persisted in calling Jackie
Robinson, had an aching back. In that ninth inning
on October 3, Cookie wasn't sure when Shotton
pointed at him that he wanted him to bat, but it had
to be. Vaughan had batted in the seventh. The only
other hitters left were nineteen-year-old Tommy
Brown, and two catchers: Bobby(.194) Bragan and
some big kid named Gilbert Ray Hodges.

"Burt says go up and hit
and I went up and hit.
I thought
Shotton was great.
Because if
Leo was around,
I don't think
I would have
been there."

COOKIE LAVAGETTO

Double off the scoreboard by Johnny Lindell drove in Yanks' second run in fourth game

"I realized I was in Brooklyn. In any other ballpark, I believe, it would have been caught. It was kind of sickening. And the next day, you had the band in Brooklyn playing, 'Lookie, lookie, here comes Cookie.'"

FLOYD BEVENS

Arm Trouble

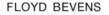

It was a good story, written for *Collier's* magazine in 1951: how Bevens had hurt his arm "midway" through his near no-hit effort against the Dodgers, and how his wife "remained up almost the entire night before the seventh game, massaging Bill's right shoulder so he would be ready for the money game if [manager] Harris needed him."

"Well, no," said Bevens, now the regional manager for a trucking company in Salem, Oregon. "Actually, I believe I hurt it in the [Oakland] Oaks' benefit game, later in the fall. DiMaggio and a lot of Bay Area guys always played in it. I had laid off almost a month, and I think that did it."

If that didn't, there was the leg he injured officiating basketball during the winter. In any case he could not make the Yankees' 1948 team, and the arm really hurt by then. "They sent me to a doctor in Baltimore and they kept me with the Newark team most of the season. But I couldn't pitch." Bevens was sold to the White Sox but couldn't make it in 1949. By 1951 he was pitching for his hometown Salem Senators (payroll $4,000 a month for 17 players) in the Class-B Western International League, where he had pitched two no-hitters for Wenatchee in 1939.

"Cincinnati drafted me," Bevens said, "and I finished the 1952 season with San Francisco in the Coast League. I pitched quite a bit; I got my turn. But I could see the writing on the wall. In '53 I gave it up. I didn't want to be a baseball bum."

The official scorers could have given credit for the seventh-game victory in 1947 to Bevens, who was "the pitcher of record when his team assumes the lead and maintains it to the finish of the game." But they didn't have to: "Do not credit a victory to a pitcher who pitches briefly and ineffectively. . . ." So they gave it to Joe Page, who one-hit the Dodgers over the last five innings.

"Sometimes," said Bevens, "I look back at it that way. They could have given it to me, and that would have been good, to win a World Series game—to have my name in the book, as a winner. But it would have been cheating Joe. He did a wonderful job, and he deserved it—more than me."

Lavagetto's double bounces off wall in
right field with Tommy Henrich chasing it

In fifth game, fastballer Rex Barney
pitched well but was beaten by DiMag homer

The Babe   When a dying Babe Ruth made his last trip to home plate wearing a camel's hair coat in warm weather and rasp-whispering his farewell to "this great game of baseball," Bill Bevens was only a few feet away.

It was a leading memory that Bevens would take away from 1947, the Yankees' fifteenth championship but Bevens' first and last. He shook the weakened hand that had been the muscle of the early championships.

"I'm satisfied," fifty-seven-year-old Bill Bevens said recently, looking back. "I got to do everything I dreamed about. I pitched in the big league, and I met the Babe."

"When I told Bevens I might have jinxed him by announcing a no-hitter in the fifth inning, he said, 'Red, you didn't have anything to do with it. Those ten bases on balls did it.'"

RED BARBER

Jackie Robinson drove in Dodger's' only run
as the Yankees took the fifth game, 2–1

DiMaggio kicks dirt after Gionfriddo's
great catch robs him of a home run

The Catch

"Carl says, 'Play him to pull,'
so I played right down the
line. So when he hit the
ball in left center, which is
415 feet away, I didn't
think I had a chance to get
it at first."

AL GIONFRIDDO

When the ball appeared to him, out of that shimmering shroud of cigarette smoke that was the left-fielder's view of Yankee Stadium on business afternoons in October, Al Gionfriddo did not think he could catch it.

When that ball hit Gionfriddo's glove, and his hat hit the ground, and "my butt hit the bullpen fence," he had three-and-a-fraction years in "the bigs," as the major leaguers put it. He never got another day, which was doubly unfortunate because on February 1 of that year, baseball's first pension plan had gone into effect, guaranteeing $50 per month minimum to every player with five years' major-league service, commencing at age fifty.

"If I never make that catch," he commented in baseball syntax, twenty-seven years later, "I figure I'd have six-seven-eight years in the majors. But Rickey capitalized on me. You know how he always thought of money."

It was possible that Gionfriddo would have failed to make the Dodger varsity on his own demerits in 1948, since the Duke Sniders of the future were arriving en masse. Gionfriddo had reached the major leagues during World War II, stroking .284 off draft-deferred pitching for the Pittsburgh Pirates in 1945. He didn't measure up in 1946—he was only five feet, six-and-a-half inches, and the big boys were back—and in 1947 he was traded to the Dodgers. Gionfriddo had one year in Brooklyn. One catch, really.

So it came to pass that, while the Dodgers' last exhibition game of the '48 spring was rained out,

*Gene Hermanski slides into third as
Dodgers take early lead in seventh game*

Al Gionfriddo and his bride heard on the radio that they had been assigned to Montreal, a Dodger farm team.

Gionfriddo, meanwhile, remained four years at Montreal, where "it wasn't bad. Buzzie was my general manager." Emil J. (Buzzie) Bavasi later moved up through the Dodger ranks to become de facto general manager of Walter O'Malley's great teams, and now is president-investor of the San Diego Padres. His *modus operandi* was to tell players that if they would be fair with him, he would be fair with them—in that order.

"They promised me a coaching job if I'd go to Fort Worth to help out Bobby Bragan." Gionfriddo went: big-league coaching counts as pension time. Then there was the chance of a minor-league managing job if Al would "help out" at Newport News for the last six weeks. "We made the playoffs and I got my release." Each move had been a step down and a put-down for a man whose star had risen swiftly.

With six children, the eldest born in the year of The Catch, the Gionfriddos are now settled in Santa Barbara. Al played out the fifties in the Class-C California League, hitting figures like .330, .348 and .368 for places like Ventura and Visalia. Late in his thirties, by then, he scouted some for the Giants, then was general-manager for the Dodgers' farm team at Santa Barbara for a couple of seasons.

"I'm hoping to get back in baseball in some capacity," Al Gionfriddo said. And then he made a sound that might have been a chuckle. "All these years," he said, "I don't know how many letters I've written to Buzzie."

Dixie Departs

An era ended in the last inning of the 1947 World Series: The Peepul's Cherce made his last out for the Dodgers. That would be Dixie Walker, aging hitting star of the mid-forties, the idol of Ebbets Field, but gone shortly after he grounded to George Stirnweiss for a final out. Walker was packed off to Pittsburgh, along with Hal Gregg and Vic Lombardi, and how could you trade a public favorite who hit .306?

·"The trade was necessary, from a purely cold-blooded standpoint," explained Arthur Daley of the Times, *"to make room for all those fine young stars who Branch Rickey has been accumulating." Well, that too. Walker was thirty-seven years old. He was also as unreconstructed as Scarlett O'Hara. He had "nothing against" Jackie Robinson, but he had been on record since 1945 with his preference not to play with Nigras; Mr. Rickey was giving him his preference.*

Walker was not alone, perhaps not even a minority. "Many of the key Dodgers," Red Barber wrote in 1969, "would put it in writing (during 1946) to Mr. Rickey that if the Negro came, they would go. After the 1947 season two of them, headliners, did go; Rickey sent them." Eddie Stanky, Philadelphian by birth and Alabaman by choice, went to Boston.

Rickey was thinking several jumps ahead, as usual. The man who broke the color line in 1947 would admit, in 1962, that he had also instituted the quota system. The quota Mr. Rickey had in mind for those early years was four.

In 1949, Robinson, Roy Campanella, and Don Newcombe played for the pennant-winning Dodgers. Only three black men, but there was no hurry. Two other stars on those "Boys of Summer" teams (as Roger Kahn called them) were Preacher Roe and Billy Cox, who both came in the Dixie Walker deal, were white, and could play just a little baseball, too.

*Dodger fans gave Dixie Walker new
car in 1948 ceremony at Ebbets Field*

LONG LIVE THE REVOLUTION!

Lou Groza says a few words into the winning shoe

Cleveland Browns/ Los Angeles Rams NFL Championship Game December 24, 1950

By Dave Anderson

owadays new sports leagues are as common as fast-food stands and shopping centers—an endless landscape of new franchises, new nicknames, new heroes, new money. Sometimes the leagues achieve parity; sometimes they disintegrate.

But the new sports leagues have their roots in the sports boom that followed World War II, when fans were eager to spend their postwar salaries on something called the All-American Conference. The best team was the Cleveland Browns, named after Paul Brown, their coach and creator. Brown was such a skillful leader that by 1950 his team was actually playing the electrifying Los Angeles Rams for the championship of professional football.

The fans who braved dreadful Cleveland weather saw an epic game—a match-up of quarterbacks Otto Graham and Bob Waterfield, a match-up of great running backs, a match-up of different backgrounds. And the game was still in doubt when a strong-armed young quarterback stepped back and heaved a pass in the closing seconds.

Dave Anderson, sports columnist for the *New York Times*, has written extensively on pro football, going back to earlier jobs with the *Brooklyn Eagle* and the *New York Journal–American*. Anderson was one of the early reporters to pay attention to the predictions of brash Joe Namath before the 1969 Super Bowl. More recently, Anderson has written *Always on the Run* with Larry Csonka and Jim Kiick—the story of their Super Bowl heroics, leading up to their planned defection (in 1975) to—yes—a new sports league.

G.V.

e hasn't changed that much. Paul Brown is still standing on the sideline on Sunday afternoon, still peering out from under his snap-brim hat, still sending in the next play. As the sixty-six-year-old coach of the Cincinnati Bengals of the National Football League, he is the essence of the establishment. But once he was the rebel of professional football. In the years just after World War II, coaching in a rebel league, he created a monster that was so brutally efficient it destroyed the element of competition and virtually the league itself. But his team, the Cleveland Browns, along with two other teams from the All-America Conference, were absorbed by the NFL for the 1950 season. The San Francisco 49ers won three games that year; the Baltimore Colts won one; but the Browns—named after their coach—emerged as the NFL champions. The rebel emerged as the ruler.

The image of the rebel in pro football today involves Larry Csonka, Paul Warfield, and Jim Kiick signing contracts to jump from the Miami Dolphins to the new World Football League in 1975 for $3.3 million. Or it's the memory of Joe Namath's provocative life-style while guiding the New York Jets of the American Football League to a Super Bowl III victory.

But in his time and in his way, Paul Brown was just as much a rebel. Perhaps significantly, he was also involved in establishing the credibility of another league —or at least the credibility of the team that had dominated that league. In the beginning he was a rebel primarily because of his philosophy of organization. Until he formed the Browns, pro football franchises had been operated casually. The coaches and players disbanded when the season ended and regrouped at training camp. Scouting consisted mostly of studying the college football magazines. Paul Brown changed all that. He popularized the organizational approach to pro football.

Many of the techniques that are accepted procedure today were unknown until Paul Brown introduced them: year-round coaching staffs, notebooks and classrooms, film scouting, grading players from film study, lodging the team at a hotel before home games, specific pass patterns, face bars on helmets, intelligence tests for players to determine learning potential, switching college offensive players to defense, using messenger guards to bring in the next play from the sideline. He also exercised complete control over the Browns' organization.

"Complete control," he said when he returned to football with the newly formed Bengals in 1968, six years after he had been dismissed by Arthur Modell, the Browns' owner, who had intruded on his control. "There is no other way for a team to operate and be a winner."

In the Bengal organization, says a club official, "There is only one vote and Paul has it." And there was only one vote in the Browns' organization when he ran it. His one vote was enough for his four AAC teams to win forty-seven games against only four losses and three ties, plus one playoff and four championship victories. In the 1948 season the Browns were undefeated in fifteen games, including a 49-7 rout of the Buffalo Bills in the championship game. Over a ten-year span through 1955 that included the Browns' first six years in the NFL, his teams won a divisional title each season, four AAC titles and three NFL titles. But when the Browns joined the NFL in 1950, skeptics snickered.

Nearly two decades later, Joe Namath had skeptics, too. He was the quarterback of the Jets, who were about to be sacrificed to the Baltimore Colts, the NFL champions, in the Super Bowl game. At a Touchdown Club dinner in Miami during the week, Namath took a sip of scotch out of a napkin-wrapped old-fashioned glass and stood up to address an audience that included many Colt followers. During his short speech, he said, "And we're going to win Sunday, I guarantee you." The skeptics snickered. But the Jets fulfilled his prophecy, 16-7.

At another Touchdown Club dinner, in Washington in the early months of 1950, another guarantee was made. Otto Graham, the Browns' quarterback, was on the dais with O. O. Kessing, who had been the AAC commissioner. When he got up to speak, Kessing sounded grateful for the invitation.

"It's unusual," Kessing said, "for the head of a defunct league to be invited to such an affair."

"The AAC isn't defunct," Graham insisted a few minutes later. "We simply absorbed the NFL."

Most of the audience laughed derisively, but George Preston Marshall bristled. The president of the Wash-

ong Live the Revolution!

ington Redskins, who had once owned a prosperous laundry, had mentioned earlier that the Browns wouldn't dominate the NFL as they had the AAC. Now, noticing Marshall's displeasure, Graham turned toward him.

"Mr. Marshall," the quarterback said, smiling, "maybe you better buy back a piece of that laundry business if we play the Redskins."

"You probably won't even have a job next winter," the Redskin owner snapped angrily. "Maybe you'd like to drive one of my laundry trucks."

Graham laughed. His guarantee hadn't been quite as explicit as Namath's, but he was clearly confident.

Yet, so was the NFL establishment. When the 1950 schedule was announced, the challenge to the Browns

was obvious. In their season opener, the Browns would oppose the Philadelphia Eagles, the NFL champions the preceding two seasons. And the game would be in Philadelphia, providing the Eagles with a hometown edge. Not that the NFL types were concerned.

"Our weakest teams," George Preston Marshall often said, "could toy with the Browns."

Earle (Greasy) Neale, the coach of the Eagles, minimized the Browns' football skills. "To me," Neale sneered, "the Browns are a basketball team. All they can do is throw."

True, the Browns had dominated the AAC with their passing attack. Graham's favorite targets were his ends, Dante Lavelli and Mac Speedie, and he also threw often

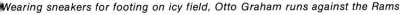

Wearing sneakers for footing on icy field, Otto Graham runs against the Rams

to Dub Jones, a running back who occasionally lined up as a flankerback. But the Browns did more than throw. With 238-pound Marion Motley as their fullback, they ran. And if their offense stalled, they salvaged field goals, with Lou (The Toe) Groza as their placekicker. They also played strong defense, with Len Ford as a feared pass rusher and Bill Willis at middle guard.

But as the Browns-Eagles opener approached, the NFL mystique prevailed. Oddsmakers established the Eagles as a three-point betting favorite, even though the two-time NFL champions were without their most

devastating runner, Steve Van Buren, limping on a broken big toe.

When the Browns won the opener easily, 35–10, they astonished NFL partisans. Graham threw for three touchdowns on plays of 59 yards to Jones, 26 yards to Lavelli, and 13 yards to Speedie. He also scored a touchdown himself, on a one-yard quarterback sneak. He completed 21 of 38 passes for 346 yards as the Browns accumulated 487 yards of total offense.

In the Eagles' locker room, Greasy Neale was asked about the "basketball" team. "They've got a lot of guns

Hard-running Marion Motley barrels into the Rams' "Tank" Younger

don't they?'' Greasy Neale said. "And they use them."

But the most perceptive words were uttered by Pete Pihos, an Eagle pass receiver who had been on their two championship teams. Pihos had showered and dressed, and now, outside the locker room, he walked over to where his wife was waiting.

"What in the world happened?" asked his wife, echoing the reaction of millions.

"Honey," said Pete Pihos with a shrug, "we met a team from the big league."

Not that the Browns breezed through all the NFL teams. Two weeks later they lost to the New York Giants, 6–0, and three weeks after that they lost to the Giants again, 17–13. But these were the only games the Browns lost during the 1950 season. Their 10–2 won-lost record included two victories over the Washington Redskins, 20–14 and 45–21, keeping George Preston Marshall quiet. But the Giants also lost only two games, forcing a playoff for the Eastern Conference title. The Browns won, 8–3, on two field goals by Groza and a safety, qualifying them for the NFL championship game in Cleveland against the Los Angeles Rams, the Western Conference winner. The match-up involved many elements beyond the basic football game.

- The Browns still symbolized the AAC, while the Rams hoped to uphold the NFL's honor.

- In an unusual rivalry, two Cleveland teams were actually involved. The Rams had once played alongside Lake Erie, even winning the 1945 NFL title. But despite the championship, the Rams claimed to have lost $50,000 that year, and Dan Reeves, the Rams' owner, became the first major-league sports entrepreneur to transfer to the lucrative West Coast market. Twelve years later, the baseball Dodgers and Giants would move to Los Angeles and San Francisco—but the Rams had been the pioneers. Now in 1950 they were returning to the city they had abandoned to the Browns and the AAC.

- The contrast in coaches was obvious. Paul Brown was a career coach, an icy disciplinarian. Joe Stydaher of the Rams, once a feared six-foot, four-inch, 250-pound tackle for the Chicago Bears, was a bourbon drinker and a tobacco chewer.

- The Browns were composed primarily of virtual unknowns who had been on service teams coached or scouted by Paul Brown during World War II, while the Rams flaunted such famous college All-America players

as quarterback Bob Waterfield from the University of California at Los Angeles, pass receiver Elroy (Crazy Legs) Hirsch from Wisconsin, and running back Glenn Davis, the Heisman Trophy winner from Army, his service hitch finally over.

As a youngster growing up in Waukegan, Illinois, Otto Graham had not appeared likely to develop into a six-foot, one-inch, 195-pound quarterback. He played the piano, the violin, the cornet, and the French horn. He also played basketball better than he played football.

He went to Northwestern as a basketball player, but the football coach, Lynn (Pappy) Waldorf, saw him throwing passes in an intramural game and suggested he join the varsity. He was a tailback in the single-wing offense when Paul Brown, then coaching Ohio State, first noticed him. After his graduation in 1944, he entered a Naval pilot training program. He was also drafted by the Detroit Lions of the NFL, but during the 1944 season he played for a Naval preflight team attached to the University of North Carolina. He later was transferred to the Glenview, Illinois, Naval Air Station, where Paul Brown visited him.

"When the war is over," Brown said, "I'm going to coach the Cleveland team in a new pro football league. I want you to be my T-formation quarterback."

Except for a few plays installed by Ray Bray, a guard for the Chicago Bears, on the Naval team in North Carolina the previous season, Graham had never been exposed to the intricacies of the T formation, then a relatively new offense.

"I'm not a T quarterback," Graham said.

"Don't worry about that," Brown said, "You've got the ability and we'll teach you the rest."

"But the Detroit Lions have drafted me."

"That's the NFL, we're a new league, the All-America Conference. We're hoping the war will be over soon so we can play in the 1946 season. If you sign, we'll pay you $250 a month as a bonus until the team is ready to play."

"You've got a deal," Graham said.

At the time he visited Graham, Paul Brown was coaching the Great Lakes Naval team. Before that he had been the head coach at Ohio State for three years, and before that, as a high-school coach in Massillon, Ohio, he had an 80–8–2 record over nine seasons.

Brown wasn't selecting players at random or on newspaper headlines. He was building the Browns with players he knew from personal observation. Dante Lavelli, for example, had arrived at Ohio State as a running back but was switched by Brown to end.

"He saw something in my stride," Lavelli once recalled. "I think my steps weren't short and choppy enough to suit his idea of how a back should run."

Lavelli had only one varsity season in 1942 before entering the Army, where he was a sergeant in a rifle platoon during the European campaign. After his discharge, he returned to Ohio State, but not to play football. Paul Brown remembered him and signed him. Paul Brown also remembered another end, Mac Speedie, from the Fort Warren team that opposed his Great Lakes squad. "They have two things in common," Brown once said. "They can catch anything they can touch and after they catch it, they can run like halfbacks."

Lavelli was a six-foot, 192-pounder. Speedie was six feet, three inches and 205 pounds. Ray Flaherty, the coach of the New York Yankees and the Chicago Hornets of the AAC, described them as "those two track stars," but the Browns' pass receivers, each selected to the All-AAC team in 1948, had different styles. "Lavelli has the strongest hands I've ever seen," Brown once said. "Nobody can take the ball away from him once he gets his hands on it. Speedie is more instinctive and more deceptive."

Speedie's speed was remarkable. When he was eight

Rex Bumgardner makes difficult catch of Graham pass as the Browns drive downfield in game's final minutes

years old, he was a cripple. Because of a bone problem since babyhood, his left leg was two inches shorter than his right leg. He was ordered to wear a steel brace on his left leg from his hip to his ankle. Each week for four years he visited an orthopedist, who adjusted a screw on the brace to stretch the leg to its proper length. When the brace was removed, he quickly developed into a star running back and basketball center in Salt Lake City, Utah, then emerged at the University of Utah as a world-class hurdler.

"I don't suppose I ever would have been ambitious enough to excel at athletics if I hadn't been a cripple as a kid," Speedie once said. "I spent so much time eating my heart out because I couldn't play normally that when they took the brace off and I found I had legs that matched, it was like turning a frisky colt out to pasture after a year in a box stall."

Paul Brown remembered Lou Groza, too. Groza had played on the freshman team at Ohio State in 1942 but then entered the Army, which shipped him to the Pacific.

"I was on Okinawa and in the Philippines," recalls Groza, "but wherever I was, I used to rig up something that looked like goal posts and practice kicking."

Paul Brown was perceptive in signing virtual unknowns. He was also lucky. He had remembered Graham, Lavelli, Speedie, and Groza but he had forgotten Bill Willis, who had played at Ohio State for him. Willis was an All-American in 1944, Brown's first year as the Great Lakes coach. During the 1945 season, Willis disappeared into an assistant coach's role at Kentucky State, but when he heard that Brown was organizing an AAC team, he asked his former coach for a tryout.

"Is it all right?" Willis wondered.

"It's all right," Brown assured him.

Brown knew what Bill Willis meant. Bill Willis was black. Many years earlier there had been black players in the NFL, but none had competed in recent years. Late in 1945, the baseball Brooklyn Dodgers had signed Jackie Robinson, who was playing on their Montreal farm team in the International League when the Browns opened their 1946 training camp. In the NFL the Rams, now in Los Angeles, were preparing to sign Kenny Washington and Woody Stode, two black running backs. Willis joined the Browns and impressed the coaches with his agility as a middle guard.

"He's offside," the Browns' center kept insisting whenever Willis sped past him. "He's got to be offside."

Bill Willis wasn't offside. He simply moved faster than the center after the ball was snapped. Middle guard, although the forerunner of the middle linebacker, was a different position with different requirements. The middle guard was considered to be a defensive lineman. Unlike a middle linebacker, he had no pass-defense responsibility. Although a muscular six feet, two inches and 210 pounds, Willis was small by comparison with today's middle linebackers. But in the Browns' programs, he was listed at 225.

"That was a psychological thing," Willis once said. "Paul Brown didn't want the other team to know I was only 210."

Not long after Brown signed Willis, the coach remembered another virtual unknown, another black player. Marion Motley had been a fullback at nearby Canton McKinley High School when Paul Brown was the Massillon coach. Later he had been a fullback when Brown coached the Great Lakes team. When he heard about the Browns, Motley wrote for a tryout.

"Paul wrote back," Motley often has said, "that he thought he had enough backs."

But after the Browns had been in training camp, Motley got a phone call one night.

"I was told," he recalls, "that if I still wanted to try out, to come to their training camp at Bowling Green. But I think I know why they called me. They had signed Bill Willis and I believe they thought they needed a black roommate for him. I don't think they really felt I'd make the team."

Marion Motley not only made the team, he *made* the team. He provided the Browns with a devastating runner to complement their passing. He was also a brutal pass blocker, and was inserted as a linebacker in the goal-line defense.

"He was a great, great linebacker," says Blanton Collier, an assistant coach with the Browns then, later the successor to Paul Brown as head coach in 1963. "Marion Motley was the greatest all-around football player I ever saw. He had no equal as a blocker. And he could run with anybody for thirty yards."

Motley's speed created the draw play, in which the quarterback fades back as if to pass, but hands off to the fullback.

"Most of the people who talk about how great Marion was are thinking of when he came into the NFL with the Browns in 1950 when he was thirty and had two bad knees," says Lou Saban, the Browns' defensive captain during their AAC reign, now the Buffalo Bills' coach. "But he was just a shadow of himself then. They should've seen him in 1946 and 1947, he was really something then."

Even with two bad knees, Motley led the NFL in rushing in 1950 with 810 yards. In one game that season, he galloped for 188 yards in only eleven carries—a 17.1 average that still stands as a one-game NFL record for ten or more carries.

Graham, Speedie, Lavelli, Motley, Groza, and Willis formed the nucleus of the Browns' teams that dominated the AAC. By the time Cleveland joined the NFL, the team had added other talented performers. Dub Jones, an obscure running back with the Miami Seahawks and the Brooklyn Dodgers, was obtained in a 1948 trade. Len Ford, the first towering defensive end at six feet, five inches and 260 pounds, was acquired when the Los Angeles Dons disbanded in the AAC collapse. Meanwhile, Brown was recognized as the dominant genius who sent offensive plays to his quarterback by shuttling guards on every play.

Clearly, the Browns were ready. But the Rams arrived in Cleveland for the championship game with the most explosive offensive team in NFL history. They had set twenty-two records for season offense, scoring 64 touchdowns and 466 points and gaining 5,240 yards total offense in the course of compiling a 9–3 won-lost record.

Those people in Cleveland who remembered the Rams knew it was not an accident. They knew the Rams' quarterback. Bob Waterfield had directed the Cleveland Rams to their 1945 title, the last NFL championship team with a rookie at quarterback. Waterfield was chosen as the NFL's most valuable player that season, a rare honor for a rookie. And by 1950 he had emerged as the symbol of the Los Angeles Rams, not only as their passer, placekicker, and occasional defensive back, but also as the husband of Jane Russell, the glamorous movie star.

He had a quietly firm personality. "Old Stone Face," his wife called him. His teammates spoke of his "inner strength," and they didn't argue with him in the huddle. Once, after Elroy Hirsch had requested a pass that was intercepted, Waterfield glared at him.

"If you don't know what you're talking about," Waterfield said sharply, "keep your damn mouth shut."

During the 1950 season Waterfield had shared the

quarterback position with Norm Van Brocklin, then in his second season. Van Brocklin had the more impressive statistics, completing 127 of 233 passes for 2,061 yards and 18 touchdowns. Waterfield had completed 122 of 213 passes for 1,540 yards and 11 touchdowns. But in the Western Conference playoff with the Chicago Bears the week before the championship game, Van Brocklin suffered broken ribs. Although weakened by intestinal flu, Waterfield threw three touchdown passes to Hirsch and kicked a 43-yard field goal in the 24–14 victory.

Besides Hirsch, Waterfield had another spectacular pass receiver in Tom Fears, who led the NFL that season with 84 receptions, then a record. And behind Davis, a swift runner, the Rams had four big backs—Dick Hoerner, Deacon Dan Towler, Tank Younger, and Vitamin Smith.

Despite the Rams' formidable offense, oddsmakers had established the Browns as a three-point betting favorite—the reverse of their role against the Eagles in the season opener. Moments after the game began, however, Waterfield whipped a pass to Glenn Davis near midfield for an 82-yard touchdown play. In vast Municipal Stadium, only 29,751 customers had shown up, ready to endure intermittent snow flurries, 25-degree cold, and a 30-mile-an-hour wind whipping in off Lake Erie. The Rams' score after just twenty-seven seconds astonished the Browns loyalists among them. But the Browns and their coach remained calm.

"Don't worry about it," Paul Brown told his players. "Just stick to our game plan."

Quickly moving 70 yards in only six plays, the Browns produced the tying touchdown when Graham collaborated with Jones on a 31-yard pass play. But the Rams retaliated with an 80-yard drive in only eight plays, with Hoerner smashing three yards for the touchdown and a 14–7 lead. Early in the second quarter, Graham found Lavelli for a 35-yard touchdown play. But on the extra point, with Lou Groza poised for the kick and Tommy James crouched as his holder, a gust of wind blew the ball away from James's outstretched hands. James lunged and caught the ball, but with the Rams rushing him, there wasn't enough time for him to spot it. Groza stood by helplessly as James tried to throw the ball to a teammate in the end zone. But the pass misfired, and suddenly the Browns, spoiled for five years by Groza's automatic extra points, trailed, 14–13.

Not that the Browns were discouraged. They realized that the Rams weren't perfect, either. For one thing, Waterfield had missed a 16-yard field goal. Shortly after the second half began, Graham and Lavelli generated another touchdown on a 39-yard play. But the Rams rallied for two quick touchdowns to go ahead, 28–20. Hoerner completed an eleven-play drive by scoring from the one. And on the ensuing kickoff, Larry Brink of the Rams scooped up Motley's fumble on the seven and trotted into the end zone. In the span of only twenty-one seconds, the Rams had taken an eight-point lead with about five minutes remaining in the third quarter.

Early in the final quarter, Graham whipped a 14-yard touchdown pass to Rex Bumgardner, one of his running backs. That narrowed the Rams' lead to 28–27, the difference being the wind-blown snap on the extra point.

With about three minutes remaining, the Browns seemed to be on their way to scoring again, either a touchdown or a field goal. But pressured out of the passing pocket by the Rams' rush, Graham ran and fumbled on the Rams' 25-yard line. Milan Lazetich recovered for the Rams, who were jumping up and down in anticipation of the NFL title. In front of the Browns' bench, Graham's head was down. He avoided his teammates' eyes.

"That's all right," Paul Brown assured him. "We're going to get the ball back. We're still going to win. We've got time."

There would be enough time only if the Browns' defensive unit prevented the Rams from getting a first down. And the Browns did just that. Waterfield had to punt, and Cliff Lewis returned it 18 yards to the Browns' 32-yard line.

Up on the scoreboard clock, one minute and forty-eight seconds remained. This time, Otto Graham knew, there would be no second chance.

Pressured out of the pocket on first down, Graham ran, as he had when he fumbled. But this time he ran 14 yards for another first down, and he didn't fumble. Graham didn't have to select the plays, since Brown was sending them into the game with his messenger guards. But the play selection was obvious. Sideline passes. If the pass was completed, the receiver immediately stepped out of bounds, stopping the clock.

In quick succession, Graham hit Bumgardner at the

Rams' 39, Dub Jones at the 22, Bumgardner again at the 11. Sure field-goal range.

But with the ball on the left hashmark, Graham realized that Groza would be attempting the winning field goal from a difficult angle. Brown sent in a running play on which Bumgardner would carry the ball in front of the goal posts. But when Graham called it in the huddle, Bumgardner had a suggestion. "Why take the chance of fumbling a handoff?" he said. "You can run a sneak without as much risk."

Graham agreed, without knowing why Bumgardner had preferred not to carry the ball on such a vital play.

"My hands were wet and cold from falling in a snow-bank after catching the pass on the previous play," Bumgardner confessed later. "I was afraid I might fumble. I knew Otto wouldn't."

Otto didn't. He even gained one yard, moving the ball to the 10. Then he turned and waved for Groza.

This time the wind didn't destroy the snap. Tommy James placed it perfectly, and Lou Groza kicked it perfectly for the 16-yard field goal that put the Browns ahead, 30–28. But there were still twenty seconds remaining—time enough for a miracle play. Jerry Williams returned the kickoff to the Rams' 47. Strangely, though, when the Ram offense took the field, Bob Waterfield remained on the sidelines. With time for one play, Joe Stydahar wanted Norm Van Brocklin's stronger arm. Predictably, the young quarterback faded back and threw a long pass. Warren Lahr, one of the Browns' defensive backs, intercepted it at the five-yard line. The Browns had won, 30–28.

"This was the greatest football game I ever saw," NFL Commissioner Bert Bell said, "and the Browns are the most intensely coached team I ever saw."

Strategically, the Browns had proved that the forward pass was the most potent weapon in pro football. Otto Graham had completed 22 of 32 passes for 298 yards and four touchdowns in freezing, windy weather. Waterfield had been intercepted four times, but he had completed 18 of 31 for 312 yards and one touchdown. Between them, the Browns and the Rams had shown the other NFL teams that there was a new way to play the game. More than that, Paul Brown had shown the other NFL teams that there was a new way to coach the game. And the skeptics had been silenced, because the Cleveland Browns, from the All-America Conference, were now the National Football League champions.

The rebel had emerged as the ruler.

Rams' Dick Hoerner goes over from the one-yard line in third period, to put the Rams ahead, 21–20. Overleaf: Browns and Rams watch Lou Groza's last-seconds field goal try

Glenn Davis (left) grabs a Waterfield pass and scores on an 82-yard play. Otto Graham (above) fakes a pass and runs instead in Brown scoring drive that covered 70 yards

"I wanted to crawl into a hole. But on the sideline, Paul Brown actually put his hand on my shoulder and said, 'Don't worry, Otto, we're still going to beat them.'"

OTTO GRAHAM

The Pot Grows

For winning the 1950 NFL title, each member of the Cleveland Browns was rewarded with a $1,114 share of the championship-game receipts. Each member of the Los Angeles Rams was consoled with $686.

In nearly a quarter of a century since then, the championship bonanza has increased about twentyfold. The Miami Dolphins, who won the 1974 Super Bowl, each collected approximately $25,000—$15,000 for winning the Super Bowl, $7,500 for winning the American Conference title, and one-fourteenth of their annual salary as a game's pay for the conference playoff.

Waterfield (left) mixed passes and runs as Rams scored again to lead, 14–7. Lavelli (above) grabbed Graham pass to score, but Browns missed extra point, and Rams were ahead, 14–13

Coaching the Redskins, Graham talks to Sonny Jurgenson

Coaches

Weeb Ewbank, the only coach to have won championships in both the NFL and AFL, is among twelve men who have been head coaches in pro football after having been either assistant coaches or players in the 1950 NFL championship game.

Ewbank, then in charge of the Browns' offensive line, went on to guide the Baltimore Colts to the 1958 and 1959 NFL titles. He later took over the New York Jets, who won the 1968 AFL title and upset the Colts, 16-7, in Super Bowl III.

Blanton Collier, the Browns' offensive coach in 1950, followed Paul Brown as head coach in 1963 for nine seasons. Hamp Pool, the Rams' offensive-backfield aide in 1950, succeeded Joe Stydahar as head coach in 1952 for three years. Of the players, five Browns and four Rams became head coaches—Otto Graham with the Washington Redskins, Abe Gibron with the Chicago Bears, John Sandusky with the Colts, Mac Speedie with the Denver Broncos, Lou Rymkus with the Houston Oilers, Bob Waterfield with the Rams, Norm Van Brocklin with the Minnesota Vikings and the Atlanta Falcons, Jerry Williams with the Philadelphia Eagles, and Tom Fears with the New Orleans Saints and the Southern California Sun of the new World Football League.

"A lot of people used to think that Paul Brown used to holler at us and shout at the half. But actually, it was a very quite thing, like a schoolroom session."

DANTE LAVELLI

Waterfield hands off to Dick Hoerner for the touchdown that put Rams ahead by 21–20

The NFL's greatest place-kicker, Lou Groza displays perfect form. As Bob Neal, the Browns' broadcaster, described the locker room scene after the game, "Lou was kissing his kicking shoe. It was like a bunch of high school kids who'd won a city championship."

Flankers

In an added irony to their 1950 NFL title, the Cleveland Browns used the new flankerback formation that the Los Angeles Rams had installed the previous season.Clark Shaughnessy, the Rams' coach in 1949, had converted Elroy (Crazy Legs) Hirsch from a running back into a flankerback in order to make the best use of his talents as a pass receiver. Hirsch lined up wide, as a third end, so to speak—the flankerback formation that is now a standard NFL offense. In 1950, Paul Brown installed Dub Jones as his flankerback, providing Otto Graham with another talented pass receiver.

The Toe

In April of 1974, the NFL altered its rules to make field goals more difficult. In effect, it was legislating against a trend begun by Lou Groza of the Cleveland Browns in the 1950 season. Groza set an NFL record with 13 field goals that season, plus two in the Eastern Conference playoff, plus the winning field goal in the NFL championship game.

Groza's success convinced other coaches that the three-point field goal was an offensive weapon that had been overlooked.

During his NFL career, which lasted through the 1967 season, the six-foot five-inch, 250-pound Groza, who also played offensive tackle, produced 1,349 points on 234 field goals, 641 extra points, and one touchdown. (Groza's totals were the all-time record until George Blanda kept kicking into his mid-forties with the Oakland Raiders. Blanda had 1,842 points going into the 1974 season.) During Groza's four seasons in the AAC, he contributed 250 points on 30 field goals and 160 extra points.

"Lou Groza," said Paul Brown, "shortened the field from 100 yards to 60 yards."

"That defeat was the lowest point in my pro career, and I think all the Rams felt that way."

ELROY HIRSCH

With the score 28–27 Rams and less than two minutes left, Graham starts Browns on scoring drive with sideline pass to Bumgardner (left). Lou Groza boots game-winning field goal (above) from the 10-yard line with 20 seconds left

Paul Brown

Hall of Fame

Ten members of the Browns' and Rams' organizations at the time of their 1950 NFL championship game are now in the Pro Football Hall of Fame at Canton, Ohio.

The four Browns are coach Paul Brown, quarterback Otto Graham, running back Marion Motley, and placekicker Lou Groza. The Rams are the team's late owner, Dan Reeves, coach Joe Stydahar (selected as a tackle for the Chicago Bears), quarterbacks Bob Waterfield and Norm Van Brocklin, and pass receivers Elroy Hirsch and Tom Fears.

Groza and Hirsch were also named to the sixteen-man all-time NFL team selected in 1970, the league's fiftieth anniversary. Van Brocklin, Stydahar, and two Browns, wide receiver Dante Lavelli and defensive end Len Ford, were chosen as reserves on the fifty-six-man all-time squad.

Hidden Rib

During the week before the 1950 NFL championship game, the Los Angeles Rams hid knowledge of quarterback Norm Van Brocklin's broken rib—a breach of conduct now punishable by a fine from the league office.

Van Brocklin had suffered a broken rib early in the Rams' playoff victory over the Chicago Bears the week before. Under NFL rules now, the Rams would be required to announce Van Brocklin's injury and his condition for the next game—probable, possible, questionable, out. But at the time there was no NFL rule covering injury information, so the Rams remained mum. Van Brocklin didn't appear in the NFL title game until he was inserted to throw a desperation pass on the last play.

The NFL changed its rules because injuries play such a vital role in football, and league officials do not want opposing teams and fans misled. The practice of revealing all grades of injuries also reduces criticism by gamblers that facts about a game are being withheld.

THE HIT HEARD
'ROUND THE WORLD

Confetti begins to fall as Thomson's home run sails into the stands

New York Giants/ Brooklyn Dodgers National League Playoff October, 1951

By Steve Jacobson

here are apartment houses on the sites now. People live in co-ops, high in the air, many not knowing what once happened on patches of grass long since destroyed. In the Flatbush section of Brooklyn, there are few reminders that Jackie Robinson once played in Ebbets Field for a team called the Dodgers. Alongside the Harlem River in Manhattan, few people recall that Willie Mays once played center field in the misshaped Polo Grounds for the New York Giants.

Bobby Thomson and Ralph Branca still live in the New York area, still remember the intense rivalry between the Dodgers and Giants, the passions that players and fans could feel when they walked out of the subway. Thomson and Branca remember what New York was like before the businessmen-owners slipped out of town, with the ball clubs in their pockets.

Thomson and Branca also remember the last pitch of the 1951 National League season. Branca threw it; Thomson hit it; and several hundred thousand fans will swear they were present in the Polo Grounds on that October day.

Steve Jacobson was not there. When Branca made that pitch to Thomson, Jacobson was walking across the campus of Indiana University, listening to the game on a portable radio (no transistors then). There is no sense in revealing his mood after Thomson swung the bat; he remains neutral in the following article.

In 1960, Jacobson became a baseball reporter for *Newsday*, near his home in Long Beach, Long Island. He has traveled with the Mets and Yankees, covered the 1968 Olympics in Mexico City, and writes an occasional column. When he runs into the old Dodgers and Giants, he invariably asks: "What was it really like?" By now, Steve Jacobson *feels* as if he had been there.

G.V.

". . . Hartung down the line at third base, not taking any chances. Lockman with not too big a lead at second, but he'll be running with the wind if Thomson hits one. Branca throws. Thomson hits a long drive. It's going to be, I believe—the Giants win the pennant! The Giants win the pennant! The Giants win the pennant! Bobby Thomson hits one into the lower deck—of the left-field stands. The Giants win the pennant! They're going crazy. They are going crazy! Ooooh, boy!"

—Russ Hodges, October 3, 1951

That was the final, wildly delirious shot of the most dramatic pennant race ever run. It may be the single most memorable play in sports history, forever making 1951 "the year Thomson hit the home run." It's a milestone of life from which memories are measured. Where were you when the Japanese bombed Pearl Harbor? Where were you when John F. Kennedy was shot? Where were you when Thomson hit the home run? People remember as if it were yesterday.

Anybody who was old enough to understand was at a television set or radio, if it was at all possible, that autumn day in New York. People took radios to work or to school. Students begged for information between classes. The Brooklyn Dodgers and the New York Giants, at the peak of the greatest sports rivalry, were providing triumph and despair in the same throb. The end came in an explosion that ticked off the final seconds of the pennant race, before the world had learned to count backward to zero.

The accepted starting point of the Giants' great comeback was August 11. Between games of a double-header, the Dodgers led the Giants by a seemingly insurmountable 13½ games. That figure is immortal, left behind as an epitaph. Then, after 154 games, the two teams were tied, and the National League was forced to have a best-of-three playoff for the second time in its half-century. The Dodgers lost two straight to St. Louis in 1946. This time, they dropped the first, won the second, and took

a 4-1 lead into the ninth inning of the ultimate game.

Then Thomson hit the home run—one swing that would make his name the symbol of baseball heroes forever, even if someone would ever do something comparable—which nobody has. And it would forever brand Ralph Branca, a gentle man who threw the pitch, as a tragic figure.

"People connect me with one event," says Robert Brown Thomson, now an executive of a paper company. "That's the change it's made in my life. If not for that, Ralph and I would be pretty well forgotten by now. We played our careers and the next guys came along—except for that."

To appreciate the magnitude of the event, you have to feel the rivalry flowing between the Giants and the Dodgers in the 1930s, 1940s, and 1950s. Maybe no real understanding is possible—except for the people who were there, New York's baseball fans. This was a sports rivalry unlike any that ever was or probably will be. For most of their existence, the Giants had been a dominant team in the National League while the Dodgers were creating an image that caused the mere mention of Brooklyn to send radio audiences into peals of laughter. William Bendix was the strong, gentle, bumbling Brooklynite through a career on film.

Dodger fans, in their annual disappointment and continuing faith, said, "Wait 'til next year."

In the 1940s, the two teams reversed places in the standings, but it was still all right to make fun of Brooklyn and Brooklyn accents. As they turned into the fifties the Yankees, Giants, and Dodgers were the best teams in baseball, each having a hold on a part of the city. For a real fan, there was no vacillating between two teams. In Thomson's family, while he was growing up on Staten Island, his father was a Dodger fan, his brother a Yankee fan, and Thomson always rooted for the Giants.

Haughty Yankee fans waited for their team's appearance in the World Series while the Dodgers and Giants met twenty-two times each season and each meeting was an angry collision. Those games were carried on two radio stations (later also by two television stations), the commentary supplied by broadcasters paid by each team. The fans rode the subway from their homes to the turf of the other team and cheered their raving hearts out. And sometimes it was close to hatred. The police blotters of the time reported incidents where a Giant fan and a Dodger fan argued until one of them was dead.

he Hit Heard 'Round the World

"There were times we stopped playing to watch a fight in the stands," says Pee Wee Reese, the Dodger shortstop for two decades.

The players felt it. "You felt it when you got on the subway to the park," recalls Bill Rigney, who has managed three teams since, but was then an infielder on the Giants. "You knew there was going to be a fight or somebody was going to get knocked on his fanny by a pitch."

The ball parks, too, had personalities. The Polo Grounds, home of the Giants, was in Harlem, crammed between Coogan's Bluff and the Harlem River. Polo was never played there, but it was shaped for polo or football, anything but baseball. The center-field bleach-

ers were 483 feet from the plate, and until the New York Mets gave up two long home runs in 1962, only one homer had ever been hit into those bleachers, by Joe Adcock of the Milwaukee Braves. The size of center field gave Willie Mays a perfect showcase for his brilliant fielding.

In right field it was measured in inches—257 feet, eight inches. At the left-field foul line the distance was 279 feet—and the upper deck hung closer than that. It was common to see an outfielder move back to the fence and poise to catch a ball, only to see it brush the overhang above him. From that came the expression "Polo Grounds home run"—spoken with contempt.

The final game: Sal Maglie pitches the first ball to Carl Furillo at the Polo Grounds

"In the eighth inning, Newcombe threw bullets." LEO DUROCH[ER]

Ebbets Field in Brooklyn was compact and constantly in tumult. "Anything can happen in Brooklyn" was the cliché, except that it was hardly a cliché. Players could recognize individual voices of fans. Hilda Chester was there with her cowbell, and there was a man known as Jake the Butcher, who would sit behind first base wearing his straw hat. When a visiting pitcher threw to first base and failed to pick off the runner, Jake would holler, "Late again." And all the crowd expected it. Gladys Goodding ("one more D than God") was the organist, and she made her immortal contribution. One afternoon, after a painful day before, she greeted the entrance of the umpires with "Three Blind Mice."

Ebbets Field was an ideal shooting gallery for the greatest hitters of the Dodgers in the fifties. Legends were made by the right-field wall, forty feet high, wire mesh atop fifteen feet of concrete, sloped at the bottom, giving an unpredictable rebound. At the base of the scoreboard in right-center there was an advertising sign that said, "Hit Sign, Win Suit." Almost nobody ever hit the sign. The Dodgers had great right fielders, as if selected by the politican-clothier Abe Stark himself.

At Ebbets Field there was also a small, vaguely musical group that paid its way into the games and called itself The Dodger Sym-Phony. Their specialty was piping a visiting strikeout victim back to his bench with a tune entitled "The Army Duff," but commonly known as "The Worms Crawl In—." The last beat was timed for the moment the player's butt touched down. Often a player would try to avoid that moment by moving about for a prolonged time, only to find that the Sym-Phony still had that last beat ready on the bass drum.

"All the ball parks today, you could be any place and never know where," Reese says. "Then I'd go to Ebbets Field by subway and walk the last part of the way. All the little shopkeepers knew you and wished you luck. I'm glad I had the opportunity to play there at that time."

Hold that rivalry against the tone of America in 1951. National Airlines was advertising service between New York and Tampa in five hours and five minutes. Baseball teams traveled largely by train. Bacon was 49 cents a pound, and Macy's was selling fourteen-year-old Chateau Lafite Rothschild at $4.29. America had its poor people and times were as hard as ever for them, but hardly anybody thought about the poor besides the poor. The black player was accepted generally, four years after Jackie Robinson broke the color line with the Dodgers, but Willie Mays remembers leaving the Giants' spring training hotel in Phoenix because blacks weren't served in the dining room.

America was fighting a war with hand grenades and flamethrowers in Korea, but the country accepted that without protest and without disrupting its daily life. Civil-defense authorities warned us that an atom bomb could kill half a million in one blast, but casualties could be reduced fifty percent with proper civil-defense techniques.

Television was still a relative novelty. It hadn't yet brought death on the battlefield into the living room. Radio had its "Lux Radio Theater," "The Halls of Ivy," and "Suspense," which encouraged us to imagine without visual bounds. Jackie Gleason, Arthur Godfrey, and Perry Como were television stars, but many newspapers didn't publish television listings yet. No series of sports events had been telecast from coast to coast before the 1951 playoff. Even so, Russ Hodges' voice of history came from a radio.

As the playoffs took place, Senator Joseph McCarthy's Communist witch-hunts were beginning to be condemned. "I have never seen a more arrogant or a more rude witness," Senator William Fulbright said one day. The headline on Eleanor Roosevelt's column read: "Women Can Combine Job, Home Life." *A Streetcar Named Desire* and *A Place in the Sun* played in movie houses, but so did *Rhubarb,* the story of a cat who inherited a baseball team. And *Angels in the Outfield* had a cast that included the Pittsburgh Pirates, thought by many to be as comically fumbling as the original Mets.

Movies then weren't supposed to explore the injustices of life. Americans found greater identification with winning and losing on a baseball diamond. (Professional football was still a game played between baseball seasons.) There were sixteen baseball teams, just as there had been since the turn of the century. There was agitation for major-league status for the Pacific Coast League and the growing cities of Los Angeles and San Francisco, but who ever dreamed the Dodgers and Giants would move there? Businesses moved, not historic teams.

The hostility between the Giants and the Dodgers was

Gil Hodges is safe at home as Wes Westrum reaches for the throw in the second game, won by Dodgers, 10÷0

very real. Baseball teams normally gossip with each other on the field every chance they get, but not the Giants and Dodgers. The Giants were managed by abrasive Leo Durocher, who had managed the Dodgers three years before. The Dodgers had the great Jackie Robinson, the ultimate competitor, who had emerged from the protective shell of being the first black player as an articulate, outspoken man with a flair for the dramatic. Robinson and Durocher had lightning crackling between them. Robinson would always be the last Dodger down the clubhouse steps at the start of the game at the Polo Grounds. "You hated to see him come to bat in a situation," Willie Mays recalls with reverence.

The Giants had Eddie Stanky, a virtuoso at irritating. And the Dodgers were managed by Charlie Dressen, who always said the right thing to make people angry—either the other team or his own.

At the July 4 holiday, the Dodgers swept a three-game series from the Giants, and Dressen crowed with his 9½-game lead: "We knocked them out. They'll never bother us again."

The Giants had been preseason favorites on the basis of their fast finish in 1950. Durocher had taken a brawny, plodding team that broke the home-run record in 1947 while finishing a distant fourth, and remodeled it for speed and hustle until he could call it "my kind of team." They won on opening day, lost, won again, and then lost eleven in a row.

The Dodgers lost on opening day—a fact they would not forget—but won ten of their first fifteen. They were in the process of assembling a super team, which by the mid-fifties was established as perhaps the finest ever to play in the National League. They had won in 1947 and again in 1949. They had been edged out on the last day of 1950 (and would go on to win pennants in 1952, '53, '55, and '56 before being carried away in a carpetbag to Los Angeles.)

They had all-stars at almost every position. Catcher Roy Campanella was voted Most Valuable Player in the league for 1951; he batted .325 with 108 runs batted in. At first base, Gil Hodges hit 40 home runs and drove in 103 runs. Reese was the leader at shortstop, and Billy Cox was a legendary fielder at third base. Carl Furillo, with 91 RBIs, was in right field. Duke Snider, the center fielder, had 101 RBIs. In June, to the dismay of the league, the Dodgers got Andy Pafko from Chicago to play left field, and he drove in 93 runs. Preacher Roe set

a record for percentage with a 22-3 pitching record, and Don Newcombe was 20-9.

At second base was Robinson, batting .338 and inventing more ways of winning a game than perhaps any man who ever played. Sometimes it was not enough for him just to win. On August 9 the Dodgers beat the Giants for the twelfth time in fifteen meetings that season, and somebody on the Dodgers opened one of the two doors that separated the home clubhouse from the visiting clubhouse at Ebbets Field. Through the thin partition the Dodgers taunted the Giants.

"Eat your heart out, Leo. So that's your kind of team," someone yelled, throwing Durocher's own line back at him. The Dodgers sang, "Roll out the barrel, we've got the Giants on the run." Listeners thought they detected Ralph Branca's noted clubhouse baritone among the voices. Branca says he doesn't remember.

Meanwhile Robinson sat next to the door pounding a fearful din into the Giants' ears with a baseball bat on the partition.

"Stick that bat down your throat, you black nigger son of a bitch," Stanky yelled.

Seated next to Stanky was Monte Irvin—like Robinson a recruit from the Negro leagues. But now Monte Irvin was a Giant. He added: "That goes for me, too."

Twenty-three years later, Irvin, an aide to the commissioner of baseball, reflected, "I could have gone along with anything they said, I was that mad. We respected Jackie. He was a hell of an athlete. But none of us Giants had any love for him."

Two days later the lead grew to that historic 13½ games, which stands now the way Pickett's Charge at Gettysburg stands as the high-water mark of the Confederacy.

Then the Giants began to come back.

Just as Durocher said, the Giants were a fine collection of players. They were to finish second in 1952 and win again in 1954. Catcher Wes Westrum was a good handler of pitchers and an expert at stealing signs. Whitey Lockman was at first base, and the infuriating Stanky, collector of 127 bases on balls that year, was at second. Alvin Dark, tither to his church and master of hitting behind the runner, was at shortstop, batting .303. Irvin was the left fielder, batting .312 with 24 home runs and leading the league with 121 RBIs. In right was Don Mueller, Mandrake the Magician with a bat.

In center was Willie Mays, twenty years old and recalled in May from Triple A with a .477 average. He wasn't *the* Willie Mays yet, but the Giants saw great things in him. "Henry Thompson, Irvin, they all took care of me," Mays says. "They put me to bed at 9:30 and then they would go out."

The pitching staff produced the best team-earned run average in the league. Sal Maglie wouldn't shave the day before he pitched so he would look mean on the mound. Then he would throw his fastball high and inside and his curve low and outside, which was as mean as could be. Larry Jansen was 23-11 and Jim Hearn was 17-9.

And on third base, moved there to make room for Mays in center, was Bobby Thomson, born in Glasgow, Scotland, on October 25, 1923. He played fifteen years in the major leagues. In 1951 he batted .293, with 32 homers and 101 RBIs. The last hit, the last home run, the last three RBIs are the golden ones.

In addition to physical talent, there was a special kind of character to the Giants. Westrum, Lockman, Stanky, Dark, and Bill Rigney went on to become managers. So did Herman Franks, a coach on that team. Jansen and Maglie became pitching coaches. And they had the extra spur of their feeling for the Dodgers and the memory of that embarrassment in the clubhouse. "When you're that far out, you have no idea of winning it," Thomson says. "But we wanted to get as close as we could."

Things began to come together. "Every night on the road we'd get together in somebody's room, have a sandwich and a beer, and talk," Rigney recalls. "I remember Larry Jansen telling us, 'Don't you guys know? Just to tie—if they play .500, we have to play .700.' Somebody said, 'Okay, Larry,' and we'd go over the game we had the next day. I kept a book that year of every pitcher we could read something on. We looked for anything we could to help us steal a game."

Two days after the embarrassment at Brooklyn the Giants swept a double-header and continued until they won sixteen in a row, thirteen at the Polo Grounds. They swept three from the Dodgers, and in a little more than two weeks the Dodger lead was cut to five games.

Whatever needed to be done, the Giants did. Durocher, a renowned clotheshorse, wore the same clothes day after day to preserve the Giants' luck. Thomson recalls wearing the same undershorts beneath his uniform "until they had ants in them." One day Durocher was late getting out of the clubhouse for the start of the game so he sneaked under the stands to the dugout—and he continued to do that.

In the midst of the streak Stanky would remind the team how it was doing. "Hey boys, don't get nervous now," he would say. "Remember, we're not playing for our lives."

Things began to snowball. At Pittsburgh, late in August, the Dodgers started their ace, Newcombe, in the first game of a double-header against the seventh-place Pirates, and they knocked him out. Dressen masterminded the situation by starting Clyde King, his best relief pitcher, in the second game, and the Pirates knocked him out too. Then the Dodgers flew home, and Billy Cox, who covered all that ground at third base but hated to fly, took a train. He arrived late for the game the next night, and a ground ball eluded his replacement, costing two runs. The Dodgers lost a close one.

Other things happened that were overlooked at the time because the Dodgers still had a good lead. They were short of pitching and Erv Palica, who was thought to have a world of stuff, had an undefinable sore arm. Dressen publicly called him "gutless" and started him against the Giants. Bud Podbelian relieved in the first inning with the score 3-0, and the Dodgers lost, 3-2

Branca shut out the Cubs and had to start again on two days' rest in Pittsburgh. He had a 5-0 lead, and the game had all the signs of a no-hitter. Pirate pitcher Mel Queen got what looked like a line-single to right to break it up, but right fielder Carl Furillo charged it and threw Queen out at first. "I had never pitched a no-hitter and I really went after it then," Branca recalls. The Pirates got two meaningless hits in the ninth, But Branca remembers straining something before it was over.

"I would pitch five or six good innings after that and then I'd get tired," he says.

Still, the Giants were seven games behind as they turned into September. "No one thought it could happen," Reese says. "We had too fine a club for that."

Of all professional sports, only baseball has something called a pennant race. The game is played every day. The pressure is constant, it becomes a way of life.

September began with the Giants beating the Dodgers three of four games at the Polo Grounds. The Giants pulled a triple play in the first game, and Mueller, a singles hitter, hit three home runs. He hit two more in the second game. Newcombe pitched a two-hitter to salvage one game for the Dodgers. Then Sal Maglie beat Branca, 2-1.

"I remember thinking, 'Hey, wait a minute, we got a chance,'" Thomson says.

Then things were tight. "That last month we lived or died every night," Rigney recalls. "But it seemed when we lost, the Dodgers also lost. We'd get to thinking we were going to catch them and then we lost a game on the road and they won. Oh, oh, now the momentum is going to shift, but then it started all over again."

Something else happened to the Dodgers. Roy Campanella was hit on the ear by a pitch and couldn't play for two weeks.

When the Giants returned from their last western trip—which meant St. Louis, Chicago, Cincinnati, and Pittsburgh—they had six more losses than the Dodgers

Charlie Dressen has a conversation with umpire Larry Goetz after Goetz called Duke Snider out at home in second game

and had only seven games to play. The Dodgers had ten games remaining. The Giants had made it close, but the Dodgers needed to win only five of their ten games to clinch the pennant. They won four.

The Giants won in Philadelphia while the Dodgers lost two in Boston, and the lead was only one game. "That's when it really got exciting," Thomson says. "It was in the air. The newspaper men from out of New York picked us up. Fans came down from New York. We got the feeling."

The next night, September 26, Jackie Robinson stole home while the Dodgers were mauling the Braves, 15-5. The Braves were just playing out the string until they could go home, but that made them angry. There were several former Giants on that team, and they didn't care for the Dodgers from their last movie. They came back the next day ready to play.

On September 27, plate umpire Frank Dascoli ruled Boston runner Bob Addis had eluded Campanella's tag at the plate, and the Braves beat the Dodgers, 4-3. Campanella was thrown out of the game. Preacher Roe kicked in the door to the umpires' room after the game.

"I remember that better than the playoff game," Branca says. "Campanella would have batted with the bases full the next inning, and who did we have to hit? Wayne Terwilliger. That call was terrible, but you never hear of that."

Friday, September 28, Carl Erskine had a 3-0 lead for the Dodgers at Philadelphia, and Andy Seminick's home run in the ninth beat them.

The 13½ games were all gone.

"Saturday morning we were in the lobby in Boston and nobody said anything," Thomson says. "We'd look up and our eyes would meet and we would burst out laughing."

Both teams won Saturday. Amazingly, the Giants won their game first on Sunday and clinched a tie. They had to wait for the Dodger final to know if they had won the pennant or if there would be a playoff. While the Giants were riding the train home from Boston and grabbing scores at station stops, Robinson was preserving the Dodgers for a later torment.

In the gathering darkness of the autumn afternoon, Robinson made a marvelous diving, skidding catch of a line drive in the twelfth inning to save the game. Then he won it, 9-8, with a home run in the fourteenth. The Giants got word of it in Providence. And in Philadelphia,

Roy Campanella said to Pee Wee Reese, "Now we got to hit against that damn Maglie again."

What the Giants did makes it unfair to say the Dodgers blew the pennant. The Dodgers won 24 of their last 44 games. But the Giants won a staggering 37 of their last 44.

On Monday the playoff opened in Brooklyn. "I remember walking out onto that field to take batting practice," Rigney recalls. "Jackie was in there hitting. Some of us walked over to the cage behind him and said, 'Hey, guess who's back.' He wouldn't turn around. Did he ever play ball that series. I don't believe I ever saw anybody play harder."

When Jim Hearn was named on the train to start the first game for the Giants, his wife's reaction was: "But Jim doesn't like to pitch at Ebbets Field." Rigney remembers somebody's reply: "Tomorrow he'll have to."

Hearn produced what Rigney calls "the game of Hearn's career." The Giants won, 3-1, with Thomson hitting a completely forgotten but vital home run, and the commissioner warning both teams to watch their language.

The Dodgers won the second game, 10-0, as rookie Clem Labine came out of the bullpen with his jug-handle curve to start and win when the Dodgers absolutely had to have him. "It was unbelievable how good Cox played at third," Monte Irvin says. Other people asked, if Labine was good enough to pitch a game like that, how come Dressen didn't discover it sooner?

The third game matched the great Don Newcombe against the great Sal Maglie. The two teams had played 156 games, and now they needed to play one more.

Robinson singled in a run to put the Dodgers ahead in the first inning, and the Giants missed a chance to tie on a blunder by Thomson in the second. Lockman was on first when Thomson lined a hit down the left-field line and kept running. "I was so determined," Thomson recalls with urgency in his voice twenty-three years later. "I guess I wasn't always that determined. There are certain times you know you have to do things within your power. I never thought Whitey would stop at second." Thomson was caught between bases and tagged out.

Thomson's fire burned in both teams. Both dugouts could hear the way Dodger manager Dressen and Giant shortstop Alvin Dark were shrieking at each other. Dressen was yelling, "You'll boot it when it counts,

Dark," Thomson recalls. "I've never seen Dark so mad. I never heard Dark swear before."

The Giants tied it at 1-1 in the top of the seventh on Irvin's double and a sacrifice fly by Thomson. It was the first run off Newcombe in 21 innings. "Newk was exhausted," Reese remembers. "He said, 'I can't make it.' Jackie and I talked him into staying in."

As it turned out, Maglie gave way first. In the eighth inning Reese and Snider singled, and Maglie wild-pitched the tie-breaking run across before walking Robinson. Pafko ripped a shot over third and off Thomson's backhand. Then Cox drilled one to Thomson's left. "I tried to block it with my chest," Thomson says. "If it had hit me flush I think it would have killed me. I never tried to stop a ball that way before."

The two hits made the score 4-1, and Newcombe seemed to recover his great strength.

"When I pinch-hit in the eighth," Rigney says, "Stanky told me Newcombe was losing it. I took one pitch, walked to him on deck, and whistled." Rigney struck out, and Newcombe looked untouchable going into the ninth. He had allowed only four hits. "My gosh, it looked like we had won it," Reese said later.

"I don't think I ever felt lower," Thomson says. "I thought, 'We just weren't good enough to go that last mile.' Newcombe had been so good in the eighth inning,

Jackie Robinson is out at second as Stanky completes double play in first game, won by Giants, 3-1

it was inconceivable that I'd come to bat again. It was a bad feeling."

Win or lose, the Giants had every right to be bursting with pride, they had come so far. "Pride is intangible," Thomson corrects twenty-three years later. "What was tangible was the numbers on the scoreboard."

Rigney found an intangible—or at least an inscrutable—thought to hang onto. He was sitting on the bench next to Clint Hartung when four pigeons alighted on the top step of the Giant dugout. "I never saw any pigeons the whole game," Rigney says. "Hartung said maybe it was an omen."

Durocher said: "We've gone this far, let's give them a finish."

Dark led off with a single, and Mueller guided a single off Gil Hodges' glove at first base. Hodges, among the finest fielders ever at first base, usually handled chances like that. The tying run was at the plate in the person of Monte Irvin, who had produced under pressure all season. Newcombe rallied and got Irvin on a pop fly. One out.

"We all had to die a little then," Rigney says.

"Actually, I thought I did them a favor by not hitting into a double play," Irvin says.

Then Lockman doubled down the left-field line, scoring one run. But Mueller sprained his ankle sliding into third. The tying run was on second base and Thomson was coming to bat—welcoming the break in the action as the Giants helped carry Mueller to the distant clubhouse. Hartung ran for him, establishing his place in historic trivia.

And Dodger manager Dressen looked to his bullpen.

"Erskine just bounced a curve, but Branca's fast and loose," coach Clyde Sukeforth informed Dressen over the phone.

Willie Mays, twenty, waited on deck, praying he wouldn't have to hit. "I was scared to death," Mays says.

So it was Branca and Thomson, about to become Siamese twins of fate.

Branca, born in Mount Vernon, New York, on January 6, 1926, grew up a Giant fan. At the age of 21, he had won 21 games for the 1947 pennant-winning Dodgers. Oh, yes, he wore number 13 on his shirt.

Branca and catcher Rube Walker—playing because Campanella was hurt in the first game—made plans at the mound: get a strike, move Thomson back with an inside pitch, then throw a curve low and away.

Branca's first pitch was a fastball inside, and the Giants jumped up in the dugout when Thomson took a strike on a pitch they thought he could have driven. Then Branca tried to get a slider inside, hoping Thomson would go for a bad pitch and hit it on the handle or be set up for the outside curve.

The pitch was inside, off the plate, but Thomson fell away and got the head of the bat around on it.

Left fielder Andy Pafko faded back as though he had a chance, and then the ball was in the stands. The sun exploded. The Giants poured on the field to pound each other near home plate, waiting for Thomson.

"I danced and jumped all around the bases," Thomson says. "I couldn't stop myself. I took a jump and a leap at the plate. All those people were there. I think I touched the plate, but I couldn't be sure."

"I couldn't believe we had lost," Reese says.

Burned into Monte Irvin's memory is the image of Robinson, the ultimate enemy, standing at second base, watching Thomson to make sure he touched the bases. "He didn't give up until Bobby touched the plate," Irving says. "Then Jackie turned away."

Mays was still waiting on deck. In his anxiety he'd missed the point. "I didn't know what happened until everybody passed me," he says.

Then the crowd was there, threatening to kill the Giants with love.

"All I could think was that we beat the Dodgers, we beat the Dodgers," Thomson recalls. "You have to understand the feeling between those teams zeroed in on each other. That's what I thought: we beat the Dodgers. I never for a minute thought of anything but that.

"I knew it was something special, exciting. I could feel it. I wanted to get home. My family was waiting. I wanted to be with them."

Thomson's wife, Winkie, was not yet his fiancée then. She was a nurse at a hospital in Plainfield, New Jersey, watching television with the doctors that day. Thomson paused for an appearance on the Perry Como television show and then went to join his closest fans.

"I had still thought of it on no terms other than beating the Dodgers," Thomson says. "Then my brother-in-law says to me: 'Bob, do you realize something like this might never happen again?' Then I began to realize what it was."

In the Dodger clubhouse, Branca sat slumped on the concrete steps, his head buried in his arms, hiding his

er have play for him." LEO DUROCHER

eyes. He says he doesn't remember going from the mound to the clubhouse. "Everyone said something," Reese says. "What good did it do? He just felt like he did it all."

The Dodgers sat on their little three-legged stools, seeing nothing but grief. "We are three runs ahead going into the ninth inning," Jackie Robinson said then. "We see ourselves in the World Series. And then—boom—five minutes later we're sitting in the clubhouse."

In the Giant clubhouse, waiting for the end to come, were Rigney and owner Horace Stoneham, who was there for a drink of appreciation if they lost, or for champagne if they won. It turned out champagne. "Duke, Pee Wee, Preacher, and Jackie came into our clubhouse," Rigney remembers. "We understood. We fought them tooth and nail. We wanted to kill them all our lives. But we admired the talent we were fighting."

On that day the Soviets exploded an atom bomb, yet hardly anyone remembers that. The world has gone on to other things. But we still remember Thomson's home run and the feeling it gave us.

"It's hard to believe those teams are no longer here," Thomson says from his office in New York. "I think back to those days. There will never be a place like Ebbets Field. Crazy. The Polo Grounds, too. It was such a great thing, that rivalry."

Thomson's home run. Overleaf: *Robinson surveys the scene, Branca walks off, and the Giants begin their new life as National League champions*

Bobby Thomson is waved home by Leo Durocher after hitting homer in first game of the playoff, which Giants won by a score of 3–1

"As we went back in the dugout for our last outs, I never felt worse in my life . . . just total dejection . . . I remembered I was about the fifth hitter and I thought, gee, you know, the way Newk was throwing out there, I figured, we're dead, I'm dead, I'm not ever gonna get a chance to hit."

BOBBY THOMSON

Togetherness

History and empathy have forever bonded Bobby Thomson and Ralph Branca and made them friends. It's the nature of the men, for one thing, and it also would have been cruel for them to constantly replay that great drama of their lives with hostility. The outcome is always the same.

"I suppose I hated him for a while," Branca says, "but it didn't last. Bobby is a good guy."

Both men have prospered and have raised good families. They say their one great event hasn't changed their lives. "Sometimes I meet people in business who don't know me," Thomson says, "and a third party tells them. They say, 'So you're the guy.' That event got me in the public eye, maybe made a few extra dollars for me, but it hasn't changed my life."

Thomson had a fine professional career. He played in the major leagues from 1946 to 1960 and compiled a strong .270 batting average. Eight times he hit 20 home runs or more. Four times he batted in more than 100 runs. But he is unforgettable because of the one event.

"I don't resent it," he says. "Now I'm a private citizen who had the good fortune to play ball. I consider myself fortunate to have had one thing like that. I was more than a one-home-run guy, but I've got a sense of humor. I don't take it that seriously now. Working helps you grow up. That event has its place in my life. It's a nice little thing that happened to me. I'm glad it happened."

Thomson calls it a "nice little thing." He remembers it fondly. He was twenty-seven years old at the time; it didn't make his whole career, it just gave him something that would be replayed as long as he lived. "Branca and I speak at affairs occasionally," Thomson says. "It's kind of fun."

For Branca it was more than a "little thing" in his life. And years later, it's never fun. He's not the kind of man who can keep the bitterness alive so long. He even admits that he enjoys the fact that he isn't forgotten, like so many who had their taste at the top and were gone. But it's still not fun.

He was in the big leagues with the Dodgers in 1944 at the age of eighteen. He was a 21-12 pitcher with the 1947 Dodgers at the age of twenty-one. Three other times he won 13 games or more. He won 88 games in the big leagues and lost 68. He was gone at thirty, with that one massive memory.

Thomson's son, Robert, has a photo in his room of his father running his home run home. The photo of Branca, his arms folded across his knees, his face buried in his arms, is on microfilm in newspaper files. It's not the kind of picture a man puts on his wall.

"I was the youngest guy since Christy Mathewson to n twenty games in the National League," Branca says. Only five other pitchers ever won twenty games by the e of twenty-one. They're all in the Hall of Fame. I rew the pitch to Thomson.

"On Friday night before the season ended, Andy minick hit a home run off Carl Erskine in the ninth ning to beat us. Wednesday before that, Frank Dascoli lled a man safe at the plate and the man hasn't uched the plate to this day. But those things aren't membered."

Branca never won 10 games again in a big-league ason. But, he says, the home run meant nothing to his reer. In the spring of 1952 Branca hurt his back and uldn't throw well. "When it straightened out fourteen onths later, I pressed to make good," he says. "I tched when I shouldn't have. I pitched when I had a re arm to show Thomson's home run had no bearing my psyche."

In 1953 he was traded to Detroit, and later to the nkees, but he never really came back. He said it was arm. "I had really gotten over it," Branca says. "A y hits a home run and we lost the pennant because of He hit a good pitch. I don't mean to belittle it, but it s a Polo Grounds home run. What I think of it was that Dodgers sent in their best pitcher. I could live with t."

Perhaps Thomson was an unlikely hero. He had flow- grace on the field, but he never reached the level ected of him. He ran with long-legged strides and od erect at the plate with his feet spread and his bat d high, like Joe DiMaggio. But Bobby Thomson was ver really a star.

Perhaps the moment in history should have been writ- for Monte Irvin, who drove in all those runs in 1951, an who had spent the best years of his career in the scurity of the Negro leagues. Perhaps it should have en written for Willie Mays, the electric rookie who was stined for twenty-two years of greatness. But maybe omson was the man for the time.

"All his life Thomson lived in the area," reflects Bill ney, the quick-minded infielder with that Giant team. Maggio was his hero. He even hit like him. Maybe it s destiny's way. Bobby had dreamed of something like t all his life. Willie's time was yet to come. Monte had e it for us all year. No, that was the right man."

nd Branca must forever feel he was the wrong man the bullpen when Erskine was rejected because he inced his curve. "In all honesty," Branca reflects, "I h it were me that bounced the curve instead of Er- e. I wish Bobby's home run happened to someone e."

Jackie Robinson hits first inning, two-run homer to put the Dodgers ahead 2–0 in the second game

"I think ultimately it was a blessing in disguise. Had I gotten him out, people would have forgotten me. Subsequently, I hurt my back and didn't pitch much after that. Had I gotten him out, I would have just disappeared and been another guy who played in the big leagues."

RALPH BRANCA

Duke Snider is out at home in close play after trying to score from third on Gil Hodges' infield trickler in third inning of second game

Russ Hodges

"We had a meeting at the mound. Charlie came out to the mound. We called Pee Wee and Jackie and Billy Cox. And Dressen said, 'How do you feel?' And I said, 'I'll do whatever the fellows decide to do.' And Pee Wee said, 'Charlie, get a fresh man out here.'"

DON NEWCOMBE

"Oooh, Boy!"

While the words of the late Russ Hodges were coming over radio and history was being made on the field, history was being made in the television booth. But there's no record of it.

There was no such device as videotape at that time, and the only record of Thomson's home run and the giddy reception at the plate comes from newsreel film. The man doing the telecast was Ernie Harwell, Hodges' partner with the Giants, formerly a Dodger broadcaster and most recently with the Tigers.

"When the ball was hit, I said it was gone," Harwell recalls. "Then I saw Pafko going back on the wall and I began to have second thoughts. My wife saw me on the screen and she said I looked stunned, like I did when I got married or when the kids were born."

It was the first series of games ever telecast nationally. Championship fights and Kentucky Derbies had been seen on TV, and the 1951 World Series was scheduled to be the first series to be telecast across the country, but the playoff beat it. The first game of the playoff didn't even have a sponsor.

Hodges' voice crying, "The Giants win the pennant. . . . Oooh, boy!" was taped as a kind of accident, too. Harwell remembers that Hodges got it months later in the mail with a letter from a Dodger fan.

"He said he taped Russ in the ninth inning only to hear him cry," Harwell says. "Then, I guess he felt guilty and sent it on to Russ. Russ sent him ten dollars."

The voice of Branca recorded on a record entitled "Great Moments in Sports" was less an accident. On it, Branca sobs, "Why me . . . why did it have to be me? . . . Leave me alone, will you . . . "

That, Branca revealed not long ago, was recorded at a restaurant some months later. The sounds in the background of the Dodgers suffering their defeat were customers eating dinner.

Dodgers won second game, 10–0, behind the pitching
of Clem Labine, helped by Andy Pafko home run (above)

Third game, last of the ninth: Mueller sprains his
ankle after sliding into third on Lockman's single

"Branca came
in by me,
coming in relief,
and I said,
'Go get 'em, Ralph,
the champagne's
getting kind of
cold in there.'"

DUKE SNIDER

Where Were You?

Where were you when Pearl Harbor was bombed? Where
were you when Bobby Thomson hit his home run? Herb
Norman happened to be at Pearl Harbor when Thomson
hit his home run—and he had a bet on the Dodgers.

Norman is now the equipment manager for the New
York Mets. Then, he was a Yankee fan from Connecticut,
a twenty-nine-year-old chief pharmacist's mate at the
submarine base at Pearl, listening with 150 other sailors
in the torpedo shop to Jack Rose's re-creation of the
game on the Honolulu station, HULA.

The station carried the games at normal afternoon times
in Honolulu even though they were already completed
stateside. Normally an enterprising fellow could find out
the score before the broadcast and occasionally make a
clever bet. This time the score was a secret when Chief
Norman discovered there were so many Giant fans around
that he had to bet the Dodgers.

"I went out of the room early," Norman recalls. "There
was no way the Giants could win. I went back again at the
start of the ninth inning and couldn't get any more bets.

"The inning starts with Rose reading off the ticker
and the Giants get a couple men on. Then Rose says: 'I'm
not going to jerk you people off. Thomson has just hit a
home run to win the pennant for the Giants.' I'll never
forget that."

Norman also remembers the aftermath around the submarine base and the telephone messages that cropped up
for Dodger fans that night. The messages would all leave
the same return phone number.

"When you called the number," Norman says, "What you
got was the city morgue. Later, or the next day, somebody
would come over to you and say, "Hey, did they bury your
stiff.'"

Dodger fans and bettors had to learn to live with that.

The unbelievable moment: Giant teammates wait to greet Thomson at home plate after his home run (above), and joyful Ed Stanky wrestles Giant manager Durocher to the ground (right)

Rained Out

After Bobby Thomson's home run, it seemed that nothing man-made could stop the Giants. And it was true. The only thing that beat the Giants that fall was the rain.

The day after the historic playoff ended, the Giants launched the World Series at Yankee Stadium against the inevitable American League champions. The Giants won two of the first three games. But it rained on Sunday, October 7, giving Allie Reynolds of the Yankees a much-needed day of rest. Reynolds beat the Giants on Monday and somebody else beat them Tuesday and Wednesday. But Giant fans will always blame the rain.

There were still some reminders of the playoff during the Series. In the World Series program, printed weeks ahead, the blurb for Yogi Berra said something like ''. . . this will be his fourth World Series, third against the Dodgers. . . .''

G.V.

> "Something hit me behind in the neck, and it was Stanky, and he kept kissing me, saying one thing, 'We did it, we did it.'"
>
> LEO DUROCHER

Political Scorecards

While the Dodgers and Giants were struggling on the field, the City of New York was split by its allegiance to two baseball teams. Politicians did their best.

Abe Stark, the clothier who had his sign on the wall in Ebbets Field, was president of the City Council then. He was waiting at Grand Central Station the Sunday the pennant race ended in a dead heat. When the Giants' train arrived there from Boston, Stark officially greeted them and wished them good luck. Then he scurried across town to Penn Station, where the Dodgers' train was due from Philadelphia. He then officially greeted them and wished them good luck.

Back in Brooklyn, Judge Samuel Leibowitz made no pretense of neutrality. ''I hope,'' the judge said, ''the Dodgers beat the hell out of them.''

Picture of a hero: Thomson races to the clubhouse, dodging fans on field

SUGAR
SHATTERS
ROCK

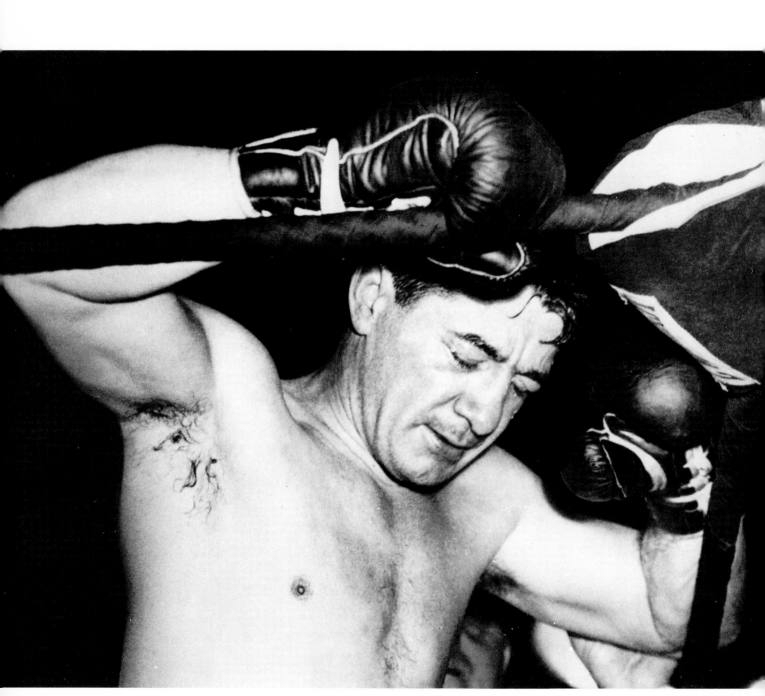

The dream is over: Rocky weeps against the ropes after the fight

Ray Robinson/Rocky Graziano Middleweight Championship Fight April 16, 1952

By Vic Ziegel

oxing is a very personal sport. You either love it or hate it. Some of the finest people would not take a free ticket to see Frazier or Ali fight, on the basis that watching two men hit each other is barbaric. Some other finest people find boxing a magnificent showcase—where the best and worst in human beings come out in the open.

One of the attractions of boxing is that it matches two men of certain known qualities, and the outcome is based on these qualities. Yet, too often in boxing, the best of men are defeated outside the ring. Within one month in 1973, there were reports of two great fighters, Kid Gavilan and Mickey Walker, both down on their luck. Unlike the professional sporting leagues, boxers have no pension plans, no player representatives to guide them. While boxers must worry about their safety in the ring, they must also develop the sophistication to hire competent boxing and financial advisers.

With this massive vulnerability always present, boxing becomes one of the great showcases for writing. It is no accident that many fine writers have done some of their best work on boxing, ranging from Robert Lipsyte's columns in the *New York Times* to A. J. Liebling's essays.

Some of the best stories are retrospective—examining what the fighters were when they met, discovering what they have become since. In the following pages, Vic Ziegel profiles two of the most exciting men ever to enter the ring—Sugar Ray Robinson and Rocky Graziano.

Vic Ziegel is the boxing writer and occasional columnist for the *New York Post*. He has been included in *Best Sports Stories* and has written for several magazines and anthologies. He has covered championship fights in Japan and Venezuela, and is also familiar with the sweaty practice gymnasiums of his native New York City.   G. V.

he greatest championship bouts are often fought in saloons, where the matchmakers never have to worry about financial arrangements, or the size of the ring, or the television contracts, or which contestant is entitled to wear white trunks.

Joe Louis vs. Jack Dempsey is typical of the dream battles that are staged with right hands wrapped tightly around a drink, left hands used for nothing more than emphasis, and footwork consisting of the ability to remain standing.

If not for those olive-stirring debates, we would never have these fights at all. This is one of boxing's shortcomings: the schedule of matches isn't neatly drawn up and dropped into the mail at the start of each year. That simply isn't possible, although there are some experts—those who specialize in suspicion—who would have us believe that boxing's painful dances are, more often than not, choreographed. These are the same people who are willing to suggest that the reason the Comet Kohoutek made such a poor showing was to boost its odds for the next millenium.

But there are fighters, like comets, who pass each other in differing orbits, like the young Rocky Marciano drubbing the old Joe Louis, proving little. And there are the stars of differing magnitude who brighten the ring with their glow. This was the case with Sugar Ray Robinson and Rocky Graziano.

Robinson, the artist in trunks; Graziano, who worked with hammer and nails. They had nothing in common but the ability to fill arenas. If they'd met in their primes, the ring ropes would have quivered, the barroom debates would have been answered. But when they stepped into a ring in Chicago on April 16, 1952, they staged a rousing slugfest that excited their fans all the same.

Robinson was three weeks away from his thirty-first birthday and had been fighting professionally for a dozen years. Graziano was four months older, a street fighter inside the ropes whose finest battles had come five years earlier. It is difficult to trust any fighter over thirty. There have been too many punches thrown and, worst of all, received. Reflexes have begun to disappoint, the eyes are not as sharp, and the legs are a step behind the beat that the next generation is moving to. The brain understands more—but the messages are received a bit slower. That split-second difference is one of the reasons referees learn to count to ten.

They should have fought in another time, Robinson and Graziano. This was a match that would have made, say, 1946 a very good year. Back then, Robinson had lost only once in sixty matches. And the most incredible part of his record was his failure to get a title chance. He was later to be known as the greatest fighter of all time, pound-for-pound. That last phrase is mandatory. If a boxing fan was asked to play a word association game, "Ray Robinson" and "pound-for-pound" would be the example to start the game.

In his first fight in Madison Square Garden, Robinson called the knockout round against Maxie Shapiro

Sugar Shatters Rock

Robinson's earliest struggles had everything to do with survival. Robinson's father had been a cotton farmer in Dublin, Georgia, until he was told about the salaries being paid by construction companies in Detroit. Walker Smith, Sr., went north by himself and then sent for his wife and two daughters in the spring of 1921. Their youngest, Walter Smith, Jr., later to be known as Sugar Ray Robinson, was born a few weeks later on the first floor of a two-story wooden frame house in Detroit's black ghetto. "It was known as Black Bottom," Robinson said in his autobiography, *Sugar Ray*, written forty years later with Dave Anderson. "Black because we lived there, Bottom because that's where we were at."

When he was eleven his mother, divorced, brought the kids to a new city, another ghetto, Harlem. He was boxing in Police Athletic League tournaments by the time he was thirteen years old, a tall, rail-thin eighty-five pounder. ("You had to look twice to see me once.") At fifteen, he walked into a church cellar that was the home of the Salem-Crescent Athletic Club. George Gainford ran the club with an iron tongue and was the leading figure in Harlem's amateur boxing. Walker Smith, Jr., became one of his fighters.

Because Gainford's new boxer didn't have an Amateur Athletic Union (AAU) card—and because Gainford always traveled to AAU tournaments with more cards than fighters—Walker Smith's name for one tournament, Ray Robinson, became his name forever. Gainford also stayed, working in Robinson's corner his entire career.

Robinson was undefeated in his 85 amateur bouts, accumulating 69 knockouts, 40 in the first round. He was nineteen years old when he began his professional career. A year later he was a main-event fighter in Madison Square Garden. The legend may as well begin there. Sugar Ray's opponent, the first time his name appeared on the most prestigious marquee in boxing, was Maxie Shapiro, a durable welterweight. Here is the story Shapiro tells about that fight, September 19, 1941.

"We came out for the third round and Sugar Ray puts his hands out like he wants to touch gloves. That ain't supposed to happen until the last round so I say to him, 'This ain't the last round.' He says to me, 'It is for you, Maxie!'"

The story might be apocryphal. What the record book says, very clearly, is that Maxie Shapiro was knocked out in the third round. A week later, Robinson was in Philadelphia to defeat the previously unbeaten Marty Servo, who would later become a world champion. Five weeks after that Robinson returned to the Garden, still pound-for-pounding, to beat Fritzi Zivic, who had lost the welterweight championship only three months earlier. In another three months, in a rematch at the Garden—where they couldn't get enough of his wonderful stuff—Robinson knocked out Zivic. Sugar Ray was twenty years old.

Rocky Graziano had not yet begun to fight. At least not under Marquis of Queensberry rules. He had other reasons to use his fists, other ways to make money. A few were legal.

Rocco Barbella, now Rocky Graziano, made his first appearance on New Year's Day, 1921, in a cold-water

In second fight against Tony Zale, Rocky scored knockout in ferocious battle

tenement on New York's Lower East Side. There had been five other children born into the family, but only Graziano and an older brother survived more than the first few months. His father, a professional boxer who quit at nineteen after some seventy fights, rarely worked. The family moved to Brooklyn soon after Rocky's birth, but that only meant a change in geography. "We lived in a wooden house," was how Rocky remembered it for *Somebody Up There Likes Me*, the autobiography written with Rowland Barber, which was later made into a movie—Paul Newman disguised as Graziano. "It was all right in the summer, but we froze in the winter. There were cracks in the walls and rat holes in the floors. As soon as we nailed tin covers over the holes, the rats chewed new ones."

He remembers an uncle named Danny Bob. "The family tough guy. I never knew him, but I felt like I did. He got mixed up in the rackets and he didn't live very long. They found him dead one morning, his chest full of lead. It was a mob killing and never solved."

Rocco was eight years old, a truant officer's nightmare. His father was having the same old problems finding a job, and his mother was in the hospital after a nervous breakdown. Rocco was running wild in the streets, and the only answer seemed to be a return trip to the East Side, a little farther uptown, where his grandparents could keep more of an eye on him. This was the neighborhood in which he was to spend most of his adolescence, when he wasn't in jail.

Rocky was a thief, a gang leader because his fists earned him all his titles. He and his friends broke into subway gum machines, robbed candy stores and Chinese laundries. On the few days he spent in grade school he took milk money out of cigar boxes in his classroom and stole pencils, reselling them. A subway cop caught him using tools on a penny gum machine, and his punishment was the night he spent on a bench in children's court. When Rocky's grandmother came to take him home, she heard a detective tell a court attendant, "Well, there goes another little guinea on his way. Good-looking kid. But I can tell his kind. Look in his eyes, you see the devil himself. Ten years from now, the death house at Sing Sing." Rocky was eleven years old.

A stolen bicycle meant his first of three rides to reform school, the Catholic Protectory. He learned to read and write there. (On one of his returns, the hearing officer

was the former baseball star, Lou Gehrig, months before his death.) When he was free Rocky was staying away from home, sleeping on subway trains, on docks, on tugboat decks, "and if I had a whole dollar, in a one-night furnished room. For a buck we would do anything. Like the man once said about us, we would steal anything begun with an A. A piece of fruit. A bicycle. A watch. A pair of shoes. Anything." An early hero, Dillinger, was killed, and Rocky remembers sitting on a curb and crying.

Not long after his third visit to the Protectory, he was talked into entering a local boxing tournament, the first time he would punch with gloves on his hands. He knocked out the other boy in the first exchange, returned to the dressing room, and was caught going through his opponent's pants pockets. Rocky was thrown out of the tournament. His opponent went on to become the club champion.

Rocky was released on bail after a break-in at a school netted a typewriter and a movie projector. He took advantage of his temporary freedom to burglarize a coffeehouse. For that he spent five months in the Tombs, New York's aptly named prison. There were several more trips to prison farms, but boxing was something Rocky began doing when he was out. He won a Metropolitan AAU tournament, went to jail, became a professional boxer under the name of Robert Barber, went back to jail, went into the army, and was jailed for being AWOL.

He spent part of his unauthorized army vacation in Stillman's Gym, the center of the city's boxing activity. A successful sparring session impressed Irving Cohen, a boxing manager, and he began finding bouts for Rocky. After eight fights in two months the army caught up with him: a year in their prison at Leavenworth. When he was released, twenty two years old, his boxing career was all he had.

Rocky moved his brawls into the ring. His style thrilled crowds and packed the New York fight clubs—St. Nicholas Arena, Ridgewood Grove, Broadway Arena, Fort Hamilton. His first main event in Madison Square

Garden came late in 1942, and he was the building's most popular boxer for the next two years. When he sparred in Stillman's his all-out performances meant the admission was raised from twenty-five cents to a half-dollar.

"He was selling out the Garden every time he fought," says his manager, Irving Cohen. "He always wanted to fight Sugar Ray, especially at that point in his career. But I didn't think he needed the fight. Yes, there was a lot of talk about a fight between Rocky and Ray. Why wasn't one made? Well, it was probably my fault. I thought Sugar Ray was the greatest and why should Rocky take a risky fight?"

And there was other work available. Freddie (Red) Cochrane came out of the navy. He was the welterweight champion of the world, a title he hadn't defended during his three years in the service, a title Ray Robinson was aching for. Cochrane decided to step out of his weight class with a middleweight, Rocky Graziano. Rocky usually weighed close to the middleweight maximum of 160; he had a thing for people escaping the 147-pound world of welterweights. The nontitle bout was a knockout for Rocky and so was the rematch, two months later. It was obvious that Cochrane's career was ending, and Robinson was anxious for the fight that would bring him a crown. But Marty Servo—whom Robinson had beaten twice four years earlier—was given the chance with Cochrane. Servo scored a knockout, finishing the work begun by Graziano.

Sugar Ray campaigned for a match with the new champion, but Servo, putting Ray off, went after a payday with a middleweight: Rocky Graziano. The Rock put Servo away in two rounds and seriously damaged his nose. ("I can still see the Rock," W.C. Heinz was to write more than twenty years later, "holding Servo under the chin with his left hand and beating him with the right with a fury I've never seen before or since....") Servo retired not many weeks afterward, and there was no champion for Robinson to fight. A vacant title meant two contenders would have to be found. Sugar Ray Robinson and Tommy Bell, fifteen rounds, December 20, 1946. Robinson was dropped in the seventh round, Bell four rounds later. It wasn't until the decision was announced that George Gainford was able to yell at the Garden's special police, "Clear the aisle. We got to get the champ out of here."

The victory over Servo earned Graziano a chance at the middleweight crown, held by a steelworker from Gary, Indiana, named Tony Zale. Rocky was training for the fight—a new habit for him—when he was reminded about some of his old habits. His apartment in Brooklyn was broken into and robbed, twice within two months. ("So now I was one of the others, I was one of them that got stole off, instead of them that stole.") Rocky's third loss came in the fight with Zale, considered one of the bloodiest, most bruising battles in ring history. Zale survived an early knockdown, and when the fight was over, after the fighters had staggered each other repeatedly, he was still champion: a sixth-round knockout. Their second meeting, in July, 1947, was another colossal struggle. Rocky's eye was practically shut tight after Zale's punches had swelled the area below his eye. Frank Percoco, one of Graziano's cornermen, pulled a quarter out of his pocket and broke open the swelling. After six grueling rounds, Rocky Graziano was middleweight champion.

His reign lasted five days short of eleven months. Zale won the third fight—the last and least of their three struggles but the only one filmed; disputes over movie

Graziano and Robinson check the contract for their fight. Robinson got 30 percent of the gate, Graziano 25 percent

"My plan was not to get hit with that right hand." RAY ROBINSON

rights to the first two matches were never resolved, and the punches thrown will never again be seen. The Graziano–Zale series set records, to that time, in attendance and gate receipts for middleweight boxers. Only one middleweight title fight has ever drawn more fans into an indoor arena, and that happened on April 16, 1952, the night Rocky Graziano and Ray Robinson were finally matched.

The phone call was from Graziano's manager. "Rocky, how would you like a title fight?" (The manager has to ask, even if he knows the answer.)

"Geez, I don't know, Irving. What do you think?" (The fighter takes orders. That way there's somebody to blame.)

"It's up to you, Rocky. It's your life. Maybe you better think it over. They're saying around the gym that you're too old for Robinson, you slowed down too much." (The manager in his Knute Rockne imitation.)

"Who's talking abot me like that?"

"Oh, just guys who hang around. You know how they always talk when a guy stops fighting so many bouts." (The psychological ploy, fully extended.)

"Irving, get me that bum Robinson." (The answer the manager was after when he invested his dime, three and one-third cents of which comes out of the fighter's purse.)

The one-word explanation for this tardy bit of match-making is television. This was 1952, remember, when the little box with the people inside was showing the John Garfield movies for no more than the second or third time. Very often, the people in the box were wrestlers wearing zebra masks or villains with German accents who told the announcers that "dis iz eggsectly vat vill hoppen" to next week's opponents at this same time, same station, folks. The networks contributed boxing shows on Wednesday, Friday, and Saturday:

From the start, Graziano had trouble with Robinson's smooth, quick style

plenty of work for the main-event fighters, plenty of opportunities for the at-home fight fans. Television did wonderful things for boxing, for several years, and then, because too much wonderful is sometimes called over-exposure, television roared on to new roads. Boxing was left behind, covered with tire marks, dying. (Example: A Brooklyn fight club, the Broadway Arena, staged bouts every Tuesday night. Uncle Miltie came along on the same night, and there weren't enough customers to buy the tickets at the Broadway Arena. So there was no more boxing and, soon enough, no more Broadway Arena.)

Where were you in 1952? Well, if you owned a little box you were probably sitting in front of it to watch the middleweight champ and the challenger, the champion of five years before, live from Chicago Stadium. The largest audience ever to tune into a boxing match was out in televisionland that night.

Sugar Ray and Rocky were still magic names, even though much of their performance was now illusion. Graziano's especially. He stayed away for almost a year after the third fight with Zale and then fought 21 times in the next four years—20 victories, 18 knockouts, a draw, no losses. But the opponents were delicately selected, and Rocky was willing to admit, a few days before the Robinson fight, "I don't know how good I punch any more. . . . I been knockin' over salamis."

The toughest nights were his three with Tony Janiro. A draw and a split-decision success came in New York, Rocky's hometown. Janiro's fighting address was Youngstown, Ohio, and the third fight—the winner would be promised a title chance with Robinson—was in Detroit, closer to home for Janiro. The midwestern fighter was well ahead on the three scorecards, and there was less than a minute remaining in the last round when Rocky began an all-out attack. Graziano punch-battered Janiro to the canvas, and the referee dashed in, stopping the fight. He never bothered to count over the fallen Janiro, who insisted he would have been on his feet in time. The technical knockout came fourteen seconds before the final bell.

The crowd responded with angry boos, just as the audience had done a month earlier in Boston when Graziano was awarded a fight because his opponent was disqualified for slapping. A month before that Rocky was a third-round winner in Kansas City, but the other fighter was fined and suspended, and a member of the state athletic commission said, "There was something rotten in Kansas City, not in Denmark."

July 10, 1951, the same night Rocky was cutting into that particularly odorous salami in Kansas City, Sugar Ray was in London, losing the middleweight title he had annexed a year earlier. Randy Turpin, the new champion, had sixty four days to celebrate before being knocked out by Robinson. Ray's next match was another fifteen rounds with Bobo Olson. And the sports pages began hinting, for the first time, that Robinson was feeling his years.

When he had fought Charley Fusari in 1950 it was a Cancer Fund benefit, and Robinson said he had wanted to give everyone a good show, the full fifteen rounds, as advertised. Teddy Brenner, president of Madison Square Garden Boxing, asked Robinson later what his toughest fight had been. Robinson's answer was Fusari. "You've got to be kidding," Brenner argued back, recalling Robinson's generosity to Fusari. "He never touched you. How can you say that was your toughest?" "Because I had to fight thirty rounds," Ray said. "Fifteen for me and fifteen for him."

His reputation was enlarged. "The greatest job of carrying since Momma Dionne," came from sportswriter Barney Nagler. "Ray has carried more fighters," wrote Dan Parker, "than the credit manager at Stillman's Gym." Added Lester Bromberg, "the greatest carrier since the Lexington." And an anonymous wag credited Ray with being "the most dangerous carrier since Typhoid Annie."

It was that part of his reputation that bothered columnist Jimmy Cannon before the fight with Graziano. "The gamblers are disturbed by the fight in Chicago," Cannon wrote, "and insinuate it may be a polite concert by a couple of business associates who might be governed by commercial instincts. Greed produces pacifism in fighters. They recollect Robinson's chivalry in his match with Fusari and remember that Graziano pampers an aversion to his trade by fighting guys who behave more like friends than opponents. It is the gamblers' theory that Robinson will act with the violence of a cotillion leader making a pass at his dancing partner. Their conception of the fight appears to be unfounded, but the rumors have been published."

And if the odds said Robinson, 3-1 and up, here's what the favorite was saying: "I know they say he can't punch any more. Do you think I'm going out of my way

"I really thought I could knock him out." ROCKY GRAZIANO

to make him prove it? If there's anything I should be better than Rocky at, it's moving, stabbing, piling up points. Any time I open up I give him the one big chance he's in there for . . . to get over his Sunday punch.''

At the contract signing, Rocky had joked, ''Robinson's scared of me. Yeah, he's scared to death he'll kill me.'' In the final weeks of training, his speeches grew serious. ''Listen,'' he said, ''I never been a great fighter, but I'm a game bum. I got no reputation to lose. I'm the fighter nobody is betting on. I read it in the papers: 'Rocky's Last Stand.' I know this is a helluva fighter I'm fighting, but I'm gonna be throwing punches. I'm not gonna use no science. If I still got something, and I get him right, I'll have him on the floor. He ain't a kid anymore either, and maybe I'll get lucky and keep him there.''

More than twenty years later, in an interview for this article, Graziano's lines weren't very different. ''I just about had it as a fighter,'' he said, ''but I wanted to take a shot at that SOB. Forget my language, I don't mean it the way it sounds. We're good friends, really. But I always thought I could flatten him. If I hit anybody on the chin I can flatten him. That's what I thought about everybody. I felt I should have knocked him dead. That was the attitude I had from 1943 until the end.''

Graziano's remarks were passed along to Robinson. ''You know, Rocky,'' Ray began, before interrupting himself with an extended chuckle, ''Rocky'' (more chuckling), ''he's really something.''

The opinion was shared by enough ticket buyers to sell out Chicago Stadium. Gross receipts were $252,237, and the attendance was 23,740 (according to the Stadium publicity man, who was interested in breaking the record for an indoor fight and therefore counted the special cops and the working press.) The athletic commission reduced the total the next day to 22,264 (because a man from the Chicago fire department had come by when he heard the first numbers announced), and it comes down to 22,008 now (through the listing in the Ring Record Book), which would be the largest indoor crowd until they built the Astrodome in Houston.

Wild right by Graziano decked Robinson in third round. Overleaf: *Cool in victory, Robinson turns away from fallen Graziano*

Chicago Stadium was already thirty years old when Graziano met Robinson. Had it ever really been new? The sounds of a crowd—Chicago Bulls basketball and Chicago Black Hawks hockey—bring it to life today, just as they did for the two middleweights then. Rocky was popular with the Italian fans on Chicago's West Side, and the $20 price for ringside seats meant it wouldn't be difficult for their loudest throats to be heard.

Sugar Ray was the perfect fighter, coolly brilliant, the people's choice when it was time to look back at the bout. During the action, though, the roars were for Rocky, his curly hair carefully ignored, his cocky smile in place. Sugar Ray was handsome, a trim six-footer with a twenty-eight-inch waist, the artist as well as the model. When Tony Zale was introduced by the ring announcer, the old champion merely touched Robinson's glove. But he visited with Rocky, made a fist, and held it in front of the face he had bloodied in the past. Graziano laughed, jabbed Zale on the chin.

The crowd roared for that bit of by-play, just as they roared in the first round when Rocky landed a few shots in the first minute—before the referee, Tommy Gilmore,

warned him that those punches to the back of the neck would have to stop.

Early in the round, Ray connected with two strong lefts that may have hurt Rocky. And so the rabbit punches bought the challenger a little time. Rocky, bending from the waist, resembling a man pushing forward against a high wind, tried a lunging left. Robinson was moving too smoothly, punching Rocky into the ropes, ripping in with both hands. The best Rocky could offer was a wild right, and Robinson—"Any time I open up I give him the one big chance he's in there for, to get over his Sunday punch"—backed away. At the bell, Robinson finished with two convincing lefts and a right to the stomach. Rocky was left lunging.

The puncher, Graziano, was moving forward in the second round when Robinson connected with a right that sent Graziano to the ropes. Ray was measuring his man. And hitting him too. After the bell, the brawler, frustrated, used his left against Ray's shoulder. The crowd scored that against Rocky.

The third round wasn't much better for Graziano, unless you count the time he knocked Robinson down.

That came after Ray was totally in command, hurting the shorter fighter with both hands and sending him, once again, into the ropes. It was time for another of the Rock's what-have-I-got-to-lose right hands. This time it worked, sort of, crashing against the side of Robinson's neck. Ray was thrown off balance, sideways, and then, perhaps to his advantage because Rocky was at his best battering a helpless opponent, the champion's knee grazed the canvas, and the referee moved in to brush off his gloves.

"The referee got in the way too fast," moaned Rocky. "I could of done something. . . . one more bomb and I got it. That is what I think."

His golden moment was gone. All the punches were from Robinson now. Rocky was against the ropes, and Ray was starting a right hand to the body—"but I saw his chin just hanging out there"—and so the punch exploded on Rocky's chin. His mouthpiece flew out and he crumpled. At the count of six, he began to stir, pawing for the rope. ("I didn't hear the count until it reached seven or eight. Even then I thought I had time to get up.") Seven . . . Eight . . . ("When I tried to get up I couldn't") . . . Nine . . . ("The count went so fast, but I guess I was mixed up") . . . Ten . . . Rocky still reaching for the middle strand of rope with his right hand, the left glove pushing off the floor.

There was one more punch Rocky would land. He was standing now, kicking his left leg to restore the feeling taken away by Robinson's fists, and the crowd was cheering the champion's electrifying win. Rocky moved behind Ray and delivered an affectionate poke to his ribs. A few seconds later he was telling the television audience, "anyone who talks against this guy is a creep."

Rocky wasn't hurt. And Robinson was unmarked. The checks came to $79,631.25 for the winner, $67,192.71 for the loser. The little box had been fed two fighters for another Wednesday night, and the promoters had done best of all, even if they had waited too many years.

"Rocky was in better condition than he had been at any time since his third fight with Zale," Frank Graham wrote, reviewing the fight for the *New York Journal-American*. "He couldn't beat Robinson. He never could have beaten Robinson, even when he was at his best, for Ray was at his best then too. But he gave it a rousing try, and losing to Robinson was better than beating bums. Paid better too."

Rocky tags Robinson with a left hand in the first round as fighters follow their plans, Rocky to move in hard, Sugar to stay away

Pushing hard, Rocky connects with another left to Sugar's head in the first round

Hanging Them Up

"Sooner or later you come to the end of the road," Ray Robinson was telling the reporters after defending his title against Rocky Graziano. "I think two or maybe three more fights and I'll call it a career."

There was a question, from the same reporters, about a fight with Joey Maxim, the light-heavyweight champion, a chance for Sugar Ray to win his third championship. "I want no part of Maxim," Robinson told them. He turned to his manager, George Gainford, and said, "Let George fight him."

Seventy days later, the Maxim–Robinson match was fought in stifling heat in Yankee Stadium. A thermometer placed on the ring apron read 104 degrees. After the ninth round Ray remembers telling Gainford, "I'm getting sleepy." That was the last thing he remembered.

Ray, the lighter man, was the aggressor throughout the bout, setting a punishing pace—for Maxim and himself. He was safely ahead on all three scorecards when he missed a sweeping right hand in the thirteenth round and fell flat on his face. His cornermen dragged him to the stool and pressed ice packs against the back of his neck. The bell rang for the fourteenth round, but Robinson was unable to continue. Maxim was the winner, a knockout, the only mark of that kind on Robinson's record of 202 fights.

His physician suggested a long rest; Robinson was thinking about longer than that. He retired, and stayed retired for twenty-eight months. Until the money ran out.

At thirty-four, eleven months after returning to the ring, he regained the middleweight title. He was to lose it three times in the next five years, winning it back twice.

He was forty-four years old and there were ten fights left for him when he was beaten in Tijuana. The next-to-last score was a three-round knockout, the last of his 109 KOs. The ring was in Steubenville, Ohio. Three weeks later, on November 10, 1965, a quarter of a century after he began, he tried Joey Archer, who was later to become the top-ranking middleweight. Ray lost. And retired. To stay. He had fought 65 more fights since predicting his retirement thirteen years before.

On the night he lost to Ray Robinson, the reporters visited Graziano to ask if he would keep on fighting. "I want to fight him [Robinson] again," he said, but it was only to give them something to write. On the train ride home to New York he was wondering if he should quit.

There was one more fight, five months after Sugar Ray, in the same Chicago Stadium ring. The television people were building a golden boy, Chuck Davey, a young southpaw. He beat Rocky easily: "a shell of his former self," the Associated Press story called the loser.

"That one don't count," is what Rocky says now. "My last real fight was with Robinson."

Name-Dropping

The ring announcer at Chicago Stadium could have pointed to the fighter jiggling on his toes in one corner and introduced him this way: ". . . and at 157¼ pounds, the middleweight champion of the world, Walker Smith, Junior." And his opponent, at 159¾, in the black trunks with the white stripe, could have been introduced as the former champion, Rocco Barbella.

Walker Smith, Jr., had not been called that in public for around fifteen years, back to when he was fighting in AAU tournaments without the required amateur's card. His manager, George Gainford, pulled a card out of a stack, the card for a drop-out boxer named Ray Robinson, and told the people in charge of that week's show that, yes, this was the same Ray Robinson.

Ray/Walker was sitting on a table in the dressing room—the bout was in Watertown, New York—when the doctor assigned to the amateur show came into the room and called out the names of the fighters he wanted to examine. There was no answer when he said Ray Robinson.

Suddenly, Ray/Walker knew whom the doctor wanted. He was that kid Robinson. The fight might have been the easiest part of that night. He scored a first-round knockout. And when he was leaving the ring, the sports editor of the Watertown *Daily Times,* Jack Case, told Gainford, "That's a sweet fighter you've got there, a real sweet fighter."

As Ray remembers it, a woman at ringside then hollered out, "Sweet as sugar." That was what Case called him in the paper the next day: Sugar Ray Robinson.

Rocky Graziano was the second name Rocco Barbella invented for himself. His first ring name, for two professional fights, was Robert Barber, an Americanization of Rocco Barbella. That career was interrupted by a call from the army. By then, Rocky was a nickname. Rocky Barbella, absent without leave, was hanging around Stillman's Gym, his fists impressing in sparring sessions. When manager Irving Cohen found a fight for the boxer he knew only as Rocky, he asked for the rest of the name.

The Graziano brothers, Rocky recalled, were out of circulation. That meant jail. "Tommy Graziano," he told Cohen. It wouldn't do to advertise a name the army was after. The first bout for the AWOL soldier was in Brooklyn's Fort Hamilton Arena. His audience, cheering him after he scored a second-round knockout, was 2,000 soldiers.

That other Graziano? The last Rocky heard he was still in prison.

His face bared in the famous Graziano scowl, Rocky rushes in, trying to tag Robinson, who evades the punch with a flick of his head

"This here guy was like a racehorse . . . he was slipping all over the ring. You couldn't hit him."

ROCKY GRAZIANO

On the attack, Robinson works on Rocky's
midsection with a left in second round

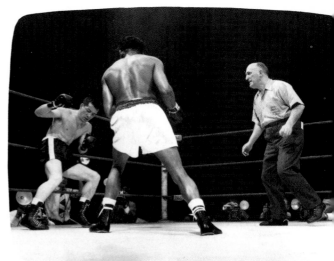

The plan changes, as Robinson catches
Rocky with a right that sends him down

"When you fight Rocky, you
see sharp or you be flat.
You get the message if this
guy hits you."

RAY ROBINSON

Perfect Casting

A few years ago, the casting director of the television series
"Mod Squad" needed an actor for a boxing manager's role.
The part went to Rocky Graziano. The casting director also
needed somebody to play an older middleweight attempting a comeback. The role went to Sugar Ray Robinson.

Neither man was exactly a stranger to show business.
When he had retired from boxing and was looking for a new
career, Rocky had been approached by the television writer
Nat Hiken. The writer was looking for somebody to play
Martha Raye's boyfriend on her show. The producers had
been looking for a "Rocky Graziano type." Rocky recalls
Hiken telling them, "Why don't we get Rocky Graziano?"

That was the beginning, his Brooklyn voice and manner
winning him laughs. ("If I talked like you," he tells people,
"I'd be broke.") The appearances led to commercials, the
first one in 1957, where Rocky smoothed on Vitalis and
told the audience: "You have to be pretty to look good."

These days Rocky sells beer in several cities and has a
long-term contract with a national auto transmission
dealer. Rocky estimates that his income from the commercials and the residuals approaches $200,000 a year.

Rocky left the ring, he says, "in good shape. Not a
rich man, but OK." There was a $100,000 annuity—paid for
with small percentages taken out of his biggest purses. His
manager, Irving Cohen, had made sure Rocky would have
money when he stopped fighting, thus assuring one of boxing's infrequent happy endings. Rocky's wife, Norma, had
known about the annuities while he was fighting—but
Rocky hadn't. They have been married more than thirty
years and have two daughters, Audrey and Linda.

They live the good life on New York's Upper East Side.
The terrace outside his apartment is where Rocky putters
around his small trees. ("He's becoming an Italian gardener
in his old age," Norma says.)

Graziano is helpless as referee Tommy Gilmore sends Sugar to a neutral corner

On his feet after the count, Graziano still wants to fight, is restrained by Gilmore

Rocky the actor

"I'm doing better and I'm happier than I ever was," Rocky says. "And I'm making money without getting my nose broke in."

Sugar Ray had money when he retired the first time, stepping out of ring shoes and into dancing shoes. He earned as much as $15,000 a week for his earliest appearances, his boxing career still fresh in his audience's mind. After a year, his asking price was considerably lower. But no one was asking.

Sugar Ray tried to keep the same life style as an entertainer. It couldn't be done. There was an accountant who took the money and ran, and Ray was forced back into the ring. He fought until he was forty-four years old, earning close to $4,000,000 from his battles. At the end, all that remained were the zeroes.

He and his third wife, Millie, live in California now, involved with the Sugar Ray Youth Foundation, a sports program growing out of a modest two-story frame house in a Los Angeles black neighborhood. There are chapters in Las Vegas and Orange County and Ray is hoping "to go national . . . stimulate a junior olympics.

"That's my life dedication now. I'm a firm believer that recognition is what all kids look for. They look forward to being Joe Louis, Babe Ruth, and we can give them that incentive, that direction, to carry it out."

He has had small parts in a few films—The Detective, Candy—and occasionally visits Las Vegas as part of a troupe that includes Nancy Sinatra and Frank Sinatra, Jr. He dances.

"You know that you get paid well in Las Vegas," he says, and now that his needs are simpler, "that carries me a long time. I couldn't be happier.

"Fights? I very seldom go. Just to watch a fight? I don't dig that. It's like a mailman going for a walk."

The man who once startled New York by driving a flamingo-colored Cadillac now drives a Pinto station wagon; "Sugar Ray Youth Foundation" are the words on the door.

"Hey, man," he says, "that car creates a lot of attention, too."

Robinson the dancer

Louis McCance 1974

THE GREAT INTERNATIONAL HOCKEY WAR

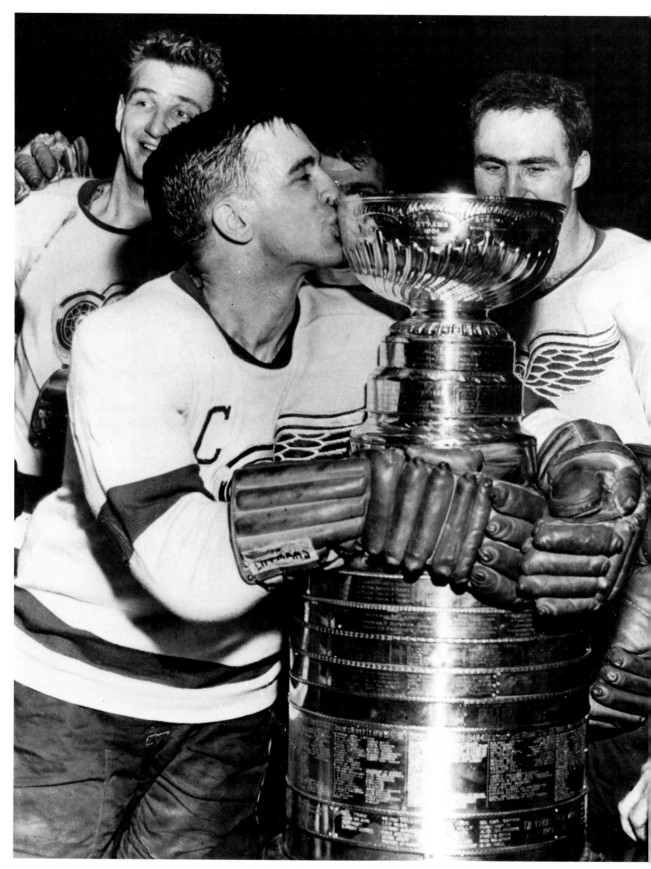

Red Wings' captain Ted Lindsay shows Stanley Cup joy

Detroit Red Wings/ Montreal Canadiens Stanley Cup Playoff April, 1954

By Gerry Eskenazi

The most recent glance at the sports pages disclosed sixteen teams in the National Hockey League, as well as twelve teams in something called the World Hockey Association. Teams from such frigid ports as Atlanta and Los Angeles were playing before packed houses.

Not only that, but all over North America parents were waking up before dawn to drive their children to hockey practice—because predawn is the only time when peewee teams can find room on the ice.

Yet it was just a decade ago when hockey seemed to be played only by rugged youths from Canada, and followed by a tiny but loyal bunch of fans in a few northern cities. The National Hockey League was the most exclusive club in North America—six teams. playing each other fourteen times— so inbred that club officials didn't bother to scout each other. Instead, they scouted the junior players in the Canadian provinces. What was the sense in scouting the Montreal Canadiens or the Detroit Red Wings? They never changed. The Canadiens were master stylists; the Red Wings were rugged aggressors. Everybody knew what to expect.

In this heightened atmosphere, the Montreal–Detroit battles came to symbolize awakening ethnic impulses in the French province of Quebec. The result was a rivalry unlike that existing in any sport in the United States.

Gerald Eskenazi, author of six books on hockey, was born in Brooklyn and attended City College, where the only skating was done on roller skates on city pavement. In 1963, Eskenazi became a sportswriter for the *New York Times*. A resident of Roslyn, Long Island, he now specializes in feature reporting for the *Times* sports section.   G.V.

The 500 French Canadians sat in coach seats, many of them singing the old Montreal fighting song, "Les Canadiens Sont Là." They were comfortable, even though it would be a twenty-two-hour train ride from Montreal to Detroit. They were accustomed to riding second class.

A few cars back, the Stanley Cup had a stateroom to itself. Tomorrow, somebody would win the gleaming silver trophy that, for Canadian hockey fans, had a higher value than a Super Bowl or World Series victory for Americans.

The National Hockey League's 1954 final playoffs were tied at three games apiece between the Detroit Red Wings of Gordie Howe and the Canadiens of Maurice Richard—perhaps the finest two teams in NHL history. For the sixth straight season, the Wings had finished first during the regular season. And for the fourth time in that stretch, the Frenchmen had finished second.

For these 500 Frenchmen, riding west through the night of April 15, 1954, even their language sometimes finished second. The language of power in Canada was English. The language of Les Quebecois was French— preserved even in the spelling of the team name "Canadiens." Yet a Frenchman in Quebec had to visit an English-speaking banker and attempt, with hat in hand and tongue tripping over the gutteral Anglo words, to get a loan. The highest executives in Montreal didn't have to master two languages. They spoke English. The French worker? He was referred to as a "Pepsi," going back to the days when Pepsi Cola gave you "twice as much" as Coke for the same nickel. The classic stereotype of the French worker showed him munching a sandwich plucked from a brown paper bag and drinking his Pepsi. It was a cheap drink.

The fans on the train were intensely proud ethnics— long before the word achieved its current fashionability. Although virtually every player in the NHL was born in Canada, only one team was predominantly French. And the Canadiens had some part in the rekindling of the French spirit, even the yearning for separatism, that was symbolized in the Fleur de Lis, the symbol of "La Belle Province." Another visible symbol was the picture of the Canadiens' great star, Maurice (Rocket) Richard. "I sup-

pose that, after the prime minister and the Cardinal of Quebec, Richard's face is the best-known in the province," said the president of the league, Clarence Campbell. And he may have been indulging in good manners to list them first and second.

The other clubs welcomed the Canadiens' identity for the sake of the box office. Indeed, they helped nurture it. Every youngster of French background in Quebec was considered within the draft priorities of the Canadiens. The other teams had a smattering of French players, but it was in Montreal that they really wanted to be. On the other teams, the French players were referred to as "Gorfs." "Gorf" is "frog" spelled backward, and "frog" was the supreme insult to a French Canadian.

The French found an antidote to insults in the heroics of their hockey team, known as "Les Habitants," which included such worthies as Rocket Richard, Bernie (Boom Boom) Geoffrion, Jean Beliveau, Jacques Plante, Doug Harvey, and Dickie Moore. The Red Wings, heavily oriented toward western Canada, where seldom a French word is heard, countered with the incomparable Gordie Howe, Ted Lindsay, Red Kelly, Alex Delvecchio, and Terry Sawchuk. The Red Wings stood for power. They were owned by the Norris family, the big grain merchants whose ships caused the biggest waves on the Great Lakes. And they had Howe, whose nickname was "Power."

The battle was not only between the two cities and two teams. It was also between the electrifying, so-Gallic Rocket Richard and the cool, effortless Howe. Who was the greater? The controversy raged. For the last four seasons, Howe had been named the right wing on the first-team all-stars; the Rocket had been picked number two. The Rocket had again led the league in goals during the 1953–54 campaign with 37. But Howe led in total points—and the NHL gives prize money only for the point leader.

The respective coaches also differed. There was the moody, gaunt Dick Irvin behind the Montreal bench. He suffered recurrent headaches, brought on when pressures aggravated a World War I injury. He was a no-nonsense, somber sort who once chased the great Geoffrion off the ice in a practice because the Boomer wasn't executing properly. Tommy Ivan led the Wings, an immaculately groomed sort who gave the impression that if he fell asleep with his pants on, he would wake up with the crease in the right place. Ivan was cool, not easily

he Great International Hockey War

ruffled. He was the sort the Norris family could invite to dinner.

Both teams had moved effortlessly into the finals. In those days, before hockey exploded in the U.S. and expansion teams proliferated geometrically, there were only six major-league clubs. They played seventy-game seasons in order to eliminate two teams. This year, New York and Chicago had failed to qualify for the playoffs. In the opening round, the Canadiens had disposed of the Boston Bruins in four games while the Red Wings toppled the Toronto Maple Leafs in five. Now came the showdown in the best-of-seven finals.

Immediately, Coach Irvin broke hockey tradition by predicting his Canadiens would win in six games. You never do this in hockey. You never bad-mouth the opposition; you never say you're better. It wasn't a question of sportsmanship (every loser always rapped the refereeing). It was simply a question of not making a fool of yourself if you turned out to be wrong. And, besides, coaches loved to tack up negative newspaper stories about their teams on the bulletin board, hoping to motivate the players.

Great things were expected from the Canadiens. After

One of NHL's great goalies, Terry Sawchuk was matched against rookie Jacques Plante as Stanley Cup began

all, they had disposed of the Bruins so easily in the first round, and the Rocket—the greatest playoff performer of them all—hadn't scored one point in the four games. He was due. True, Plante was complaining of stomach problems. But the asthmatic goalie was always complaining about something. He kept a vaporizer-inhaler in his pocket during the game in case his larynx muscles needed relaxing. Some believed Plante was a hypochondriac.

Plante said, for example, that he suffered from allergies. Some people are allergic to cats, or cigars, or eggs. But Plante was, among other things, allergic to Toronto. He even figured out a way to beat his allergy. Whenever the Canadiens had a game in Toronto he would simply spend the night at a motel on the outskirts of the city. Then, shortly before game time, he'd grab a cab and head directly for Maple Leaf Gardens. One night, though, he dreamed he was in Toronto—and woke up wheezing.

The spiritual force behind the Red Wings was Ted Lindsay, his battle scars causing half his face to tilt to one side, his prominent incisors giving him an almost Dracula-like appearance when he took the ice without his bridgework. He was the most penalized player in history, who took every check as a personal insult on his manhood. He was also the best left wing in the business.

Red Kelly, on the other hand, was an easygoing defenseman, also an all-star, who never cursed. His strongest expletive was "hang," as in "they checked the hang out of us." Sawchuk, crew-cut, was a bundle of nerves. Howe, of course, was Mr. Everything. If you needed forty minutes of "two-way hockey"—rushing forward on offense, coming back quickly to cut off your opposing wing when the other team had the disk—Howe was your man. He was perhaps the most sneaky-dirty player in the game, too—a man of enormous strength who could flick out his stick and separate a man from his collarbone—and the referee couldn't even see it.

"You'd skate by and see a guy in agony on the ice and you just knew that Gordie did it. But you couldn't prove it," referee Vern Buffey once said of Howe.

The Canadiens hoped their equalizer would be the supreme Doug Harvey. No defenseman—perhaps no player—had ever had his ability to slow down the game to his deliberate tempo. On the surface, it would appear to be an impossibility in the swift, almost formless-looking game that hockey is. Players skate close to thirty miles an hour. Their slapshots can zip from the blue line

155

to the goal, sixty feet away, in a fifth of a second. Yet, Harvey, a bear of a man wearing his beer-barrel stomach like a blue ribbon, would cajole the puck to do his bidding. He was in no hurry. He never thought much of training. And when he wanted to take things nice and easy, perhaps when the other team was pressing, he'd simply shift into low and suddenly the game was a slow-motion ballet. He was a perfect neutralizer for the Red Wings. But he was attempting to conceal an injured knee that was making him miserable.

Despite their western-Canada orientation, the Red Wings did have two highly regarded French players, Marcel Pronovost and Marcel Bonin. Pronovost happened to be one of the game's best defensemen. Bonin had knocked around amateur hockey for years. He had also wrestled bears in carnivals. In an exhibition game against the Red Wings he fought with Ted Lindsay. That appealed to "Jolly Jack" Adams, the impresario of the Wings, who grabbed Bonin from the obscurity of senior hockey. For a Frenchman to make the Red Wings, he had to be something special.

The 1954 finals started at the Detroit Olympia, an antiseptic building where the box-seat holders wore tuxedos and minks. But in the far reaches of the building, in the standing-room sections, only French was spoken by more than 700 fans from Montreal. When the first game was over they were disconsolate, because Kelly's final-period goal, while the Wings were a man short, helped guarantee a 3-1 Detroit victory.

"We won the big one," Ivan gloated afterward.

The next day the irritable Irvin locked himself in his hotel room. He saw no one until supper time, when he went to the dining room alone, pecked at his dinner, and returned to the isolation of his room.

The Wings were a great club, all right, with overwhelming skills. But they knew they might need an extra ingredient against the Canadiens: muscle. Around the league the "gorfs" were known, charitably, as men who would rather skate than fight. It was the *beau geste,* the tricky little maneuver, that brought rapture to the fans in the Montreal Forum, rather than the well-placed elbow. And if hit, the Frenchmen wouldn't fight back. The explosive Rocket was the exception. He had been fined more times than any player in history.

So Howe and Lindsay set out in the first game to batter the Canadiens, hoping to intimidate them, make them hesitate a split second, thus neutralizing their obvious

superiority in skating and passing. The Wings even gave a full shift on the ice to Tony Leswick, a five-foot six-inch marginal player whose greatest attribute was his tenacious hounding of the opposition. Ivan didn't care if Leswick scored—as long as he bothered the opposition.

The battle plan remained the same in Game Two. Soon, Howe was sent off for high-sticking, and Leswick,

who slashed at a Canadien, joined Howe in the penalty box. The Wings were two men short—and they would remain that way for two minutes. When you committed a penalty in 1954, you didn't return to the ice if the other team scored. You sat in the box and just hoped your penalty killers could do the job.

Immediately, the Canadiens grabbed their opportunity.

Moore put in a ricochet shot against Sawchuk. Then Richard went to work. In a twenty-nine-second span he scored twice. The three·goals took fifty-six seconds—the fastest three goals in the history of Stanley Cup play. This was what the Canadiens were all about. Champagne corks popped back in Montreal, where the Habs' followers were watching the game on television. (The

Canadiens' goalie Gerry McNeil, who replaced Plante after the fourth game, goes sprawling as he blocks shot by Glen Skov (left) in sixth game. Canadiens won, 4–1, to tie the playoff at 3–3.

"We kept on Richard all the time." TONY LESWICK

Canadiens were the highest-rated TV show in Canada, outdrawing even Ed Sullivan and Dinah Shore and Sid Caesar.)

There was nothing new about the Rocket rising to the occasion, of course. Ten years before, against Toronto, Richard had become the first—and still the only—Stanley Cup performer to register a five-goal game. He had more overtime goals than anyone else in Cup play, and he had scored more than anyone else in playoff competition.

But the Canadiens' 3-1 victory in Game Two was costly. Beliveau was blindsided, and his knee swelled up. He would miss Game Three, back at the Forum. Although this was only his first season in the NHL, Beliveau already had earned the nickname of "Le Gros Bill," after a Bunyanesque French-Canadian folk hero. Beliveau was willowy and the most graceful player in the league. He had been cajoled into turning pro by the Canadiens after receiving $20,000 a year as an "amateur." In Canada you were an amateur if you were called an amateur. Beliveau, noncombative, happy just to relax at night with his pipe in front of his television set, had no reason to turn pro. His picture graced most of the milk cartons sold in

Eyeball to eyeball in the second game, Red Wings and Canadiens wait for someone to throw the first punch as linesman Doug Davis (10) restrains Red Wings' Tony Leswick (8) and Canadiens' Tom Johnson (far left)

Quebec. He turned down speaking engagements. He was a hero. To get him, the Canadiens had pulled a simple ploy. They bought his amateur league and turned it professional. Beliveau thus belonged to Montreal.

Harvey also injured his knee in the second game, and he did not play. He was missed. The Wings shot to a 3-0 lead and skated away with an easy 5-2 decision. Now the Wings weren't distressed with the officiating, as they had been after the second game. After the Montreal victory the Canadiens' general manager, Frank Selke, had jokingly told Adams: "[Referee] Red Storey is on the Forum payroll." The story was splashed over the Detroit newspapers, and the Wings' management did nothing to indicate that Selke had simply been trying to make a joke.

Although Believeau and Harvey returned for Game Four, no one on Montreal could solve Sawchuk. The Frenchmen became unglued, almost hysterical. Irvin tried everything. He even activated Elmer Lach, at thirty-six the oldest man in the playoff. It was Lach's last season, following an outstanding career as Richard's center. But Lach was only a part-timer now, not even employed in the easy victories over Boston in the first round. Now Irvin reunited him with Richard. Nothing happened. The Wings nursed a 1-0 lead late in the game, and then Irvin tried another switch. He took defenseman Tom Johnson (the club's best, with Harvey hobbling) and switched him to center. It didn't help. With seven seconds remaining in the game the Wings' Kelly slammed the puck into an empty net to secure a 2-0 victory.

The Canadiens were down, three games to one. They would have to win three straight games. No club had ever recovered from such a deficit to take the cup since the Maple Leafs had done so against the Wings twelve years earlier—and that was the only time it had been accomplished.

Since one team was only a game away from victory, the Stanley Cup had to be readied for presentation. The three-foot-high punch bowl had been around since 1893, when the Governor-General of Canada, Frederick Arthur, Lord Stanley of Preston, paid $48.67 to a silversmith and had it created. Then he donated it as a prize to the top amateur team in Canada. Lord Stanley never desired—or even imagined—that it would one day go to those who weren't simon-pure.

During the season the Cup was on display at various places, usually Eaton's department store. But during the playoffs it was kept in a carton at the NHL offices. Prices had gone up over the years. To engrave the names of the players on the winning team on the cup base now cost more than $100—twice what the cup itself had cost. To get your name on the Cup you had to actually sit on the bench, at the very least, in a Cup game. If you were the star of the club and got injured in the last game of the regular season and missed the playoffs—well, your name didn't appear.

Meanwhile, Irvin was receiving pressure from the opinionated French-Canadian press, a gaggle of newspapers that devoted much of their sports pages to hockey 365 days a year. They began the rumor that the great Plante was to be replaced by Gerry McNeil. Plante was only a rookie. But after McNeil's nerves gave way late in the season Plante stepped in, played seventeen games, and turned in five shutouts.

Few people mentioned McNeil's name once Plante took over in the nets. McNeil had been the Frenchmen's number one goalie since the 1950 playoffs, when Bill Durnan suddenly decided he couldn't take the pressure of stopping pucks and quit. Harried goalies were a tradition in Montreal. McNeil and Durnan both spoke continually of having to win in the tense, electric atmosphere the Canadiens carried with them. After all, the team represented an identity—almost a people. Ultimately the goalie shouldered the blame for a losing game.

Now, in Game Five, McNeil reappeared—high irony. Just a few years before he had taken over for a distressed colleague. Then he himself was sidelined. Often, very often, a change in goaltenders reunites a team. The defense plays tighter, checks anyone in an alien uniform, so it is good psychology—when it works. And the Canadiens knew that if they didn't win with McNeil they would have, as hockey players put it, "an early summer."

So McNeil responded. Sawchuk was superb, too. In fact, the teams were scoreless after three regulation periods. That meant sudden-death overtime—the game would end as soon as the first goal was scored. An overtime period puts twelve players on the ice, in front of 15,000 spectators, along with a time bomb. The bomb is the puck, the frozen slab of vulcanized rubber that suddenly takes on a larger identity. Every time the puck is simply nudged in an overtime period it brings gasps or cheers from the crowd. One shot is all it takes.

Yet, Ivan didn't want his Wings withdrawing into a shell. "Win it as quick as you can," he told his team. He knew that the club had an advantage. It was playing before a home crowd—and in hockey the visiting team considers itself lucky if it can get a draw on enemy ice. Ivan didn't want his club to get sloppy, to take chances, but he also knew that even if the Wings lost they still had a commanding edge in games.

owe almost won it for him after thirty seconds. He cruised in on McNeil and snapped his wrist—the strongest wrist shot in the game. McNeil crouched frozen. Suddenly he pounced on the disk as it headed between his knees and smothered it two inches from the goal line.

The save inspired the Canadiens, and Ken Mosdell. He was the all-star center but had not scored a goal in the playoffs. After five minutes and forty-five seconds of overtime he got his first one—and it won the game. Now the Wings' edge was cut to three games to two. The teams were going back to Montreal for a sixth game. Campbell, Stanley Cup in tow, had to write a second speech. His first one, prepared for delivery in the Olympia, would have to be translated into French. If the Wings won the Cup at the Forum, Campbell would make the presentation first in French, then in English.

Over 85 percent of the Forum fans were French-Canadian. No photograph of English royalty hung from one end of the building, as in Toronto's Maple Leaf Gardens. The announcements in Montreal were made first in French, then in English. It was the focal point for Quebec, and a season's seat was a precious commodity. Men made sure their wills provided that season's seats be left to their heirs.

McNeil was back in the nets, and it was like old times. Geoffrion opened the scoring in the second period (after which he was punched in the stomach and knocked out), and Floyd (Busher) Curry added two more in a seventy-eight-second span. The Rocket scored the final goal in a 4-1 victory, and the Canadiens' legend lived. Perhaps they just might do the impossible. The series was tied at three-all.

Two Montreal policemen, each holding a wide-barreled shotgun, flanked the steps leading to the first-

class train car as the Stanley Cup was carried aboard for the trip back to Detroit.

The biggest crowd in Detroit's twenty-eight-year NHL history turned out at the Olympia. The 15,792 fans saw Sawchuk again in the nets for the Wings and McNeil back for the Canadiens. But the scoring came from unlikely sources. Busher Curry lifted the Frenchmen to a 1-0 lead in the opening period. Then Kelly, who had scored only six goals in fifty-one previous playoff games, got his fifth of the series, and the score was tied. Despite the goal, the Wings appeared to be on the way out. They had seen their 3-1 bulge evaporate into a brand-new series. And they were watching the Canadiens, who hadn't won at the Olympia in the regular season, give them a battle now in the most critical game of the year.

With four minutes remaining it appeared to be all over for Detroit. Richard had the puck and was zeroing in on Sawchuk. He stared at Sawchuk for the briefest moment, his eyes burning brightly like two torches from a mountainside cave. The Rocket pulled back to shoot—and then Bennt Woit creamed him. He hit Richard so hard that as the Rocket fell he broke his stick. The puck lay at his skates. With no stick in his hand, he instinctively did the only thing he could do. He swiped at the puck with a free hand and pushed it past the surprised Sawchuk. But it didn't count. The puck had to be propelled home by a stick. The Wings were given another chance. They played the Canadiens even, and the third period ended with the score tied at 1-1. Another overtime was coming up—this time for the Cup itself.

Ivan, of course, started his top line of Howe, Delvecchio, and Lindsay. Within ninety seconds they were replaced by a second line. Hockey is the only sport that makes substitutions while play is in progress. It's a necessity. The work is so hard that forwards can go at full tilt a minute and a half at most. Defensemen might play as long as two minutes, since they don't carry the puck so often. By the time the third shift was ready, the Detroit checkers were called out. They were Glen Skov, Marty Pavelich, and Leswick. Adams liked to call Leswick "The Pest." He was the sort of player who always manages to hook onto a team—willing, self-sacrificing. The three combined had accounted for only thirty-two goals during the regular season—five less than the Rocket had accumulated by himself. Now they were all supposed to do the same thing for ninety seconds: hold the Flying Frenchmen so the Howe line could get a rest.

They may have been a marginal line, but they had one advantage over the Canadiens. They knew the lively boards at the Olympia. The Red Wings made more use of their arena than any team in the league. It was always theirs to practice on. Plays were developed using the peculiarities of the boards behind the net. A favored Detroit play saw Delvecchio lash a shot off the board. The puck would rebound right out to Howe, who timed his appearance perfectly.

So it didn't strike the crowd as odd that a rebound caromed onto Skov's stick. He spotted Leswick and fed him a banked pass off the boards. Leswick looked in front of him and saw McNeil fifty feet away covering the net too well. And in front of McNeil stood Harvey. Leswick decided to let the puck go anyway. A soft, rising shot sailed toward Harvey. Normally, Harvey might have ducked, giving McNeil more room to see the puck. But he had lost some mobility because of his bad knee. Anyway, it was a harmless enough shot. So Harvey stuck out his hand. But rather than batting it down, he touched it only with his thumb. The puck changed direction suddenly—and skipped over McNeil's shoulder.

For a second Ivan didn't move. The Detroit bench was still. The goal judge didn't trigger the red light that signifies a score.

But the crowd knew it. It let out a roar, the kind one hears when a lion has just struck for the kill and is proclaiming its dominance. And then the red light flashed, and Ivan jumped and Leswick raised his hands. His teammates did the thing hockey players always do when a puck goes in—they embraced the goalscorer.

It was over, so suddenly. And yet, automatically, the Red Wings lined up to shake the losers' hands. But no one from Montreal remained on the ice. They all walked off, following the somber Irvin into the locker room. The crowd booed this breach of etiquette.

Later, in the dressing room, between sips of champagne from the cup, Leswick said with a sneer, "Did you see how they shook hands?"

In the Canadiens' locker room Irvin dismissed the hand-shaking business as "sheer hypocrisy."

Finally, it was time to leave. Richard attempted to slip out but saw a crowd of Red Wing fans waiting near the dressing room door. They were taunting him. He stormed back and grabbed a soda bottle and shouted to the walls, "They been pushing me around this series and I won't let them do it any more."

"Drop it," Lach told him quietly.

Then Lach put his arm around Richard and the pair left a Canadien dressing room together for the last time.

"I would have given five years of my life to have scored just one more goal," said Lach.

Doug Harvey (right) and Dollard St. Laurent, caught by the camera at the moment Tony Leswick's winning shot went into the net. Shot skimmed in off Harvey's glove after he tried to catch it. Overleaf: A hockey ballet: Canadiens' Maurice Richard (9) and Red Wings' Red Kelly (4) scramble for the puck against the boards

Dutch Riley (14) scores for Canadiens with a shot that sails into the net off Ted Lindsay's stick

Red Kelly puts the puck in against Jacques Plante, and the Canadiens win the first game by a score of 3–1

The Richard temper flares in 1954 game and he is restrained after slapping the linesman

Fiery Frenchman

The tempestuous Maurice (Rocket) Richard appeared to recover from the shock of the 1954 playoff defeat. During the 1954–55 campaign that followed, The Rocket was on his way to the scoring championship that had eluded him each of his previous eleven seasons, even though he had led in goals four times.

But hockey, its moguls said, was a team game. Thus the National Hockey League never honored its top goal-getter. To win the Art Ross Trophy you had to amass the highest number of points with goals and assists combined. The assists, the league said, showed that a player wasn't selfish.

Finally, however, the scoring title was in his grasp. Only three games remained after a Sunday tilt at

> "You knew that Plante was going to be a good one."
>
> RED KELLY

Maurice Richard's shot goes past Terry Sawchuk in second game. Richard scored again seconds later

Red Wings sneak puck in from behind the left side of the goal to beat Plante and go ahead 4–1 in third game

Boston. The Rocket had amassed 74 points—two ahead of his teammate, Boom Boom Geoffrion, and three ahead of another Frenchman, Jean Beliveau.

Richard was his usual fiery self in the game. There was a collision with the Bruin's defenseman, Hal Laycoe, and Laycoe swiped at Richard. The tense Richard pushed his hand through his thick hair and felt something sticky. He looked at his hand and saw blood. Suddenly, Richard went into a frenzy. He leaped at Laycoe and started punching.

One of the linesmen, Cliff Thompson, leaped on Richard's back and tried to snare his arms. But Richard flailed wildly behind him, trying to get Thompson off. "Someone was holding me," Richard was to recall. "But no one was holding Laycoe." Richard then spun around and whacked Thompson in the face. While everyone rushed to this little scene, Doug Harvey sauntered past Laycoe and smashed him between the eyes, knocking him out.

Three days later Clarence Campbell conducted a three-and-one-half-hour hearing. Richard contended he didn't know what he was doing after being smacked on top of the head by Laycoe. But Campbell had heard this before. Just a month earlier he had fined Richard for a similar incident in Toronto.

"The time for probation or lenience for Richard is past," announced Campbell. And he suspended the hero for the remainder of the season—and the playoffs. The suspension cost Richard the scoring championship. (He never did win one.) It also provoked an incredible response from Richard's fans.

"The toughest part of goaltending is the pressure that you feel in there. Today, with the slap shots, a lot of them can score on you from the blue line. You know if you just blink your eyes, they can score on you from 60 feet out, and this is what you fear most."

JACQUES PLANTE

165

Scoreboard shows final score in third game, with Detroit beating the Canadiens to take 2–1 lead in playoff

On-the-ice wrestling match stops the action in the fourth game, which Red Wings won by a score of 2–1

"Even five, six years after he was in the league, Howe always felt that he had to earn his position on the club and always made it very rough for the left winger playing against him in camp—he never quit working for his job."

TED LINDSAY

The Riot

The night of Rocket Richard's suspension, Boom-Boom Geoffrion got a phone call at home: "If you pass the Rocket, we will kill your daughter," said the caller. Geoffrion called the police, who immediately placed a twenty-four-hour guard around his home. More calls came in, obscene ones to Geoffrion's wife (daughter of a former hockey star, Howie Morenz). Geoffrion received death threats. Always volatile, he was now near a nervous breakdown. Only three games remained, and Boomer was just two points behind Richard.

The Canadiens' next game was the following night, March 17, against the Red Wings, who were moving quickly on first place—which had been occupied by the Canadiens. Before the game Campbell received a phone call. "I'm an undertaker," said the caller, "and I'm getting ready to see you."

Extremely righteous, with a high sense of honor, Campbell saw no reason not to attend the game that night. "I would have no business being president if I let a few cranks scare me," he recalled. Campbell had a late supper with his secretary, Phyllis King (his future wife), her sister, and a friend. He wasn't aware of what was happening outside the Forum.

Hundreds of teenagers, many of them looking like motorcycle thugs out of "The Wild One," roamed in front of the building. A well-dressed woman carried a sign, almost like a cross, that read, "Injustice Au Canada Français." Much of the province accepted this claim of injustice to French Canada. The symbolism was perfect: Campbell, the Rhodes Scholar, administering justice to a French Canadian.

*Red Wings' defenseman Red Kelly scores the final
goal in fourth game to give Wings 3–1 lead in playoff*

*Boom Boom Geoffrion blazes the puck past Terry Sawchuk
in the sixth game, to put the Canadiens ahead, 2–1*

It mattered little to the French fanatics that Campbell had been a judge at the Nuremberg war crimes trial. For now, he was a hated Anglo.

Campbell parked his car a few blocks away from the Forum and told the women to go on ahead without him. The game had already started. He walked briskly through the slush and was surprised to see himself surrounded on all sides by screaming fans. They hooted in French, "Démissionne," asking for his resignation. A policemen, not recognizing Campbell, tried to stop him from entering the building.

When he finally got inside and took the few strides to his seat from the entranceway, the crowd spotted him. Immediately they began shouting and booing. Richard, meanwhile, sat quietly behind one of the goals.

The noise grew worse as the period wore on. The Canadiens were losing, 4-1. Fans tried to get at Campbell, but security guards pushed them away. Then the hail of paper and tomatoes and overshoes came. People around Campbell quickly left their seats. One man, a few rows behind, pointed to Campbell to help the aim of marksmen in the upper reaches of the building. He resembled one of those men on the flight deck of an aircraft carrier waving his arms to direct the landing planes. One fan somehow convinced the police he was a friend of Campbell's. He got close to him and stuck out his hand, as if to congratulate Campbell. The league president offered his hand and the man punched him.

Then a tear-gas cannister was tossed not far from Campbell, and the panic began. The choking smoke filled the bottom of the building, and hundreds ran

for the exits. Campbell left. Outside, meanwhile, a full-fledged riot began. Store windows were smashed in a seven-hour orgy of frustration. About one hundred people were arrested after creating half a million dollars worth of damage. As a result of the rioting, the Canadiens forfeited the game.

Two nights later, Geoffrion got three points in the first twelve minutes against the Rangers and passed Richard to win the championship. The following night, in the final game of the season, Sawchuk shut out the Frenchmen and the Red Wings grabbed first place. (In the Stanley Cup playoffs, the Wings once again defeated the Canadiens.)

Beliveau also passed the idle Rocket, and Big Jean was to say later, "I think the Rocket would have been upset if Bernie or me had missed the nets on purpose."

Maurice Richard scores for the Canadiens as they beat the Red Wings, 4–1, to even the playoff at 3–3

Skating furiously in final game, Wings and Canadiens fought to a 1–1 tie at the end of regulation time

Goalie Pressure

A year after his sensational goal tending in the playoffs, Terry Sawchuk was traded by Detroit to the Boston Bruins. He was at the height of his career, and had turned in his fifth straight season of yielding fewer than two goals a game. But the Wings had an outstanding youngster named Glenn Hall, and they figured they would trade Sawchuk at his peak and get something in return. Ironically, the Wings got no one of lasting value in the multiplayer deal.

Sawchuk never liked Boston, even though he registered nine shutouts in the 1955–56 campaign. The following year he got mononucleosis and played while sick. The bellicose Boston fans affected him with their pointed screaming, and Sawchuk suffered a nervous breakdown—an occupational hazard for goalies. In 1957, Sawchuk was traded back to the Wings in exchange for John Bucyk. The great years were over, but Sawchuk played until 1970, moving on to Toronto, Los Angeles, back to Detroit, and, finally, to New York. By then he had amassed a record 103 shutouts. He was a Vezina Trophy winner four times.

One day in the spring of 1970, after the Rangers had been eliminated from the playoffs, Sawchuk went out drinking with one of his friends—his roommate and teammate, Ron Stewart. They got into an argument over the rent and had a fight in the bar. They were taken in separate cars to their rented house on Long Island. What happened in the following moments is unclear. Stewart told a grand jury that they wrestled and Sawchuk fell over a barbecue grill. Whatever happened, Sawchuk was struck so violently that his gallbladder was ripped. He died a short time later from complications.

"It was too bad Terry never managed his private life as well as he played goal," said a former teammate.

His stick broken by a fierce bodycheck, Maurice Richard
scores illegal goal by swatting puck in with his glove

Shooting from fifty feet out, Tony Leswick gets
off the winning shot for the Wings in overtime period

Honors

Red Wings embrace
Terry Sawchuk
in locker room

Like Maurice Richard, Doug Harvey was a moody hero. There was no denying his playing credentials for hockey's Hall of Fame: starting with the 1951–52 season he was named to the first all-star team seven straight times—and in ten of eleven years. He was voted the James Norris Trophy as best defenseman seven times in eight seasons. Yet in 1972, when he became eligible for the Hall of Fame after having been out of the game as a player for three years, he was not voted in. Part of the entrance requirements was what is signified by the word "character," and some members of the committee thought Harvey lacked it. Harvey had been heard to complain that hockey had treated him badly. (Actually, he had been given coaching opportunities as his playing career neared its conclusion.) In 1973, the committee reconsidered and voted him in.

"I'll be out fishing during the ceremonies," he predicted. And he was.

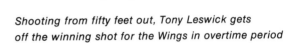

"I happened to be in the right spot at the right time and when you say I was a hero, I I don't know. Next year I was traded to Chicago."

TONY LESWICK

LYN 0 0 0 0 0 0 0 0 0
IKS 0 0 0 1 0 1 0 0

THE LAST
SUBWAY SERIES

The Series begins: fans fill Ebbets Field for the first g

New York Yankees/ Brooklyn Dodgers World Series October, 1956

By Stan Isaacs

hey had played each other so often, it seemed safe to assume that everything possible had already happened. Mickey Owens letting a third strike slip past him in 1941. Cookie Lavagetto breaking up Bill Bevens' no-hitter in 1947. Tommy Henrich slugging a homer to beat Don Newcombe in the tenth inning in 1949. And then the Brooklyn Dodgers finally whipped the New York Yankees in the 1955 World Series. What more could happen?

Don Larsen had an answer, one year later. Perfection. Tall and casual, he strolled to the mound and retired twenty-seven straight Dodgers. That effort must have destroyed the script maker. There was indeed nothing else to say. So the Yankees and the Brooklyn Dodgers never played another World Series after 1956, at least not for the price of a subway ride.

Stan Isaacs, a native of Brooklyn, laments the passing of the "subway series" and chronicles the strange perfection of Don Larsen. He covered this Series for *Newsday*, the growing Long Island newspaper. Later he wrote his own column, "Out of Left Field," a humorous and philosophical view of sports that gained him national prominence. Now a featured columnist for *Newsday*, Isaacs feels the metropolitan area has never quite recovered from the loss of the two baseball teams, the Dodgers and the Giants. A graduate of Brooklyn College, he resides in Roslyn Heights, Long Island, where he is one of the leading stoopball players. G.V.

The Last Subway Series

We didn't know it then, that the 1956 World Series would be the last "subway series"—the end of a wondrous time. At the moment, it seemed like the showcase for Don Larsen's perfect game, the only perfect game in World Series history. But it was more, much more.

For New Yorkers, it was the last time they would ride the subway to see crosstown rivals play in the World Series—no small loss. Since the World Series had begun in 1901, there had been fifteen crosstown Series: one in Chicago, one in St. Louis and thirteen in New York. Fans had grown used to either the Brooklyn Dodgers or the New York Giants challenging the perpetual Yankees in October.

It is possible to give too much weight to the impact of a sporting spectacle on a city—a metropolis of twelve million people is much more than a bunch of grown men playing a little boy's game. But nevertheless something would go out of the city, a spiritual high water mark would recede with the departure of the Giants and Dodgers to the West Coast after 1957.

In 1956, New York was still a baseball town more than anything else. It wasn't until the Dodgers and Giants skipped town that pro football had its boom and the Knicks and Rangers began to take over the metropolis for most of April. And even when the Mets were born in 1962, baseball never again really owned the town the way it did in the days of the subway series.

While the Series generally brought together opponents who were virtual strangers to each other, the Yankees and Dodgers played so often between 1947 and 1956—six Series, thirty-nine games—that their meetings were almost like adventure chapters in a serialized novel. The present was measured against the past; the fans had a keener knowledge of the opponents than was the case in most World Series.

Nobody understood the Yankee mystique better than Dodger partisans or feared it more. Having seen their powerful team beaten in five straight Series by the Yankees, they had taken ecstatic joy when the Dodgers finally in 1955, and they wanted a repeat victory in 1956 just to begin to make up for past indignities.

But the Dodgers were fated for the ultimate indignity on that Monday afternoon when they would become the first team in World Series history to make twenty-seven consecutive outs. The indignity would come from a strange source. The Dodgers had the vaunted Sal Maglie pitching against the erratic Larsen, a twenty-seven-year-old right hander in his fourth year as a big leaguer who had been the losingest pitcher in baseball only two years previous, with a 3–21 record at Baltimore. In 1956 Larsen had won 11 games, the high mark of his career. But this was the time Larsen, a not-always-dedicated athlete, came up perfect. His perfect game was perhaps the single outstanding pitching performance of all time—particularly considering the Series pressure.

Some of the greatest figures in baseball history were among the 1956 cast of characters. For the Yankees, there was, first and foremost, manager Casey Stengel, leading his team into Ebbets Field, which he had helped open as a Brooklyn ballplayer in 1913. He was in the middle of the action with his strategic wizardry, changing pitchers on the mound, and he was up all night at World Series press headquarters, replaying the games and the strategy with experts and folks, personifying his observation that, "I have been around for so long, I can get along with anybody." Yogi Berra had his greatest World Series. Mickey Mantle, forty-year-old Enos Slaughter, and winning pitchers Whitey Ford, Tom Sturdivant, and Johnny Kucks all played major roles for the Yankees.

For the Dodgers, the manager was, even then, Walter Alston, guiding the boys of summer grown older: Jackie Robinson and Pee Wee Reese (who would be playing in their last World Series), Carl Furillo, Roy Campanella, Duke Snider, Gil Hodges, and winning pitchers Clem Labine, Don Bessent, and Maglie. Also for the Dodgers there was the huge pitcher, Don Newcombe, tragic in defeat.

The 1956 Series followed the pattern of the previous fall, when the Dodgers had beaten the Yankees for the first time. The home team won each of the first six games. In the seventh game, the visiting team broke the pattern to win the Series, the Dodgers at Yankee Stadium in 1955, the Yankees at Ebbets Field in 1956. In those days, aficionados followed these home-team patterns closely. There was hardly a street-corner analysis that wasn't replete with speculation of how the day's particular battle might have gone had it been

Perfect form: on his way to pitching perfect game, Larsen delivers to the plate

played in the other ball park. A drive to spacious left-center in Yankee Stadium would have been a home run in tiny Ebbets Field; a home run down the short right-field line in the Stadium would have hit the high fence at Ebbets Field. It made a difference.

The difference in the first game was Maglie. If ever there was a player who was considered a money pitcher, it was Maglie. He was thirty-nine then, having come to the Dodgers as a castoff from the Cleveland Indians for the waiver price in mid-season. He immediately stepped into the Dodger rotation and won some big games while compiling a 13–5 record.

A few years earlier, Maglie had been the ace of the Giants' staff, the glowering, peerless curveballer who helped subdue the powerful Dodgers time and time again in Ebbets Field, where the Giants had once gone a whole season without winning a game. As a Giant, Maglie had been an ogre second only to manager Leo Durocher, an ex-Dodger. (The ultimate irony was that Maglie would eventually pitch for all three New York teams; in 1958 the Yankees would purchase him from the Dodgers late in the season to help them win the pennant.)

Maglie was a pitching craftsman whose swarthy features, heavy beard, and concentration game him a sinister presence on the mound. Also, his tendency to pitch inside to hitters who dared to crowd the plate earned him the nickname, "Sal the Barber." His great control made him seem like a brilliant tactician, and he didn't disagree when some people suggested that sometimes he intentionally went to a count of three balls, no strikes, to help set up a hitter. He had a baffling variety of low-breaking curveballs. Even while he was with the Dodgers, the mind's eye went back to his days with the Giants when he was throwing those curves on the outside corner past the Dodgers' powerful row of right-hand hitters.

Maglie, who had pitched the only no-hitter of his career eight days earlier, fell behind 2–0 in the first game on a two-run homer by Mantle. But the Dodgers tied it in the second with the help of a homer by Jackie Robinson and went ahead for good on a three-run homer in the third by Gil Hodges off starter Whitey Ford. After a homer by Billy Martin in the fourth, Maglie coasted home for a 6–3 victory, getting stronger as he went along, inspiring the cheers of the home crowd, whose faith in him was boundless. Ebbets Field, a treasured bandbox

Action in the Series: Duke Snider (left) *cracked a three-run homer in the second game as the Dodgers crushed the Yanks, 13–8. Roy Campanella* (right) *scared Larsen with a long drive that curved foul in the ninth inning of perfect game.*

of a ball park, was filled to its capacity—34,470 fans—on a day for politicians in a year of politicians.

President Eisenhower, who was running for reelection against Adlai Stevenson, made the first presidential appearance at a World Series since Franklin Delano Roosevelt threw out the first ball in 1936. Also on hand were a governor, Averell Harriman; a mayor, Robert Wagner; a former President, Herbert Hoover (who had been booed when he attended a World Series in his tenure during the Depression); and a former king, the Duke of Windsor. Henry Krajewski, the pig farmer from New Jersey who was the presidential candidate for the American Party, had requested and been sent a ticket to the opener by the Dodger owner, Walter O'Malley. Democrat Stevenson attended the second game. As it turned out, the World Series turned out to be more interesting and closer fought than the election, another landslide for Eisenhower.

The second game spectators and Stevenson got a brief glimpse of Larsen, the unlikely hero of the future. Larsen was an enigma because he seemed to have the ability to be an outstanding pitcher but also had a lackadaisical approach to baseball and to life. He was what many people called a ''happy-go-lucky guy''; he was shy, likable, popular with his teammates, who called him ''goony bird,'' and not the most difficult man in the world to take advantage of.

Ballplayers have a lot of time on their hands away from the ball park. There are many diversions. It takes a certain amount of dedication and good sense to at least stay out of trouble. Larsen didn't have this discipline. He frequently broke curfews and missed planes —earning a reputation as a playboy. It had looked for a time as if he might not even stay with the Yankees because of a notorious incident at spring training that year.

Amply fueled by alcohol, he had wrapped his car around a telephone pole at the Yankees' St. Petersburg, Florida, training site one 5:30 A.M. He confessed freely to the police. Casey Stengel warned him not to do it again and hastened him on the way to reclamation by naming him to pitch on Opening Day. Larsen was used as a spot pitcher, and he did well early and late in the season, winding up with an 11–5 record. As the starter for the second game, he was given a 6–0 lead but was then removed in the second inning. Most of the damage in a six-run Dodger rally came after he left. All the runs

Yankee first baseman Bill Skowron stretched hard (below), *but Pee Wee Reese beat throw for infield hit; Gil Hodges* (right) *blasted home run as Dodgers won the first game*

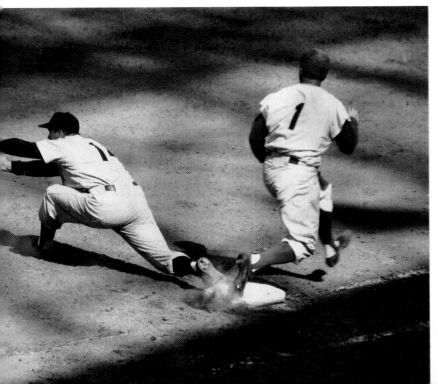

were unearned because of an error by Joe Collins at first base, and some perspicacious observers criticized Stengel for giving Larsen a quick hook. Larsen had allowed one hit and one unearned run, and the bases were loaded with two out when he was removed. The Dodgers then jumped on Johnny Kucks and Tommy Byrne for a six-run rally, highlighted by Duke Snider's three-run homer. Then Don Bessent completed seven innings of relief to nail down a 13–8 Dodger victory in three hours and twenty-five minutes, the longest Series game ever.

Ahead by two games, the Dodgers led Whitey Ford 2–1 in the sixth inning of the third game. Here the Yankees broke through with a three-run homer by Enos Slaughter, the hustling old St. Louis Cardinal hero, to beat Roger Craig, 5–3. The next day Tom Sturdivan beat Carl Erskine, 6–2, to tie the Series for the Yankees as Mickey Mantle hit one of the longer World Series home runs, a blast twelve rows into the center-field bleachers above the 407-foot sign. (Roy Campanella said, "It wouldn't have gone over the fence in Ebbets Field . . . might have gone through it, though.") Now

The manager: Casey Stengel heads for the dugout after conference with Tom Morgan and Yogi Berra

the Series was even at two games apiece. And Larsen would oppose Maglie the next day.

That night, Larsen had dinner at former Giant Bill Taylor's restaurant, and was joined by roommate W. Gary (Rip) Coleman and newspaperman Art Richman and a few lady friends at the bar. He went back to his apartment at a hotel near Yankee Stadium before midnight. Richman, who later became promotions director for the New York Mets, said recently: "There have been a million stories that Don was up all night; there are a million bartenders all over town now saying he was

sloshed in their place in the wee hours before the game. None of that is true. He had a pizza and went to bed. I recall that, as I was leaving him, he gave me some money to give to my mother for her synagogue. He wasn't religious, but he thought she might say a prayer for him. He even said in that who-gives-a-damn attitude of his, 'I might even pitch a no-hitter.' "

The crowd of 64,519 spectators for the fifth game at Yankee Stadium was a typical Yankee Stadium World Series crowd. A goodly portion of the people in the good seats were expense-account trade, the kind of people who come to a World Series game because it's a place to be. They were not the day-in, day-out baseball fans, the ones who know the game well, who anticipate situations and keep a ball park bubbling. Yankee Stadium has never been a good ball park for noise, and there was a particular calm over the great arena this day, mostly because nothing much happened for a long time. It was only in the last three innings, when Larsen moved toward the perfect game, that tension took hold.

Larsen's first pitch to leadoff hitter Jim Gilliam was wide for a ball. He then retired Gilliam on strikes. Larsen went to a three-ball count on the next batter, Pee Wee Reese, before retiring him. It was the only time Larsen would reach three balls all day. Most pitchers go through a nine-inning game throwing at least 110 pitches; Maglie threw 148 winning the first game, Larsen would throw 97.

Larsen sailed through the Dodger lineup with ease, almost effortlessly. He took little time between pitches, never having to go to a full windup. And he threw fastballs, curves, sliders, and change-ups, almost always for strikes.

The sense of ease was accentuated by the no-windup delivery Larsen had adopted in his second-to-last start of the season. Believing that Del Baker, the Red Sox coach, was getting a good look at how he was gripping the ball, Larsen had begun throwing without a windup to give Baker less time to detect the pitch. He had pitched a shutout—and adopted the motion.

The motion added to the impression of nonchalance about Larsen. A big man, six feet, four inches and 215 pounds, Larsen stood on the mound looking down at catcher Yogi Berra for his sign, nodding, poking the ball into his glove as he got set, then pulling it out and throwing, raising his left hip for leverage. He looked like a man standing on the beach, scaling stones into the water.

179

There were no base runners for the first three innings. Then, with two out in the bottom of the fourth, Mantle dented Maglie with a home run into the lower right-field stands. The Yankees made it 2–0 in the sixth on a pair of singles by Andy Carey and Hank Bauer, sandwiched around a Larsen sacrifice. Larsen kept mowing down the Dodgers. Though people would later point to four or five instances in which the Dodgers came close to a hit, not one ball should have been a hit. When good fielding was needed, the Yankees provided it.

■ In the second inning, Robinson hit a liner to third base which caromed off Carey's glove over to shortstop Gil McDougald, who threw over to first baseman Joe Collins.

■ In the fifth, with one out, Hodges hit a long drive to left-center field which Mantle tracked down after a spirited run, catching the ball with a back-handed grab. Mantle later said, "I thought it would be an easier catch than it turned out to be. I was with it all the way."

■ Immediately afterward, Sandy Amoros hit a liner into the right-field stands that hooked foul by a foot at the last moment.

■ In the eighth, Hodges hit a sinking soft liner toward third base, which Carey moved over to grab on the fly.

Each out by Larsen brought him closer to something that had never been done before. In all of baseball history, there had been only six perfect games. And of the 143 previous no-hitters since 1875, none had come in a World Series. Each out heightened the excruciating tension in the ball park. The drama of the event was intensified by the awareness that this was a close game, in which the Dodgers were capable not only of breaking through to stop Larsen, but of winning the game.

Fans recalled the only comparable game, nine years earlier—in the fourth game of the 1947 Series—between the same two teams, when the Yankees' Floyd Bevens had a no-hitter and a 2–1 lead with two out in the ninth inning, only to lose the no-hitter and the game on a two-run double by pinch hitter Cookie Lavagetto.

By the sixth inning, Larsen was aware of what he was into, which his teammates said nothing to him in the dugout. At one point Larsen's roommate, Rip Coleman, who couldn't stand the tension, ducked down the dugout steps and paced up and down under the stands. When a groundskeeper came by and blithely told him, "Larsen's pitching a no-hitter," Coleman glared at the violation of baseball custom. Mantle avoid Larsen's eyes.

The stage was set ever so nicely for the finish when Maglie zipped through the Yankees in the eighth by striking out the side, starting with Larsen on three swings. As the Dodgers came toward the dugout still trailing 2–0, Roscoe McGowen of the *New York Times,* who was in the stadium runway waiting to cover the Dodger dressing room, reported he heard Jackie Robinson call out in the dugout, "Come on guys. Let's get 'em. This game isn't over, yet."

A haze seemed to settle over the ball park, and ribbons

ove at home." DON LARSEN

---

of paper fell from the upper right-field stands as Larsen moved out for the ninth. Inexplicably, some people were already filing toward the exits, and there were some less-than-stalwart soldiers who chose to watch the finish on the television sets in the Stadium Club bar.

Carl Furillo, trying to hit to right field, was up first. He had flied to right and popped to second. He fouled off two pitches, took a ball, fouled off two more pitches into the boxes behind first, and, on the sixth pitch, raised an easy fly to Hank Bauer in right field.

As Roy Campanella moved to the plate, Yankee fans all over the park indulged in their own little superstitions to keep Larsen going. From the rear of the press section, Irving Rudd, the Dodgers' promotions director, shouted, "The hell with history, Roy, let's get on base and start something." Campanella, who had taken a third strike and popped to second, swung at the first pitch, and for a moment there was a collective gasp as the ball headed toward deep left field. It was, however, an obvious foul. Larsen then threw his only curve of the inning, and

Mickey Mantle grabs a fly ball in the eighth inning of Larsen's perfect game

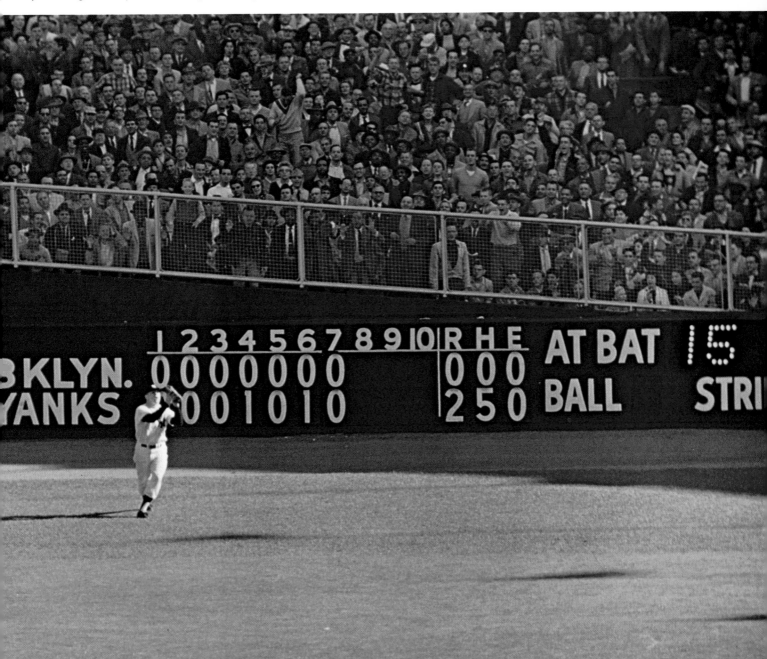

Campanella grounded to Martin at second base.

There was a delay before Dale Mitchell, the pinch hitter, an experienced outfielder, moved to the plate. Larsen recalls now that the delay scared him, the only time he was nervous, because "it gave me time to think. My knees were shaking. I sort of asked for a little help from the man upstairs. Looking back on it though, I know how much pressure Mitchell must have been under. He must have been paralyzed. That made two of us."

In the Yankee dugout, Stengel recalled, "Everybody suddenly got scared we weren't playing the outfield right. I never seen so many managers."

Mitchell took a ball wide, then a slider for a strike. With a continued nonchalance that belied the moment, Larsen threw another stone into the ocean, another fastball, which Mitchell swung at and missed. Mitchell fouled off another fastball. Berra then called for a fastball, and Larsen's pitch headed toward the outside corner. Mitchell cocked his bat to swing and tried to hold up. Plate umpire Babe Pinelli did not hesitate. He shot his right arm up for a called strike three. While Mitchell stood in the batter's box, making a feeble protest to the departing Pinelli, the Yankees, led by Berra's leap into Larsen's arms, mobbed their pitcher.

Larsen was surrounded by interviewers for almost two hours. Some of it went like this:

Question: "Are you thrilled?" Answer: "Yes, I know it happened, but I still can't believe it. I haven't had a chance to take a deep breath."

Question: "When did you first start thinking about the no-hitter?" Answer: "In the seventh. I had been aware of it before that, but that was when it really took hold, I guess."

Question: "What were you thinking in the ninth?" Answer: "I don't know."

Question: "Did you ever think of Floyd Bevens?" Answer: "Yes, I did in the eighth. I hoped what happened to him didn't happen to me."

Stengel even had one nameless reporter ask him: "Was this the best game Larsen ever pitched?"

Among the visitors to congratulate Larsen was umpire Pinelli. Pinelli, at sixty-one, was closing out a twenty-two-year career after the World Series, and this was his last game behind the plate. He said the last strike was a good one, that "Larsen had the greatest pinpoint control I have ever seen."

Even in his hour of triumph, Larsen's personal troubles intruded. While he was pitching at Yankee Stadium, his estranged wife was in a courtroom a few blocks away asking that Larsen's World Series money be withheld until he paid her back alimony. It came out that Larsen had been married secretly to protect a daughter, and the couple had not lived as man and wife. Larsen was to pay alimony for years afterward.

While Larsen was being toasted around the country, the subway series rode underground from the Bronx to Flatbush, where the Yankees had lost five straight games in two Series. Stengel, with his antennae always working, decided not to send his ace, Ford, a lefty, against the Dodgers' powerful right-handed array in a bandbox ball park. Instead, Stengel had set up his pitching order so that Bob Turley and Johnny Kucks would be ready.

In the sixth game, Turley and Clem Labine pitched a scoreless tie through nine innings—before Jackie Robinson took over. Robinson, greying and heavy at thirty-six years of age, had not been the regular third baseman in 1956, playing behind Randy Jackson. But when the Series came, it was inevitable that Robinson, one of the greatest competitors sports has known, would be in the lineup. After hitting a home run in the first game, Robinson was relatively unheard from until this game. His first three times at bat, he left five men on base. But in the tenth inning, Jim Gilliam walked, Reese sacrificed, and, for the second straight time, Snider was walked intentionally to get at Robinson. This time Robinson delivered a line drive to left field. Slaughter came in at first and then retreated too late as the ball sailed over his head. It fell at the base of the wall for a double that gave the Dodgers a 1–0 victory, evening up the games at three-all.

But Stengel and the Yankees were not done yet. At sixty-six, Stengel was at the peak of his career as Yankee manager and needed to make only a few moves to demonstrate his acknowledged juggling genius. He had benched Bill Skowron for Joe Collins after the first game, but now he restored Skowron to the lineup for the seventh game, and Skowron hit a grand-slam homer. Slaughter had a good series, but when the veteran had his troubles in the sixth game, Stengel did not hesitate to pull him for Elston Howard, who had not participated. Howard responded with a home run.

Stengel's pitching rotation also worked out neatly

up real quick." DUKE SNIDER

in the end. He gave Larsen an early hook in his first start but did not shy away from coming back with him a second time. He got a victory out of Sturdivant in the important fourth game, chose Turley over Kucks for the sixth game, and then, when it came to the seventh game, he bypassed Ford in favor of Kucks, a sinkerball pitcher, who came through with a three-hit shutout to win the Series. It was at a time like this that Stengel might have said, "I couldn't 'a done it without the players."

Umpire Larry Goetz, an observer at the Series, said, "Stengel must talk to God."

Big Newcombe, who had never won a World Series game, was the victim of the seventh-game barrage. Berra hit a two-run homer in the first inning and another two-run homer in the third. After allowing the home run to Howard in the fifth, Newcombe departed. Skowron hit his grand-slam homer off Roger Craig, and the Yankees won, 9–0, a brutal ending to such a dramatic World Series.

When the Series ended, the Dodgers went on a trip to Japan. Who would have dreamed there would never again be a World Series in Ebbets Field? There were rumors that Walter O'Malley was seeking to move to Los Angeles. But not much attention was paid to an Associated Press story from Los Angeles that month that began:

"As the Brooklyn baseball team flew away for a tour of Japan today, the prospects seemed dim indeed that the Dodgers would ever return as a permanent institution in Los Angeles." An L.A. city official said: "The Brooklyn authorities have promised the Dodgers a new stadium. If this should fall through, Walter O'Malley says Los Angeles would be the first place for him to move. But he thinks there is no likelihood of it [a Brooklyn stadium deal] not going through."

There was no stadium deal that would satisfy the grasping Dodger owner. He skipped town in 1957. The Mets came into being in 1962. Some day there will be another subway series, and New Yorkers, at least, will hearken back to 1956 and talk about Don Larsen . . . and Stengel . . . and Robinson . . . and Mantle . . . and Ford . . . and the excitement of a city.

It was the best of times . . . .

The perfect pitcher: Yogi Berra hugs Don Larsen after last out

Facing Whitey Ford in first game, Sal Maglie gave up two quick runs to fall behind

Three-run homer off the bat of Gil Hodges put Dodgers ahead, and Maglie got 6–3 win

The Teams

Posing for the traditional team portraits on the preceding two pages are the 1956 Brooklyn Dodgers and the 1956 New York Yankees.

The Dodgers: *Top row, left to right.* John Griffin, club house manager; Al Walker, Ed Roebuck; Don Drysdale; Roger Craig; Don Newcombe; Jim Gilliam; Sal Maglie; Don Bessent; Roy Campanella. *Middle row, left to right.* Lee Scott, traveling secretary; Duke Snider; Sandy Koufax; Humberto Fernandez; Charlie Neal; Gino Cimoli; Kenny Lehman; Ransom Jackson; Jackie Robinson; Dale Mitchell; Harold Wendler, trainer. *Bottom row, left to right.* Sandy Amorcs; Joe Becker; Billy Herman; Jake Pitler; Walter Alston; Pee Wee Reese; Clem Labine; Carl Erskine; Homer Howell; Gil Hodges; Carl Furillo. *Not shown.* Batboy Charlie Digiovanni.

The Yankees: *Top row, left to right.* Tom Sturdivant; Norm Siebern; Andy Carey; Tom Byrne; Bob Grim; Mickey Mantle; Hank Bauer; Maurice McDermott; Tom Morgan; John Kucks; Joe Collins. *Middle row, left to right.* Gus Mauch; trainer; Enos Slaughter; Bob Cerv; Jerry Coleman; Bill Skowron; Elston Howard; Bob Turley; John Dixon; George Wilson; Gary Coleman; Don Larsen. *Bottom row, left to right.* Whitey Ford; Billy Martin; Billy Hunter; Tom Carroll; Bill Dickey; Frank Crosetti; Casey Stengel; Jim Turner; Yogi Berra; Irv Noren; Charles Silvera; Gil McDougald. *Bottom center.* Batboys Eddie Carr; William Loperfido.

"What really got me, here I see Dale Mitchell coming up. I'd seen him in the American League before. [I was] afraid he might get one of those nice big hoppers or a line drive somewhere. He could still run pretty good . . . As years have gone by, I realized that I did it against the Brooklyn Dodgers and I'm very proud of that." DON LARSEN

Don Larsen

"It Was Nice"

There was some talk after the perfect game that Don Larsen's no-windup delivery might revolutionize pitching and that Larsen might go on to become one of the game's great pitchers. The no-windup was used by Larsen's teammate, Bob Turley, for a while, but it never caught on. The perfect game was attributed to Larsen's remarkable control and assortment of good pitches. In short, he had good stuff that day.

Six years to the day following his perfect game, he pitched in that same Yankee Stadium and received credit in relief for a World Series victory by the San Francisco Giants.

Larsen did not achieve great distinction after his perfect game, though he remained on the big-league scene for a longer period than many people might recall. He split a pair of World Series games for the Yankees against Milwaukee in 1957, and pitched seven innings of a shutout victory over Milwaukee in 1958. He was dropped by the Chicago Cubs in 1967 and retired in June, 1968, after pitching for Cub farm teams in Tacoma and San Antonio.

Larsen has been living in Morgan Hill outside San Jose, California, with his second wife and son. He is a paper salesman. "It's all right, it's a job," he says.

The perfect game hasn't affected his life much. His baseball career helped him get the salesman's job shortly after he was cut from baseball, and now it is a subject for conversation when people talk to him. "Oh, are you the Don Larsen?" they ask. "And I get back to a lot of these Old Timer's Days," he said. "That wouldn't have happened if not for the no-hitter." In 1974 Cincinnati staged an Old Timer's Day around the theme of no-hitters, in celebration of Johnny VanderMeer, whose double no-hitter stands alongside Larsen's feat as one of baseball's two premier no-hit achievements.

Larsen said, "I have the film of the no-hitter. [He refers to the game as the "no-hitter" rather than the "perfect game."] The American League gave it to me. I don't look at it too much, maybe a few times a year, when people want to see it—some clubs and groups. Yeah, I still enjoy it; it was nice."

He remains a man with whom it is not easy to plumb inner thoughts. He recalled that "pitching against that ball

Slaughter is congratulated at plate by Berra after hitting three-run homer in third game

club was pretty tough. You never expect to do something like that." He singled out the near-hit by Robinson in the second ("probably earlier in his career, when Jackie was faster, he might have beat that out") and "of course one of the biggest plays was Mantle catching Hodges's ball in left-center. You know that probably would have been a home run in most ball parks except for the Stadium."

Larsen said the game "didn't bother me mentally a bit" until the last out, when Walter Alston put Dale Mitchell up to pinch-hit. "When I had the break, a lot of thoughts went through my mind, but I couldn't pinpoint a thing." And when he struck out on three pitches in the eighth, he said he didn't do it purposefully to get ready for the ninth. "No, I was trying to hit the ball—I was a good hitter, you know—but Maglie was tough. I just wanted to help win the game."

He said he sees Babe Pinelli—the umpire who called the third strike—on the coast at banquets now and then, and they reminisce about the game. "Babe is happy. He's always happy because the game gave him a good finish to his career." There was some mild controversy that Pinelli may have been anxious to call the last pitch a strike to help Larsen get the perfect game and wind up his own career on a high note. As far as the last strike is concerned, Larsen said with a laugh: "It looks better to me all the time. Mitchell took a half-swing and almost went all the way around."

Despite all the hullabaloo and predictions that Larsen would rake in $100,000 from the perfect game, it didn't happen. Larsen made $23,000 from personal appearances.

Did he have any regrets about that now?

"No. The more you make, the more you spend," Larsen said.

187

Mantle saves Larsen's perfect game in fifth inning with spectacular catch of Hodges' drive

Umpire Babe Pinelli calls third strike on Dale Mitchell for last out of perfect game

Out by Out

This is an analysis and summary of the perfect game pitched by Don Larsen at Yankee Stadium, October 8, 1956.

Number of pitches (97):

Called strikes	23
Swinging strikes	9
Foul strikes	12
Fouls after two strikes	7
Balls	26
Groundouts	7
Fly- or popouts	13
Total Pitches	97

Outs (27):

Strikeouts	7
Pop flies to second base	3
Pop flies to third base	1
Flies to left field	1
Flies to center field	4
Flies to right field	4
Grounders to second base	4
Grounders to shortstop	1
Grounders, third-base-shortstop	1
Grounders to pitcher	1
Total Outs	27

Of Larsen's twenty-seven outs, thirteen were hit in the air, seven came on grounders, and seven came on strikeouts.

"I threw Mantle a curve and he hit the heck out of the ball in Brooklyn. Now I come back with the same darn pitch in the Stadium, so I had to be a little stupid."

SAL MAGLIE

The Barber

Sal Maglie, still a tough old bird, still replays the perfect game from his point of view. Now a liquor salesman near Buffalo, New York, Maglie after years of coaching pitchers, says he wishes the fifth game had been played in Ebbets Field instead of Yankee Stadium.

"Hodges' ball would have been a homer," he says, referring to a drive by the late Gil Hodges that Mickey Mantle caught in the endless "death valley" of left-center.

Maglie also talks about a line drive he hit behind second base in the third inning. Mantle, playing shallow, caught it easily.

"I don't want to take anything away from Larsen, because he pitched a helluva game, but if that ball had fallen for a hit, it might have been different. He might not have pitched so well if he wasn't going for the no-hitter," Maglie recalls. Does anybody expect "Sal the Barber" to be less of a competitor in his fifties than he was in his thirties?

Bob Turley (left), *like Larsen a no-windup pitcher,* *and Clem Labine* (above), *both pitched scoreless* *ball for nine innings in tightly-played sixth game*

The Jet Age

There haven't been any "subway series" since 1956. Now that teams are spread all over North America, it is much harder to produce series between geographical neighbors —although the San Francisco Giants and the Oakland Athletics could stage a Bay Bridge series, the California Angels and the Los Angeles Dodgers could stage a Freeway Series, and the Cubs and White Sox could ride the subway, as could the Mets and Yankees.

The first crosstown Series was in 1906, won by the South Side White Sox over the North Side Cubs. Then the Giants and Yankees met three straight times, from 1921 to 1923, with the Yankees winning only the third year. But they won in 1936 and 1937 to go ahead.

In 1941, 1947, and 1949, the Yankees beat the Dodgers from the borough of Brooklyn. And sandwiched in World War II was St. Louis's only "streetcar series"—with the Cardinals beating the Brownies.

In 1951, the Yankees beat the Giants. Then came four more Dodger–Yankee battles, with the Dodgers finally winning a World Series in 1955 and Don Larsen helping the Yankees get even in 1956. After 1957, the Dodgers and Giants headed for California. The Yankees met them back-to-back in 1962 and 1963, beating the Giants, then losing to the Dodgers. But jet planes were not the same as the subway, at least for New Yorkers.

CASEY STENGEL ON MICKEY MANTLE

"Of all the fellas I ever played with or ever saw that hit from both sides of the plate, there'd be some part of the day the ball would go further than anybody else . . . The ball in Washington went out of sight and the players came into town and just looked at where that scoreboard was that they hadn't touched for four years, and he went over the scoreboard."

Big Newk

For Don Larsen, the 1956 World Series was the height of glory. For Don Newcombe, the same Series was the depth of failure. Newcombe was the star Dodger right-hander, a huge man, a good hitter, just thirty years old, in the prime of his career.

He had just completed his sixth season with the Dodgers. In five of them he had won at least 17 games. He was the premier pitcher in the National League with 27 victories, the Most Valuable Player in 1956. Yet he came into the Series with something of a reputation as a pitcher who didn't win World Series games.

Newcombe had lost all three World Series games in which he had pitched. He had not been used by Alston in the 1955 Series after he was knocked out in the first game. Dugout bench jockeys called him "gutless." The charge became an obsession with Newcombe, a not-always-mature fellow who had reacted to a crucial error by a teammate during the season by demanding of manager Walter Alston, "Why don't you get somebody out there who can catch the ball?"

In the 1956 Series, Newcombe started the second game and was knocked out in the second inning, allowing six runs. The big hit was a grand-slam home run by Yogi Berra. Newcombe was a dejected figure as he trudged off the mound to the taunts of spectators. He left the ball park immediately. As he went to his automobile, a fan taunted him about folding up in the clutch. Newcombe, a volatile man when aroused, punched the man in the mouth. The incident and the impending lawsuit did little for Newcombe's peace of mind through the rest of the competition.

One man who sympathized with Newcombe in the face of the taunting by the crowd was Milton Gross, the late New York Post columnist. When Newcombe departed, Gross left the press box and followed the unhappy pitcher to the parking lot just after he had punched the fan. Gross then rode with Newcombe to his home in New Jersey and wrote a fine, compassionate story. The article was a highlight of Gross's career.

Though the Dodgers rallied to win the second game be-

Don Newcombe is surrounded by Brooklyn teammates after a 1949 victory. Rear: Carl Furillo, Gil Hodges, Roy Campanella. Front: Luis Olmo, Newcombe

Slaughter jumps high but can't reach Robinson's game-winning double in tenth inning of sixth game

hind reliever Don Bessent, Newcombe's failure intensified the criticisms about his fitness in World Series games. Walter Alston showed no inclination to use Newcombe again, choosing Clem Labine in the sixth game, when the Dodgers trailed three games to two. Alston finally picked Newcombe for the seventh game, when there was hardly anybody else, and when his rejection might have been a deathblow to Newcombe's confidence in future seasons.

Before the seventh game, Newcombe made no attempts to indulge in the vacuous "it's just another game, folks" banter of many athletes before a crucial game. He said: "I couldn't be any more ready than I am now. I want to beat them more than anything else in my life. I won't rest until I do."

A fine performance and a Newcombe victory in the seventh game would have made a dramatic climax to the World Series, but it wasn't to be, as Berra crushed him again with two homers.

So great was Newcombe's sense of shame when he left the mound in the fifth inning—again taunted by the fans— that he again dressed immediately and left the ball park.

"I feel sorry for him" Whitey Ford said. "It was awful the way the fans booed him. Why should they boo a fellow who did so much for the Dodgers this year? That business of his being a choke-up pitcher is unfair. Some of our guys yell 'no guts' at him, but only because they think it bothers him. Nobody really believes the guy can't win the big games."

Fair or not, Newcombe never did get out from under the World Series onus. He was never again a top pitcher, and was traded from the Dodgers of Los Angeles in 1958. Only the keenest observer might have remembered that just before each of the crushing two-run homers by Berra, Newcombe had reached back and thrown big third-strike fastballs past Mickey Mantle, the Triple Crown winner in the American League that year.

Yogi Berra cracks home run over right field wall in first inning of the seventh game

Bill Skowron is congratulated after grand slam home run that wrapped up Yankee's 9–0 win

Reporters try to keep up with a Stengel monologue after Series game

SUDDEN DEATH
IN THE AFTERNOON

A Colts fan walks tall into Yankee Stadium

Baltimore Colts/ New York Giants NFL Championship Game December 28, 1958

By Jack Mann

rofessional football did not come of age merely because of its first overtime game ever. But the event was a signal point, a culmination of the past, a funnel for the future.

The game matched the Baltimore Colts and New York Giants, two divisional champions of the National Football League, two teams believing themselves underdogs. Pro football had its own underdog mentality, too: the sport had only recently graduated from the class of "something to do between baseball seasons."

Then, with a national television audience watching, the two teams careened to a tie in the regulation sixty minutes. Instead of chucking off their uniforms in unconcluded frustration—the way tie football games had always ended—they went back into the pit, until somebody scored.

Jack Mann's article on that game, for *Newsday*, was included in *Best Sports Stories of 1958*. He is also author of "This Mad Set of Games" in this collection.   G.V.

ports Illustrated, which caused it to be called "The Greatest Football Game Ever Played," didn't actually use the word "greatest." Tex Maule, the pro football curator, wanted to use the word. But his magazine had a rule against it. So they settled on the word "best," and people got the idea anyway. Maule also remembers *SI* merely giving the "Best Game" a two-page, one-picture spread. "Pro football just wasn't Madison Avenue in those days," he recalls.

"Those days" included the fourth-to-last day of 1958, when the Baltimore Colts needed eight minutes and fifteen seconds of history's first sudden-death overtime to complete a 23-17 conquest of the New York Giants for the championship of the National Football League, the only pro football league there was in those days, when there was one basketball league and one hockey league.

These days Commissioner Pete Rozelle's television euphemizers would have called the extra period—over Commissioner Bert Bell's dead body—"Sudden Victory." Much more than that has changed, and much of the change began in the clammy gloaming of that December 28 in Yankee Stadium.

The game was heroically contested, a fierce confrontation between self-anointed underdogs. It was magnificently flawed: e.g., two fumbles, leading to a touchdown each, by Frank Gifford, the glamour-boy eminence, now a glamour-boy television sportscaster.

The game was exquisitely second-guessable from either side and came perilously close, several times, to being worth the routine treatment *Sports Illustrated* had planned for it. But withal, you can bet your genuine ceramic, Official, $6.95 Redskins ashtray, the very good game was the Greatest Thing that had ever happened to make pro football great: "Much above average," Webster defines the adjective, "in magnitude, intensity, etc."

Et cetera. While John F. Kennedy lived, a fad became a fixation and a coach a demigod; they played football games for money on the day a murdered president lay cold in the Capitol. Under Richard Nixon, a commercial entertainment became a public issue, and George Allen a knight of the realm.

The same wonderful people who had given us "I Love Lucy," the roller derby, and "The $64,000 Question" would have purveyed megalofootball in prime time and Living Color sooner or later. Sooner, perhaps, if the four previous NFL championship games hadn't ended up in unmerchandisable disarray: 59-14, 47-7, 38-14, and 56-10. Later, perhaps, if Baltimore fullback Alan Ameche had "thrown the goddamn ball," as teammate Gino Marchetti put it, when the '58 Colts had their sword poised at the Giants' throatlatch in the third quarter. They led, 14-3, and had a first down on the Giants' three-yard line. If the Colts scored a touchdown, channel selectors would click from palm to pine. There would be no overtime, and probably no room for Ameche's bow on that evening's Ed Sullivan Show.

Alan was called "The Horse" because he could move forward in a very powerful manner, even dragging people. Little else was expected or asked of him normally, but the Giants had an abnormally obdurate defense, the one that gave identity and glamor to the DEE-fense business—being the first defensive unit to be introduced in the pregame rites. So the Colts' planners had "put in" a play to give Ameche another option, just in case of exactly what happened. Ameche gained two, Unitas nothing, Ameche nothing. Fourth-and-goal on the one-yard line.

Jim Mutscheller was the "inside" or tight end on the right. "I guess he was supposed to throw to me. Anyway, it was supposed to work because Alan hadn't thrown all year—couldn't pass at all. The play was Flow 28, a quick pitch to the halfback. With Lenny [Moore] out wide, Ameche was in the halfback spot."

"Ameche takes pitch, goes wide right," reads the mimeograph transcript. "Hit by Livingston on 5."

Possibly linebacker Cliff Livingston had taken the bait, made the rebuttable presumption that Ameche could not or would not pass, and diagnosed the run, leaving Mutscheller as free as the Colts' strategists had hoped. In any case, Ameche never got rid of the ball. The Giants' DEE-fense (it was chanted in Yankee Stadium first) had accomplished the implausible. "Reprieved," as in the final scene of *The Threepenny Opera,* would have been the appropriate chant for the OFF-ense, which five plays and an outrageous bit of luck later had New York back in the game, 14-10.

"It was slippery down there," Baltimore coach Weeb Ewbank remembered of the goal-line stand. Indeed, it

udden Death in the Afternoon

seemed the leprechauns who often piloted the Giant-owning Mara family among the shoals of fortune were having a good day, even if people named Gifford and Conerly were not. It was slippery down there, at the dark-ling home-plate end of the Stadium, because the day of the big game had dawned on Mara Weather: sunshine, not reasonably expected in a normally lousy New York winter.

The late Jack Mara and brother Wellington likely would have sold the 64,185 tickets that day if icebergs had been sighted in the Harlem River. They remembered those hard days when five-figure crowds had been a gleam in their father's eye. Right up to World War II it *mattered* to pro football entrepreneurs whether it was sunny or cold; a heavy rain was a financial bath. In those days, or so it seemed to a lot of people, it hardly ever rained in New York on a Sunday when the Giants were playing at home. (Some Mara-watchers saw relevance in the family's connections as ranking Catholic laymen. Father Benedict Dudley is believed to be the first clergyman to go on the road as chaplain of a pro-football team, and after at least one game of that 1958 season there were seventeen priests in the Giants' dressing room, interviewing players.) So Mara Weather thawed the tundra enough that Alan The Horse, faltering like a thoroughbred on a winter track, never got footing to throw, if he planned to.

It was redemption time for the Giant offense, which was a sometime thing predicated on one of those decisions-not-to-decide that were the currency of leadership in Eisenhower's time-out decade. With incomplete faith in Charlie Conerly, because he was old, and in Don

Conerly gets off a pass over the arms of a Colt defender

Heinrich, because he wasn't, the Giants would start Heinrich, who "probed" the enemy defense for a quarter or so until, by some inscrutable criterion, it was time for Charlie.

The Colts' bearing was jaunty, like the adhesive-tape spats that made Lenny Moore's feet a white blur as he sped down the sideline in a "fly" pattern before there was such a term. And it was daring, in the why-not approach of brash young quarterback Johnny Unitas, who in the sudden death would call a penultimate play so reckless as to make the winning touchdown anticlimactic.

There were other differences. The game was no morality play, but there were neo-Dickensian overtones. The Colts were clearly the have-nots of the piece, not only because the Giants had been champions before, but for instance: Cliff Livingston, rugged-handsome if you dug that new Richard Boone thing, but no Montgomery Clift, had a TV commercial in New York. There *weren't* such things in Baltimore. Stuff like that.

The sixth biggest city in the United States was on probation as a big-league town, having opened and closed in one NFL season after surviving the anschluss that closed out the All-American Conference.

The Orioles had been in town only five years, not long enough to fumigate their past as the St. Louis Browns. The Colts came back to Baltimore as a foundling of the NFL, which had unsuccessfully placed them in foster homes, first as the New York Yanks, then as the Dallas Texans.

The Texans were Gino Marchetti's first professional team (using the term promiscuously): "[Art] Donovan and I got tired of people settin' records against us. 'Hugh McElhenny [mimicking a public-address announcer] has just broken the Forty-Niner's record. . . .' In L.A. I scored my first touchdown and I felt pretty good. Then I heard the PA system say that made the score 46-6— *at the half.*"

They still grumble in Baltimore that Commissioner Bell, a sedulous rail-splitter in the edification of the NFL, made the new owners sell 15,000 season tickets in front before they could have the Texas reject. They also griped that the 1960 owner, Abe Watner, who cried poormouth and tossed the franchise back to the league, could have made it. It's all part of being from "Ballamer," a factory city that would rather be known for white stoops and crabcakes, where that part of the populace that cares at all is aggressively defensive.

Awareness of this attitude may have moved Ballamer coach Ewbank to his finest hour, just before the kickoff. Not known before or since as a motivator of men, Ewbank came on in his pregame talk as a latter-day Marcus Antonius. Gino Marchetti, tough as his centurion's visage and blasé to the point of indelicacy on the subject of pep talks, is perhaps most objective of all the Colts who remember the speech, and they all do.

"In fourteen years," Marchetti said, "I heard 'em all. 'Win for Mother, Win for Father. . . . Don't disappoint all those people watching on TV.' Sometimes they just tell you how to act: 'Don't piss in the air with forty million people watching.'

"But Weeb really put it to us. He went down the

roster, name by name: 'Donovan, they got rid of you—too fat and slow. . . . Ameche, Green Bay didn't want you.' Yeah, he named me, Unitas. . . . He didn't miss anybody."

Colts' personnel director Fred Schubach, as equipment manager, was privy to all the incitements to riot from the '53 reincarnation through the dark angers of Don Shula to Don McCafferty's easy ride to the Super Bowl. Weeb's is the exhortation he remembers. It left him feeling that "the only way we could get recognition would be to beat the Giants *in New York*—to show that New York press. . . . It would be the first big thing that ever happened to Baltimore."

Ewbank was taking a calculated risk. The massive Donovan, for example, was on the serious side of thirty, and his boyish figure was long gone, but reminding a four-time all-pro tackle that he once was somebody's wretched refuse can bring violent reaction. "I told them they were guys Paul Brown didn't want—nobody wanted," Weeb has since said. His credentials were in order. He had been an assistant in Cleveland in March, 1953, when Brown "backed up the moving van," to use Casey Stengel's phrase, and sent ten people to Baltimore for five. That gave the Browns Mike McCormick and three of the next four division championships. It gave the Colts Art Spinney, Carl Taseff, and Bert Rechichar, who was going out to kick off when Ewbank stopped talking.

"We started from scratch," Weeb recalled. "Trades, free agents, pickups. Pellington [the Colts' "meanest" linebacker for a decade] was cut from the Browns—as an offensive tackle. Gino was one, too, when I got him.

Pat Summerall boots a 36-yard field goal in the first period to give Giants a 3–0 lead

"John was throwing the ball in real sharp." RAYMOND BERRY

Spinney and Alex Sandusky ['58 guards] were defensive ends. Nobody handed me a football team.''

''He's right,'' Hall of Fame defensive end Marchetti said years later, from the nerve center of his hamburger chain. ''Weeb was no great coach, but his great asset was a talent for recognizing ability.''

They had worked too hard and sacrificed too much, Ewbank told his poor, huddled masses in conclusion, to be stopped now. Righteously indignant, they stormed out to meet the other underdogs.

To reach the title game, the Giants had had to ''upset'' the Cleveland Browns three times: 21-17 at Cleveland, 13-10 on Pat Summerall's 50½-yard field goal in a driv-ing snow—when the 10-10 tie would have given the Browns the marbles—and 10-0 in a playoff. The last may have been the most persuasive beating a football team ever took by a score that low: Jim Brown, holder of the league record of 237 yards gained in one game, was held to eight. The Giants had beaten the Colts in New York, 24-21, but Unitas had watched lying in a hospital bed.

For the record, the ''paper'' odds on the championship game made Baltimore a four-and-a-half-point favorite. Nobody who was of betting age at the time seems to have met a man who got, or gave, more than three. By any account, the price was less than six points, which

Unitas is smothered by a Giant defender as he tries to pass

Gifford runs for nice gain as Giants move
into position for Pat Summerall field goal

Alan Ameche goes over for touchdown
after Colts recovered Gifford's fumble

Toughest Man

"Something didn't grow right" when they put his leg back together, so now and then Gino Marchetti must have "ingrown things" removed from the ball of his right foot. When he does, he thinks of number 16, Frank Gifford, standing over him, hands on hips.

"All right," Gifford was saying, "stop faking. You stopped me. You can get up now."

"Jesus Christ, I can't," Marchetti said. Trainer Ed Block, incubating the only tension headache he would have in his now threescore years, needed only to look. "Both bones [tibia and fibula, all there are between knee and ankle] were broken."

"Gifford thought I was trying for a free time-out," Gino recalled years later, not without annoyance. "Christ, Big Daddy fell on me." Marchetti and linebacker Don Shinnick had Gifford stopped when the late Gene Lipscomb threw his 290 pounds into the effort.

Vince DiPaula, one of the very big men who carried Marchetti away, is dead. The other, Bill Naylor, remembers the babel of voices: "Gino was cussing his luck, what a

helluva time it was to happen. . . . Dr. McDonnell was yelling to get him inside. . . . It was getting foggy and cold, and Bill Neill [a consulting trainer] kept yelling about shock. Gino didn't want to go at all. I still think he's the toughest son of a bitch I ever saw."

Gino Marchetti's dark face is at once handsome and fierce ("of a nature to inspire terror"), a difficult face to say no to. DiPaula and Naylor bore him into the shadows of the home-plate end of the Stadium; they had reached the end zone when the Giants' punt reached the 14 and was fair-caught. "Put me down here," Gino said, and the big men complied. His head propped on an elbow, Marchetti lay and watched the Colt machine from behind as it sputtered, then began to leap away, out of the shadows, toward the light fading on the bleachers. "He must have been hurting like hell," Naylor said, "but he didn't say anything until the field goal. Then he let out a big yell."

"I was worried," Marchetti explained. "Myhra had this habit: if you gave him too much time to stand around and think . . . well, he might'a had a problem. The sad part was I couldn't see the sudden death. I saw the coin flip and kickoff."

"Neill yelled and we had to get him inside," said Naylor, who can still see Gino on the training table, with his uniform pants cut away, a game ball in his hand, and a big grin. "I wanted to get him to a hospital in New York," Ed Block said, "but he wouldn't have it." His leg in a temporary cast, Marchetti flew back to Baltimore with his team.

"Toughest man I ever knew," Bill Naylor said again. "Didn't he have his appendix out and play a game seven days later?"

Not really. "I went into the hospital the morning after a Saturday-night game with Detroit," Marchetti said. "I missed the next game, at Green Bay."

Charlie Conerly calls John Unitas "the greatest quarterback who ever played the game," and most experts agree with that. Singling out his greatest asset, Raymond Berry said: I don't think John is ever defeated."
Against the Giants, Unitas brought the Colts back to a tie and then led them to victory with brilliant passing and great coolness. During the overtime drive to a score, Berry was open for a five-yard pass. The Colts needed eight yards for a first down. So Unitas rolled out and calmly motioned Berry downfield another three yards before he threw.
Of his pass to Mutscheller, a risky one out in the flat from the eight-yard line, Unitas said after the game: "You don't risk anything when you know where you're passing."

With no receivers free, Unitas crosses
up Giant defense and runs with the ball

"Our offensive unit was not highly regarded. When the offensive unit went out on the field, the defense shouted, 'Get in there and hold them.'" KYLE ROTE

Raymond Berry gathers in Unitas pass for
a touchdown to put the Colts ahead, 14–3

Colts threatened again in third quarter as
Moore caught Unitas pass near goal line

"You'd say, 'Hey, John,
I can do it now.' He'd
keep it in the back
of his mind, and
when the time was
right, he would call
on you."

LENNY MOORE
ON JOHNNY UNITAS

Giant coaching crew under Jim Lee
Howell (standing, center) *included*
Vince Lombardi, (kneeling, left)
and Tom Landry (standing, right)
Ken Kavanagh (standing, right)
and John Del Isola (kneeling, right)
completed the staff

After Rote grabbed Conerly pass and fumbled,
Webster picked up ball and went over for TD

In fourth quarter, with Giants ahead, 17–14,
George Myrha booted tying field goal for Colts

Sideburns

Don Maynard surely did remember that kickoff. "Yes, sir.
I was the first man to touch the football—with my hands—in
the first overtime period ever played."

And the first to drop it. "Not that I recall. . . . Least I
didn't fumble it to the other team."

As the Mara Weather faded into dusk, the ball took one
more Mara Bounce. Bert Rechicar's kick was a low line
drive, and Maynard, posted on the turf DiMaggio had pa-
trolled, swooped in for the shoestring catch and dropped it
on the 10-yard line. Of all the multifarious bounces an agi-
tated football could take, this one came back up to Maynard
as true as to a little girl playing jacks and he toppled to
the 20.

Coach Howell had need for no such brinkmanship and
said so. Next August Maynard was banished, waived, and
claimed by the lowly Packers; he went instead to Canada
for a year, as a Tigercat who caught one pass, played defensive back, and returned no kicks.

"That wasn't the reason," Maynard recalls. "Coach
Lombardi had gone to Green Bay and I had a conflict
with Allie Sherman. Gifford was quarterback and I was
running at halfback for the first three exhibitions and Allie
said I took too-long steps. I wasn't trying to be smart, but
I guess nobody had ever talked back to him. Finally he just
yelled, 'Get out of here!'"

In the fifties, almost nobody talked back to anybody. In
1958 Tony Kubek, a sophomore Yankee, had said: "They
tell me what I can and can't say, but don't write that I
said that." And nobody wore sideburns, or cowboy boots,
except this quietly exuberant twenty-one-year-old out of
Crosbyton, Texas.

"I guess the sideburns hurt me a little bit," said the thirty-
seven-year-old El Paso necktie merchant ("Garo Yep-
remian's out of my class: he gets $15 for ties I sell for $5").
"Coach Howell asked me to shave them and I kinda said
yeah. When I still hadn't, a week later, he had a lot of com-
ments. But if you'd check the pictures now, you'd see that
those sideburns weren't so long. Not really."

In 1960 Don Maynard went to work for the Titans, who
became the Jets, and for whom he caught passes for more
yards than any man ever had. He also helped the Jets win
something called a Super Bowl in 1970. The Giants haven't
made it that far yet—sideburns or not.

Maynard with Gifford

Unitas hands off to Ameche on trap play that
gained 23 yards in overtime touchdown drive

Ameche cuts outside and heads for winning
touchdown from the Giant one-yard line

The Rumble

With the mechanistic cool of a molecule
absorbing an orphaned electron, Raymond
Berry gathered in yet another pass and
minced out-of-bounds in front of the Colts'
bench. That was where Sam Huff creamed
him; the question was when.

"Oh, I saw Sam at the meeting in Miami
[in 1974] and we had a good laugh about
that," said Weeb Ewbank. "Actually he was
hitting late all day. He got Raymond five
yards out of bounds."

There was a rumble, and the way some
recall it, the five-by-fiveish Ewbank, age
fifty-one, threw a fair right hand into The
Violent World of Sam Huff. By virtue of hard
work, clean living, and a sonorous public-
address announcer who seldom read deeper
than the number 70 on the top of the pile,
Robert Lee Huff had emerged from Morgan-
town, West Virginia, at the propitious time
to be annointed pro football's first Mister
DEE-fense (teeing off some people like
Joe Schmidt, Bill George, Chuck Bednarik,
and a few Giants). As such, he was the
Giants' enforcer.

"I never hit him," Ewbank said. "An as
sistant trainer went after him; everybody wa
shoving him around." (The Giants' play-by
play record suggests in a marginal not
that Don Shinnick had a piece of Huff.) "
was played out of proportion."

Bert Bell, the Commissioner, had playe
primordial football, helmets optional, an
he empathized with Weeb.

"Hell," he told him aside in the locke
room, "You gotta fight for your team.

"I thought he was hitting a little late my
self," Bell added.

Ameche going ove

Weeb and Colts

"After the game I we
into the locker room
and I was up on a
cloud, and I didn't
come down for quite
a while."

RAYMOND BERR

210

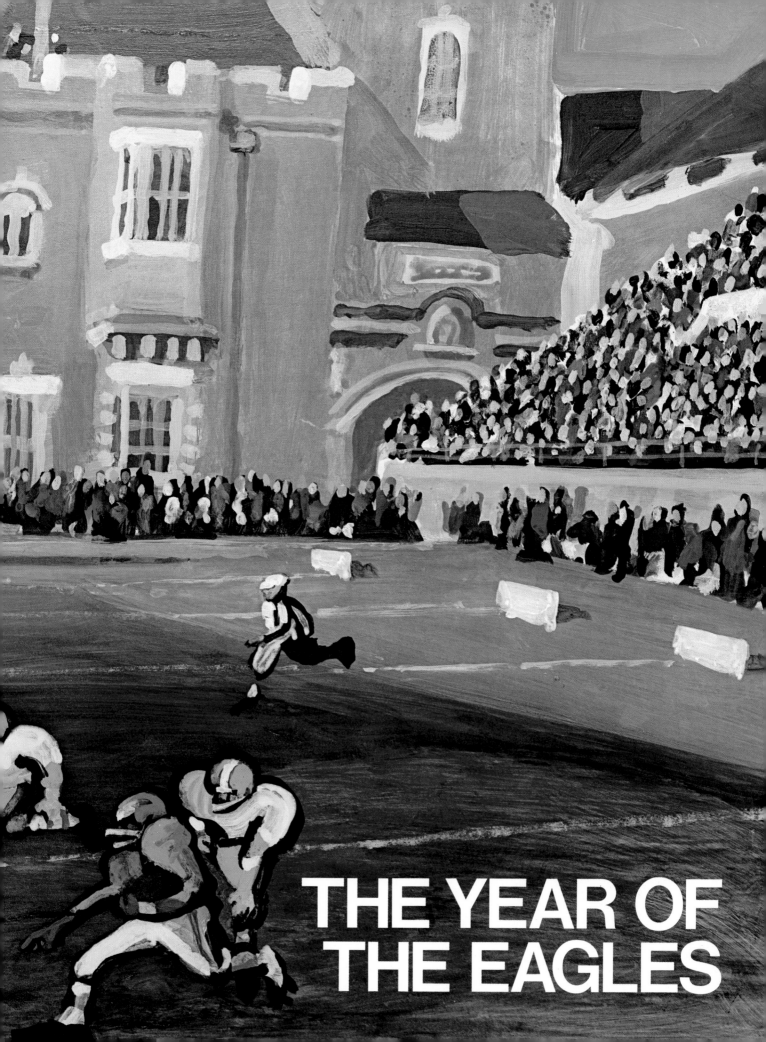

THE YEAR OF
THE EAGLES

Champion Eagles reward coach Buck S...

Green Bay Packers/ Philadelphia Eagles NFL Championship Game December 26, 1960

By Larry Merchant

It was the late boxer, Sonny Liston, who once said: "I'd rather be a lamppost in Denver than the mayor of Philadelphia." He said it while packing for Denver.

In its recent past, Philadelphia has exiled more than its share of disenchanted, controversial athletes. Dick Allen used to mark off his days with the baseball Phillies like a convict, scratching his spikes in the basepaths. Wilt Chamberlain left his hometown twice because basketball could not support him in the manner to which he had become accustomed. Norman Snead heard so many boos when he quarterbacked the Eagles that he thought the city's symbolic bird was the hoot owl. And it was Bo Belinsky who once suggested that Philadelphia fans would boo an Easter-egg hunt.

Well, let's put it this way. If there were an Easter-egg-hunting league, the Philadelphia team would probably finish last. Philly fans haven't had many winners—one basketball title from Wilt in 1967, the 1974 Stanley Cup from the hockey Flyers. And a few residents with good memories still recall the autumn of 1960, when the Philadelphia Eagles actually. . . .

In 1960, Larry Merchant was sports editor and columnist for the *Philadelphia Daily News*. A former scrub for the University of Oklahoma football team under Bud Wilkinson, Merchant is now a sports columnist for the *New York Post*. He is also the author of two books on professional football, the latest being *The National Football Lottery*.   G.V.

y calendar years, 1960 does not seem such a long way back. By National Football League years, it does. That was the year the Philadelphia Eagles won a championship.

That has become a historical embarrassment to the NFL, as though Albania had licked NATO. 1960? Wasn't that the year the American Football League came bouncing crazily, like a football, into the picture tube? 1960? Wasn't that the year Pete Rozelle was named to suceed Bert Bell, the late father figure of pro football, as commissioner? 1960? Wasn't that the year Vince Lombardi—Vince Lombardi, not just the Green Bay Packers—lost in the playoffs?

Yes, yes, and yes.

But it was also the year that Norm Van Brocklin had what many of his peers consider the one greatest season a quarterback ever had, and then retired in a bitter controversy that was related to the death of Bert Bell. It was the year, too—presumably the last year for all time to come—when one player, Chuck Bednarik, would play both offense and defense, lending an antique finish to the season.

It was a very good year, then, capped by a terrific championship game, even if it has become forgettable outside Philadelphia (which hasn't had very many good years lately), because the years immediately before and after 1960 were so unforgettable.

Only two years before 1960, the NFL had made the leap from its Middle Ages to its Enlightenment. While the Eagles and Packers were last and least in their divisions, the Baltimore Colts beat the New York Giants for the championship in a sudden-death melodrama that proved to be a hugely successful pilot show for the television-inspired football (and all-sports) boom that is still booming. In 1959 the Colts repeated over the Giants.

After a one-year interruption, by the Eagles, the Giants would pick up where they had left off. They would be losers in the next three championship games, the first two to the dynasty-bound Packers.

Thus the embarrassment of the Eagles. Unlike most teams that contend for a championship, they didn't get a good smell of another championship game in the decade before or after they won it. They surfaced momentarily and mysteriously, perhaps magically, and then, like the Loch Ness Monster, submerged, with no plausible explanation. "No one will ever know," said safetyman Don Burroughs, "how unbelievable this was."

For the Packers, of course, it was only a temporary setback on the march to empire, although they were as much of a surprise as the Eagles at the time. They hadn't won anything in sixteen years, since the regime of Curley Lambeau, who organized them in 1919 and led them to six championships, and the era of the legendary Don Hutson, who was a generation ahead of the game as a pass-catching specialist.

Enter Vince Lombardi in 1959. At the age of 46 he was getting his first head coaching job above the high-school level. He had been a guard on Fordham's "Seven Blocks of Granite" in the mid-thirties. He had been an assistant with the Giants. He was well regarded in the trade. He felt, apparently with some justification, that he had been passed by because he was Italian; there were few Italians in sports with prestigious leadership jobs. His reputation for being devoted to the running game when the passing game was supreme had probably held him back, too. The conventional wisdom was that you had to throw the ball to win, and to draw crowds. The big winners had quarterbacks named Bob Waterfield, Norm Van Brocklin, Bobby Layne, Johnny Unitas.

Lombardi inherited some excellent football players, quality studs like linebackers Ray Nitschke, Bill Forrester, and Dan Curry; ends Boyd Dowler, Max McGee, and Ron Kramer; offensive linemen Forest Gregg, Jerry Kramer, and Jim Ringo; running backs Jim Taylor and Paul Hornung. He found Bart Starr on the squad and kneaded him into his quarterback. He added defensive linemen Henry Jordan and Willie Davis in trades. This was his nucleus. He knew what to do with it.

Football wasn't religion to Lombardi, but he coached it with a philosophy that had religious undertones. He believed that pain was a concomitant to achievement. He believed that exhaustion was a spiritual high. It was not for nothing that Norm Van Brocklin, years later, dubbed him "St. Vince."

In 1960, he was just another successful coach hustling his thing, which was, of all things, an old-fashioned running attack. To run the ball required pain and exhaustion and another oldie but goodie, discipline. If you could

The Year of the Eagles

run the ball on the other guys, knock them down and trample them, intimidate them, they would respect and even fear you. Wasn't that what football was really about? Depending on the pass to win might turn you soft and the other guys contemptuous. Morally, to Lombardi, it was a cop-out.

Running had its tactical advantages, too. It was safe, providing you could do it well enough. Running teams usually made fewer mistakes than passing teams, and that usually could be translated into more wins. The master plan had one flaw: it's deadly dull football if you don't win. The Packers won, right away. They had a winning season in 1959, as a prelude to 1960.

The lens of public attention zoomed in on Jim Taylor and Paul Hornung, who were becoming the most famous ball-carrying partnership since Blanchard and Davis of Army. Taylor amassed 1,101 yards, second only to Jim Brown. Hornung scored fifteen touchdowns and set a scoring record of 174 points.

Ironically, the last team to win an NFL championship with an infantry mindset had been the Philadelphia Eagles. Steve Van Buren, a prototype of the big, fast backs of today, had powered them to championships in 1948 and 1949. Yet despite their success on the field, the Eagles had struggled financially. Sellouts were rare, television contracts nonexistent in those days. You could buy a good seat for yourself, your friend, and your coats five minutes before most kickoffs. The Eagles were sold in 1949 to a syndicate of 100 fans who put up $3,000 apiece—$250,000 for the purchase, $50,000 for operating costs. (Fifteen years later, when they sold out, the shares were worth $52,000 apiece; five years after that, when the Eagles were sold again, the market value of those shares would have been $162,000 apiece.)

One Jim Clark, a businessman and local Democratic Party boss, organized the syndicate and named himself president of the team. He was a better politician than football man. The Democrats ousted the Republican machine in Philadelphia, but the Browns and Giants ousted the Eagle machine in the Eastern Division. So Clark decided to jettison Greasy Neale, his coach. Neale, who had been a teammate of Jim Thorpe in the incubator days of pro football, compiled a record of three seconds, three firsts, and two championships in six seasons with the Eagles. A city long used to adversity in fun and games was retreating into its bosom again.

Hornung follows interference in Packer drive that led to field goal in first period

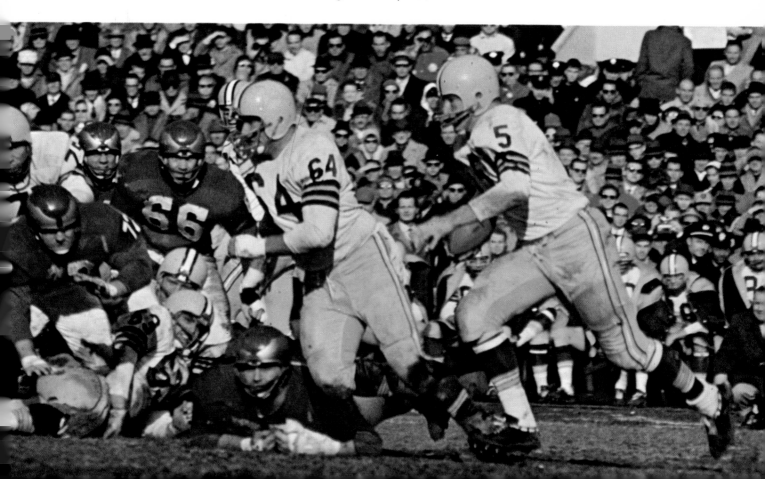

Van Brocklin looks for the open man

"Brown and Taylor were th

Enter Norm Van Brocklin and Buck Shaw in 1958. Van Brocklin's greatest claim to fame, among many, would be that he beat Vince Lombardi in a playoff game—the only time that ever happened. Shaw is the answer to a trivia question in connection with that happening: who coached the Eagles when . . . ?

Actually, Shaw had a distinguished career in football, first achieving fame as an All-American tackle under Knute Rockne at Notre Dame, then as head coach of the San Francisco Forty-Niners. Joining Van Brocklin completed a spiral cycle. Rockne popularized the pass. Van Brocklin was among the men who made it an ultimate weapon.

Van Brocklin alternated with Bob Waterfield throwing cross-country to Elroy Hirsch and Tom Fears with the Los Angeles Rams in the early fifties. Their quick-striking offense terrorized the league until defensive backs and theory learned to cope with it. Sammy Baugh and Don Hutson, who had introduced the possibilities of the pass in the thirties, were regarded as forces of nature. But the Rams, by incorporating the pass into a team pattern, were a downright threat to society. Why spend all those tedious hours perfecting the martial arts of football when one cross-country connection between two gifted athletes disarmed the burliest strongmen? The long-ball offense was such a revolutionary concept that the only defense against it was to scoff at it as another California fad. Like surfing, it was possible only in a climate with guaranteed sun. Van Brocklin threw four touchdown passes in one quarter and for 554 yards in one game, for goodness' sakes.

Like many virtuoso quarterbacks, Van Brocklin had the temperament of a singular, strong-willed artist. He hassled with his coach, Sid Gillman, frequently. "I wanted to coach," Van Brocklin deadpanned, "and he wouldn't let me." Shaw would let him. The Eagles traded a first draft choice for him.

After one season—two wins, many bruises—Van Brocklin understood that he would never realize his ambition to coach if he didn't get out of the game alive. He told the Eagles he was going to retire, at thirty-two.

Enter Bert Bell, commissioner. Bell, who had once coached the Eagles and was concerned now about the franchise's stability, talked the Eagles into promising Van Brocklin that he would take over as head coach in 1960 if he would play one more season. He agreed. When the Eagles had a winning season in 1959, Buck Shaw asked for a one-year extension in quest of his first championship. Van Brocklin agreed to that, too, proving in the end that nice guys get shafted.

But Van Brocklin played in 1960 under the impression that he would take over, officially, the next season. He announced in training camp that this would be his farewell season and repeated it as often as he was pressed to. Lombardi, at the same time, was hoping to go back to his native New York to coach the Giants in 1961. It was, he said diplomatically, not easy for a big-city boy to take root in a small town.

The Packers displaced the Colts in the Western division by winning on the last day of the season. The amazing Eagles had already clinched the Eastern Division by winning nine games in a row. Time and again Van Brocklin brought them from behind in the second half. A former Eagle with the St. Louis Cardinals, Jerry Norton, said, in recognition of the personnel with Van Brocklin, "They ought to give him all their championship shares."

That was only half of it. Van Brocklin deserved management's share as well.

Off the field, he was used by the front office to scout and recruit college prospects. His advice was sought on trades. Three starters were acquired on his recommendation: Don Burroughs, a safety man, Stan Campbell, a guard, and Joe Robb, a rookie defensive end.

On the practice field, he spent many extra hours coaching Pete Retzlaff and Tommy McDonald in end play. Retzlaff was a magnificent athlete who didn't have a position until Van Brocklin went to work with him. McDonald could catch the ball, but he had no idea of what he was doing, and at five feet nine inches he needed an idea. Van Brocklin gave it to him. Retzlaff and McDonald became all-pros.

On the playing field, Van Brocklin was a quarterback and coach, implementing and improvising game plans amidst the tumult and shouting. When all else failed, he did the punting.

Two things he didn't do were play center or left linebacker. Chuck Bednarik did them. Bednarik started the season as a center, then was forced to double up as a linebacker when a teammate was injured. "It's something I always wanted to try," he said. Having been a linebacker for most of his life, boy and man, he made eleven unassisted tackles in his first two-platoon game. One big tackle he made against the Giants in another game defined him and the position. Frank Gifford caught

a pass and, as he wheeled upfield, he also caught the full fury of Bednarik. Gifford went down in a lifeless lump. He had a concussion. The ball rolled free. As an Eagle fell on it, Bednarik pirouetted gleefully, punching a fist into the sky. He was celebrating the fumble recovery, but disappointed and horrified fans at Yankee Stadium interpreted it as a celebration of an idol's maiming. Bednarik was booed and vilified. "If he was a Giant," said Van Brocklin, "they'd build a monument to him next to Ruth and Gehrig."

The careers of Bednarik and Van Brocklin were interlocked in the ironies of the 1960 championship taffy pull. They had been rookies when the Eagles and Rams met for the championship in 1949. The run-oriented Eagles were cast as defenders of football's blood-and-guts tradition as they beat the hedonistic Rams. Now the Eagles were defending the new faith of the pass against the blood-and-guts provincialism of the Packers (who themselves had been passing fancies as champions two decades before).

The oddsmakers installed these Packers slight favorites over these Eagles. The prospect of the thirty-five-year-old Bednarik playing sixty minutes against the bruising Packers was as romantic as reincarnating the flying wedge and the Stutz Bearcat, but it also exposed the soft underbelly of the Eagles. Their defense, with two rookies, seven journeymen, a stick-out in cornerback Tom Brookshier, and Bednarik, was highly suspect. In addition, the offensive line was ordinary, the tight end was a small, once-outstanding wide receiver, Bobby Walston, and the running backs were Billy Barnes, tough but slow, and Ted Dean, a promising rookie replacing the injured Clarence Peaks. Bob Pellegrini, the first-string middle linebacker, also was sidelined.

In sum, Van Brocklin throwing to McDonald and Retzlaff was supposed to outslick a thundering stampede of young Packer bulls. Van Brocklin had so captured the imagination with his heroics that it seemed to be an entirely reasonable proposition. With the election of John F. Kennedy as President seven weeks before, during a time of peace, prosperity and stability, heroes were still possible.

The game was played on Monday, December 26—the NFL did not yet put itself on an equal plane with Christmas as a religious pageant—at Franklin Field. This ancient pile of bricks, a double-decked horseshoe, is the home turf of the University of Pennsylvania, whose foot-

"I don't think Van Brocklin ever overthrew me." TOMMY MACDON

ball fortunes had been in retreat since Chuck Bednarik All-Americaned there. Crowds of 70,000 to 75,000 had been common then, but capacity for the Eagles was 60,000, because all that peace, prosperity and stability had broadened the expectations for comfort—and also the behinds—of the fans. A temporary bleacher section was erected in the open end of the horseshoe, seating another 7,000. A few of the 67,352 paying customers were able to buy eight-dollar tickets from scalpers for five dollars just before the game. The crowd yielded a record share of $5,116.55 each for the winners, $3,105.14 for the losers.

After a week of winter and a white Christmas in Philadelphia, it came up Van Brocklin weather: sunny, 45 degrees. Rimmed by the snow shoveled off the tarpaulin that protected it, the field was in good though imperfect shape. The underfooting was soft enough to provide alibis, hard enough to ignore them. "It's going to be a nice little war," said Emlen Tunnell. Tunnell, a great defensive back with the Giants, was the only Packer with extensive playoff experience.

Then, on the first play from scrimmage, the Eagles nearly blew themselves out of the war.

Much of their offense was designed to take advantage of defensive strategy against the long pass—using screens, swing passes, draw plays. Van Brocklin flipped a quick swing pass to Barnes that popped off his fingertips into the arms of defensive end Bill Quinlan. The Packers were in business on the Eagle 14-yard line.

The series that followed prefaced a half of frustration. Taylor and Hornung, on three straight-ahead smashes, brought the ball to the six-yard line. On fourth down and a short two, standard procedure is to grit your teeth and take the field goal. Vince Lombardi gritted his teeth and gambled. Lombardi saw the moment as an opportunity, at negligible risk, to establish superiority over a defense he held in contempt. If the Packers didn't make the first down, their strong defense would still have the Eagles backed up against their goal line. Lombardi's decision to go for it was a cousin to the one he made in the 1967 championship game with the Dallas Cowboys, when he ordered Bart Starr to try a one-yard quarterback sneak, rather than take the tying field goal, on the last play. He won that one.

But he lost this one. The Eagles, led by Bednarik, jammed Taylor up. The Eagles, it developed, were establishing their ability to contain the Packers when they had to. They had to, again, right after the next commercial.

Ted Dean broke through the middle for 10 yards and fumbled to the Packers on the Eagle 22.

Hornung and Taylor got a first down on the 11, Hornung went to the eight, but Taylor's three-yard pickup was nullified by an offsides penalty. Starr tried two passes into the end zone, incomplete. The Packers had to settle for a 20-yard field goal by Hornung.

Late in the period, the Packers marched into scoring range on their own initiative. They reached the Eagle 14 when another three-yarder by Taylor was nullified by another offsides, followed by two more Starr incompletions. Hornung kicked a 23-yard field goal and the Packers led, 6-0.

Although the Eagles made only one first down in the first period, and that on an interference call, it was far from a total loss. The Packers betrayed their overeagerness with those two penalties; they were exactly the kind of mistakes they wouldn't make in the glory years, or would be able to overcome as Starr gained poise. And the Eagles, as coaches say, were making them play left-handed. By stunting and overloading defenses to slow down Taylor and Hornung, they were forcing the Packers to abandon their strength in the scoring zone. As a result, three thrusts inside the Eagle 15-yard line left the Packers still within Van Brocklin's sights, and he was drawing a bead on them.

Midway through the second quarter, Van Brocklin struck. Right-handed.

He hit McDonald across the middle for 22 yards to the Packer 35. McDonald, an irrepressible squirt, bounded back into the huddle and told Van Brocklin that the defense was converging on him in the middle, why didn't they fake that route and go outside. Agreed. The Packers went for McDonald's fake, McDonald cut for the flag at the goal line, and Van Brocklin put the ball on his hands. McDonald slid across a patch of snow beyond the end zone, Walston converted, and Van Brocklin football led Lombardi football, 7-6.

Minutes later it was 10-6. This time Van Brocklin found Retzlaff on a deep sideline route for 41 yards to the Packer 33, and came back with a swing pass to Dean for 22 more. Going for the knockout, Van Brocklin threw three incompletions. Walston then kicked a 15-yard field goal.

The Packers, like a bunch of kids trying to kick in a steel door when all they had to do was calmly unlock it

Jim Taylor climbs a mountain of players and is thrown back

and walk in, roared back to their fourth anticlimax with two minutes remaining. They marched 73 yards to the Eagle seven, Taylor and Hornung running and catching for most of it. Then, as time ran out, Hornung missed a field goal from 14 yards.

The half was marked by the failure of the Packers to cash in their opportunities and the success of Van Brocklin in cashing in his. Lombardi mourned those failures after the game. But it cannot be said that they caused the defeat, because the Packers got the lead in the fourth quarter. It can be said that the Packers didn't seize control when they had a chance to. It can be said that the failures of the first half foretold later failures. "We were a young team and it showed," says Boyd Dowler, now an assistant coach with the Eagles. "We weren't ready to win. But I can hardly remember the first half. It's the second half that stands out."

There was one graphic feature of the first half that doesn't show in the play-by-play or the game movies. On every exchange of the ball, 42 players trotted on and off the field in the familiar traffic jam of offensive and defensive platoons. Chuck Bednarik, legs and arms crossed as casually as a man at a bus stop, stood at the line of scrimmage watching and waiting. The second half would be his as much as the first half was Van Brocklin's.

Bednarik made four big plays, two in a row as the Packers continued to assault the Eagles between 20-yard lines. After Hornung got 14 and Taylor 16, the Packers had a third down and two at the Eagle 26. Hornung tried Bednarik's side, and that was the last side he tried all day. Bednarik's bear hug pinched a nerve in his shoulder, momentarily paralyzing his right arm and putting him out of the game. The Packers had a very capable substitute in Tom Moore, but Moore had not led the league in scoring. With Hornung incapacitated, Green Bay bypassed a field-goal attempt and challenged Bednarik with Taylor. He escaped in one piece, but without the first down.

The Eagles mounted a threat of their own, Van Brocklin shooting arrows of 33 yards to McDonald and 25 yards to Walston on deep slants. From the four-yard line he aimed another over the middle, but his receivers were held up and it was intercepted, by John Symank. This was the only penetration the Eagles didn't get points from, and Van Brocklin went to school on it. The next time they got that close, he had a surprise for the Packers.

He needed it, because the Packers finally scored a

touchdown two minutes into the fourth quarter. After three bad passes by Starr, Max McGee averted a possible panic with a 35-yard run from punt formation. Starr hit Gary Knafelc for 17 yards, Taylor and Moore slashed for two first downs, and Starr hit McGee for the score from seven yards out. Hornung converted. The Packers led, 13-10.

The Packers were punishing the Eagles, a young heavyweight wearing down an older one. "Taylor gives you a clean shot at him," said Brookshier, "and almost kills you." Linebacker Maxie Baughan was knocked silly. Asked by a team physician to identify himself, he had to think about it.

But the Eagles had one more big punch left in them. Ted Dean delivered it on the kickoff, bursting 58 yards to the Packer 39. "Psychologically, that put them back in the game," Lombardi said. Dean was having what would be the best day of a career curtailed by injuries.

Determined to throttle Van Brocklin, the Packers were penalized five yards for holding, their third damaging penalty. Sensing their mood, Van Brocklin elected to stay on the ground, Dean and Barnes carrying for a first down. He went back to pass and was blitzed for a seven-yard loss by Nitschke. He then passed to Barnes for 13 and handed off to Barnes for five more and a first down on the nine. Here the surprise. The Packers, expecting the pass, were blown out twice. "The line was begging me to stay on the ground," Van Brocklin said. Dean got four at guard and circled left end for the touchdown. Walston made it Eagles 17, Packers 13. So would the headline writers all over the country.

The Packers had two more shots. Bednarik was there for both of them. McGee caught a 12-yard pass on the Eagle 48 and fumbled. Bednarik recovered.

With less than three minutes on the clock, the Packers made their final bid. Starting from his 35, Starr completed four passes around a nine-yard run by Taylor, moving to the Eagle 22. Time for one play. Starr faded back, saw his receivers blanketed in the end zone, and dropped the ball off to Taylor. Taylor broke a tackle just beyond the line of scrimmage, careened past the 15-yard line, was met at the 10 by a defensive back, Bobby Jackson, and was twisting loose with no one between him and the winning touchdown when Bednarik, on the last tick of his sixtieth minute, swooped in at an angle and wrestled him down, as the gun went off.

It was a dramatically correct finish for the Packers,

agonizingly close. But they don't pay off on close. They don't pay off on statistics either. The Packers had 87 plays to 48 for the Eagles, 401 yards to 303 for the Eagles, 22 first downs to 13 for the Eagles, seven scoring chances to four for the Eagles. More revealing, six of Van Brocklin's nine completions gained at least 22 yards, while only one of Starr's twenty-one completions gained as much as 20. A ringing endorsement of Van Brocklin football. "The Packers play good fundamental football," said defensive tackle Jesse Richardson of the Eagles, "but they don't have the home run. We do."

It was a huge personal triumph for Van Brocklin, and he left them pleading for more forever. He confirmed his plans for retirement, becoming one of the few athletes ever to walk off the stage on top, at thirty-four. "This is the happiest day of my life," he said. "I've been doing this a hundred years. I never want to see a uniform again."

He meant from the inside. He intended to see the green and silver of the Eagles a lot from outside. Buck Shaw announced his retirement, definitely, at the same time as Van Brocklin.

Van Brocklin had fulfilled his part of the deal with the Eagles. But the strong-willed personality who ruled on the field was a threat to the front-office hacks whose only constructive act in a decade had been to hire him. They knew that Van Brocklin knew that they didn't know what they were doing; he would wind up ruling them, too. Bert Bell was dead. As far as they were concerned, so was their part of the deal with Van Brocklin.

They gave the head-coaching job to line coach Nick Skorich. In a year the team plunged into a malaise from which it has not yet recovered. Only the packed houses that began with Van Brocklin remain as a legacy of that championship season.

The brand-new Minnesota Vikings signed Van Brocklin as their first coach for 1961. After a brilliant start, he quit in 1966 over a public feud with his quarterback, Fran Tarkenton, who was as strong-willed as he. He moved sideways to the expansion Atlanta Falcons, where he is today. High-spirited, independent and witty as a winning player, he has a reputation as a Lombardi-like martinet as a coach. In fact, he handed out an inspirational-type book about Lombardi to his players. Like Lombardi, he is one of those driven men whose only true friend is victory. But he has yet to be embraced by another championship.

Lombardi stayed in Green Bay, of course, until he won five championships. In the process he grew to mythic stature as a symbol of right-thinking, conservative values during the generation-gap sixties. He died in 1970 after coaching the Washington Redskins for one season.

His legacy to football can be seen on any NFL field, including the ones graced by Norm Van Brocklin. In the long run, the short run won out. As sophisticated zone defenses discouraged the long pass, Lombardi football evolved as the game's dominant force. Joe Namath's dramatic championship season with the New York Jets in 1968 has been the lone reversion to 1960.

Complaints are heard in the land that professional football, with its conservative cast, is duller than it used to be. Sure is in Philadelphia.

Tommy McDonald slips away from Packer defender to score first Eagle touchdown on a 35-yard pass. Overleaf: Ted Dean runs hard behind menacing blockers

Defensive end Bill Quinlan grabs a tipped
Van Brocklin pass on first Eagle play to
give Packers the ball on Eagle 14-yard line

Tommy McDonald pulls in a Van Brocklin
pass and goes 35 yards for Eagle touchdown

"We didn't think at the start of the season that we were going to be in a championship game. After the game, Lombardi said, 'Don't hold your heads down. You had a great season. We didn't make it this year, but we'll be back.'"

PAUL HORNUNG

Lombardi's Boys

The 1960 title game proved to be just a brief tidal wave for the Philadelphia Eagles. But for the Green Bay Packers, it turned out to be the start of a long flood.

The Packers had come from a wretched low ebb—not one season above a .500 record from 1948 through 1958. Then Vince Lombardi came to the Wisconsin town in 1959 to be coach and general manager for the local stockholders, who somehow managed to keep a franchise during the big-city boom of pro football.

In one of his best decisions, Lombardi went to the movies. In game film of 1958, he saw slope-shouldered Paul Hornung wandering from quarter-back to halfback to fullback, succeeding nowhere. He inquired about the former Golden Boy from Notre Dame, who had become bitter and confused. Then Lombardi called up Hornung and said: "You're not going to play quarterback for me. You're going to play left halfback or you're not going to play at all."

Then Lombardi watched films of the last two games of Coach Scooter McLean's regime—and observed a rugged 215-pound fullback named Jim Taylor, a rookie from Louisiana State University. Finally given his chance, Taylor had gained 247 yards in 52 carries behind an uncoordinated line. Lombardi decided to build his offense around the quick slants of Taylor, the wider slashes of Hornung.

In Lombardi's first year, the Packers had a 7-5

Bart Starr led Packers to Eagle seven as first half ended with Eagles ahead, 10–6

With Taylor (31) running hard, Packers mounted drive in third quarter but failed to score

record. In his second year, Hornung set a record with 176 points in only twelve games. That same year, Taylor gained 1,101 yards, the first of five straight seasons over 1,000 yards, a record. But the Packers lost the championship to Philadelphia. They didn't know it then, but they were setting a record. Lombardi would not lose another playoff game in Green Bay.

In 1961 and 1962, they won their first NFL titles, beating the New York Giants—Lombardi's old team —both times. In 1963, Hornung was suspended by Commissioner Pete Rozelle for betting on his own team. The Packers finished behind Chicago in 1963 and behind Baltimore in 1964. Then they came back to win three straight NFL championships and the first two Super Bowl games.

But Hornung and Taylor barely survived into the Super Bowl era. Hornung was injured in 1966 and was later drafted by New Orleans, although a neck injury kept him from ever playing for the Saints.

Taylor moved to New Orleans in less harmonious fashion. He refused to sign a contract with Lombardi in 1966, so he played at a low salary in order to become a free agent. Then he signed with the Saints in his native Louisiana. But he was worn down from years of pounding the line and retired after 1967.

Lombardi always had a soft spot in his heart for the merry bachelor, Hornung, but he considered the quiet Taylor to be disloyal for jumping clubs for money. Lombardi himself grew weary of coaching, and of Green Bay, and he moved on to coach the Washington Redskins in 1969. He died in 1970.

G. V.

Vince Lombardi

227

Father of the "Steagles"

Bert Bell

Perhaps the fortunes of the Philadelphia Eagles would have been different if Bert Bell had lived longer. But how would that have affected the future of the National Football League?

Bell was the Main Line resident who had transferred the old Frankford Yellow Jackets to Philadelphia in 1933, in the early, shaky days of pro football. Besides being a pioneer, Bell was an innovator. In 1936 he organized a common draft of college stars, a practice that still exists today. (The first player drafted? Jay Berwanger, star halfback of the University of Chicago, a football power of the time, drafted by Bell's own Eagles.)

In 1941, Bell arranged one of the strangest deals ever to be made in any sport—the cross-transfer of franchises between Philadelphia and Pittsburgh, with Bell moving to Pittsburgh. That was followed by a wartime stratagem to cope with manpower shortages: the temporary merger in 1943 of the Philadelphia and Pittsburgh teams (known to the league as "Phil-Pitt" but known to fans as "The Steagles"). In 1944, Bell's Eagles merged with the Chicago Cardinals and were known as "Card-Pitt." In 1945, he went back to running the plain old Steelers.

In 1946, Bell was named president of the NFL, moving the league offices to Philadlephia, where he was a familiar figure in the stands at Franklin Field. And it was there that he died on October 11, 1959, with two minutes remaining in a game between, ironically, the Eagles and the Steelers.

By that time, the successor to Bell was Alvin (Pete) Rozelle, a smooth public-relations man from Los Angeles who had once been general manager of the Rams. Rozelle moved the NFL offices to New York with wall-to-wall public-relations men, just in time for the 1960s. During Bell's thirteen years, the league had grown from ten to twelve teams. In Rozelle's first season, the NFL was challenged by an eight-team American Football League, eager to spend money for college players. Although the NFL tried smugly to ignore the AFL, it eventually had to merge with it. Now Rozelle presides over a twenty-six-team league—and Tampa will be the twenty-seventh in 1976. The cost for the new franchise will be $16,000,000—the most ever received for an expansion franchise in any sport.

"Everything in sports is a lot of money," Rozelle said in April of 1974. "It's a matter of value received."

Those kinds of figures were not present in Commissioner Bert Bell's days, when $16,000,000 probably could have bought all ten franchises.

G. V.

Eagles came back on pass plays such as 25-yard Van Brocklin completion to Bobby Walston

"I used to love to run on fourth down. But when Vince got there, he said, 'You'll never run on fourth down as long as I'm coaching the Packers,' so you can imagine what would have happened if I hadn't made it."

MAX MCGEE

Eagles drive ended as John Symank intercepted Van Brocklin's pass from the four-yard line

McGee catches pass from Bart Starr (above) to put the Packers ahead by a score of 13–10. Max McGee takes Packers out of a hole with a 35-yard run on a fake kick play (below)

Turning point of game was Ted Dean's brilliant 58-yard kickoff return to Packers' 39-yard line

In closing minutes, Starr's passes (above, to Konafelc) almost brought Packers back

Dean goes over for winning touchdown

Jerry Wollman and Joe Kuharich

Van Brocklin's Revenge

What happened to the Philadelphia Eagles after 1960 might have come out of a script for their demise written by a bitter Norm Van Brocklin. They did challenge in the Eastern Division in 1961, but then the bad times rolled in.

After two straight losing seasons, a new owner dealt himself in: Jerry Wollman, a high roller who, in a moment of inspiration, staked his new coach, Joe Kuharich, to a fifteen-year contract. Kuharich had coached six seasons in the NFL, producing one winner. His record with the Eagles turned out to be one-in-five. But their worst loss of all came at the end of the 1968 season when they won two straight games, thereby missing the chance to finish last and draft a running back named O.J. Simpson.

A new owner came in and dismissed Kuharich, but he couldn't dismiss the fifteen-year contract. That one runs out in 1979.

G. V.

"Dean's runback was the big play of the game . . . we saw a little weakness in their kickoff coverage, and sure enough it worked, it worked for 58 yards."

CHUCK BEDNARIK

230

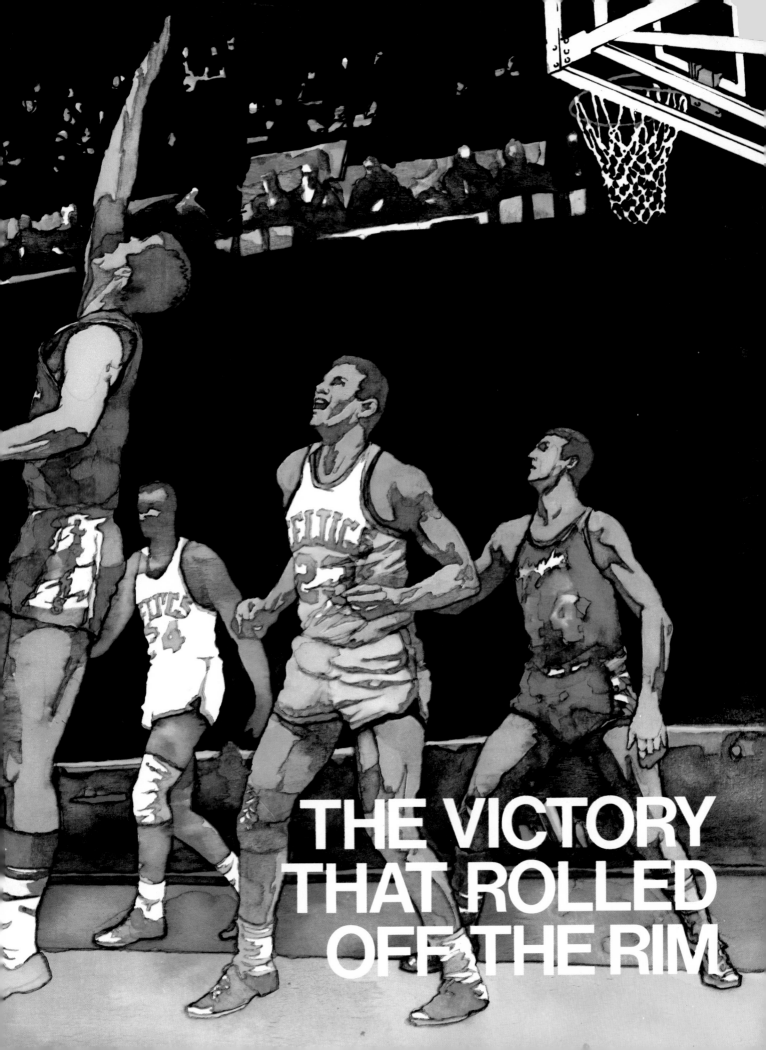

THE VICTORY THAT ROLLED OFF THE RIM

The outcome in doubt, Red Auerbach communes with his cigar

Boston Celtics/ Los Angeles Lakers NBA Championship Playoff April, 1962

By Neil Amdur

e is still highly visible, as coach of the improving Seattle Supersonics. Before that he was highly audible, as a commentator on televised games. But Bill Russell was, of course, most prominent in the thirteen years when he flew high around the defensive backboards of the National Basketball Association.

Russell was dominant—on the court, daring anybody to take a close shot; in the clubhouse, challenging the premature assumptions of some sportswriters; striding away from the arena, disdaining the impersonal autograph seeker. But in private he was also dominant in his warm laughter, his insights into America's racial problems. For thirteen years, he made the other players seem a little less like giants.

One of the toughest years was 1962, when Russell and the Boston Celtics had to take on the Los Angeles Lakers, with Elgin Baylor and Jerry West at their best. The sounds of that confrontation are still echoing.

Neil Amdur has covered a variety of sports since joining the *New York Times* in 1968 from the *Miami Herald*. His current specialties are tennis, football, and track and field—and he covered the 1968 and 1972 Olympics for the *Times*. His knowledge of basketball is sound—although one sportswriter who has played with Amdur reports that Neil's style is more Tom Heinsohn than Bill Russell. Amdur is the author of several sports books, including *My Race Be Won*, an autobiography of Vincent Matthews on which he collaborated. A native of Wilkes-Barre, Pennsylvania, he now lives in Harrington Park, New Jersey.

G.V.

He called them "Russell's Laws"—rules to live by, he said; actions that spoke louder than any jive. Like getting a rival player to do just what you wanted him to do.

Mathematical or physical laws are permanent. Prove them once and they are accepted forever. But sports laws must be proved every game, every season—if one is audacious enough to have laws in the first place. Bill Russell, center for the Boston Celtics, proved his laws by winning championships in eleven of his thirteen professional seasons—the greatest winning record of any player in any sport.

But each year was different, some harder than others. In the spring of 1962, Russell and his Celtics had to overcome Wilt Chamberlain, at the end of Wilt's greatest scoring season. Then the Celtics had to take on the Los Angeles Lakers in the first coast-to-coast championship series in the history of the National Basketball Association. The Lakers merely had Elgin Baylor and Jerry West, both in their prime, the greatest one-two punch in basketball history. And the game hung on a shot that twirled around the basket, setting up an overtime period that would drain everybody in the Boston Garden.

It was a brutal test even for William Felton Russell, the six-foot, ten-inch "eagle with a beard," as Tom Meschery, a player and a poet, had dubbed him. Yet Russell had set his standards high. The man with the infectious laugh in an interview, the man with the nervous stomach in the privacy of the clubhouse, had set himself up as a cold-blooded killer on the court, a defensive star who revolutionized the game.

"You got to have the killer instinct," Russell had once noted, another law of his land. "If you do not have it, forget about basketball and go into social psychology or something. If you sometimes wonder if you've got it, you ain't got it."

There was never any doubt in Bill Russell's mind about who reigned as chairman of the boards in the 94-by-50-foot world of basketball. A poor boy whose family had fled Louisiana, he had blossomed late at McClymonds High School in Oakland, California. Then he had won

back-to-back National Collegiate Athletic Association championships at the University of San Francisco. After sparking an Olympic Championship in 1956, he got a belated start in his rookie season with the Celtics, a team that had never quite found the championship touch. But when he claimed possession of the air lanes near his defensive basket, he made the Celtics champions.

"Russell was the key to the Celtics," noted Carl Braun, an older player who joined the club in 1962 from New York. "They always had great shooters, with Ed Macauley, Bill Sharman, and Bob Cousy, but we still could whip their ass. It was Russell who made them champions."

He didn't always do it by flicking away somebody's jump shot, either. Sometimes he did it with a closed fist. Jim Krebs, the Laker center during the 1962 series, was one of the players who tested Russell's patience. And lost. At a game in Providence, Rhode Island, Krebs pushed Russell to the limit with continued shoving and chatter.

"Put your guts where your mouth is," Russell told Krebs. Krebs lifted a right hand from the floor, but Russell uncorked a left that broke Krebs' jaw and left him unconscious for twenty minutes.

By that season, however, Russell had made most of his points by effort and guile, by making offensive players hesitate before they shot. His tactics had produced the Celtics' first NBA title in 1957. They missed in 1958, because Russell suffered an ankle injury against the St. Louis Hawks. But in 1959 the Celtics defeated the Lakers (still ensconced in Minneapolis, where there actually are lakes), and then they took the Hawks twice, in 1960 and 1961. The league record for consecutive titles was four straight. To match that record, the Celtics would have to triumph over the new Los Angeles Lakers in the 1962 championship series.

Russell was already a triumph for Red Auerbach, the abrasive, chunky, cigar-smoking coach. Auerbach had been around professional basketball as far back as the Washington Capitols of the Basketball Association of America, which preceded the NBA in the mid-forties. He had achieved a reputation as knowledgeable, and he had also refused to let ego-minded owners tell him how to coach. It wasn't until Walter Brown, owner of the Celtics, hired him away from Ben Kerner of the Tri-City Blackhawks (later to become the St. Louis Hawks) nat Boston moved from last place to second in the NBA. hey had the shooters but not the endurance.

Auerbach's greatest coup involved his old boss, erner, at the 1956 draft of college seniors. First choice elonged to Rochester, which picked up Sihugo Green f Duquesne, a smooth backcourtman. Second choice elonged to the Hawks. Auerbach persuaded Kerner o trade the draft rights to Russell for Ed Macauley, an ld star, from St. Louis, and Cliff Hagan, a future star. ut neither was, or would be, Bill Russell.

As a technician, Auerbach may have been no better r worse than many other successful basketball coaches. ut with Russell in his lineup, the Celtics seldom ran more than eight or nine basic plays. And that was enough.

Russell affected every phase of the Celtics' attack. On defense, he became such an overwhelming influence under the basket that Tom Heinsohn, Cousy, and others could afford to overplay rivals in quest of steals and turnovers, knowing that Russell would intimidate anyone who dared drive down the middle and challenge his domain.

"On no other team could guys afford to cheat on defense the way they did at Boston," Carl Braun said. "But with Russell, they could do it and get away with it. They didn't have to hang around the basket chasing

erry West drives for the basket as Tom Heinsohn moves in to guard him

ebounds and loose balls. They knew Russell would clean the board and get that lead pass out there for the fast break."

Russell's value on offense was often minimized in comparison to Cousy, Sharman, the Jones boys, Heinsohn, and Frank Ramsey. But his strength under the offensive basket prevented opposing teams from springing forwards and guards downcourt. Russell was as effective feeding and screening as he was spinning for a short, left-handed hook shot.

Before Russell came along, the Celtics' biggest star had been Bob Cousy, the smooth Frenchman from the playgrounds of New York City. No two players could have been more different in background than Russell and Cousy: black/white, big man/little man, city college/Catholic college. Yet for all these differences, and despite the usual rivalry of two superstars sharing headlines, each seemed to respect the other as a player and as a person: Russell was the supreme being on the boards, Cousy was the cocky traffic cop directing the fast break with poise and precision.

Auerbach played to the strengths of his personnel, pairing Heinsohn, the shooting forward, with a player who was primarily content with defense, like Jim Loscutoff or Tom (Satch) Sanders. He had Cousy and Sam Jones in the backcourt along with K. C. Jones, a defensive specialist who had been Russell's college teammate. Heinsohn and Frank Ramsey, another roadrunner, rarely played forward at the same time.

Auerbach also was conscious of keeping a productive, practical bench. He did not want dissidents crying for playing time and disrupting his delicate balance. He utilized Carl Braun—fired as coach of the Knicks after the 1961 season and grateful for a second chance—along with a rookie, Gary Phillips, and another hungry player, Gene Guarilia, who was to have an unexpected moment of intense pressure in the seventh game.

Auerbach was an intuitive psychologist who knew when to turn up the volume or crack the whip. Heinsohn became a favorite target for language that Auerbach seldom heaped on his more sensitive superstars, such as Russell or Cousy. But Heinsohn could take the tougher handling, and he ultimately won such affection and respect from Auerbach that he would be-

come a successful head coach at Boston in later years.

With such a diversified group of players, the Celtics were understandably not always together. Carl Braun, who was to have a brief test in the crucible of the seventh game, recalls being "really more of an observer that last season. The Celtics went different ways as individuals. But once they walked on the court, they became a unit."

Russell, deeply sensitive to other people behind his impassive mask, sometimes tried to avoid friendships with rookies, who might be cut any moment. That was fine with Tom (Satch) Sanders, a young defensive specialist from New York University. "When I first came to the Celtics, I decided Russell and I weren't going to get along," Sanders recalled. "In training camp, I was going to be mean and hard and cold, and I wasn't going to have anything to do with anyone—just concentrate on making the team. Well, that lasted two or three seconds. Russell let loose with that big laugh in this restaurant, and I decided that anyone with that much laughter wasn't anyone to be mean and hard and cold around.

"I went over and asked if I could tag along. In his inevitable fashion, he turned on me and said, 'No, hell no, certainly not.' Well, I thought, I've done it now, I've shown myself up as weak, just when I was going to be mean and hard and cold. I'd better change back fast. But then, just as I was turning away and getting set to be aloof again, he said he was only kidding. That's like him. He enjoys surprising people to keep them just a bit off-balance."

Perhaps Russell had noticed that the slender Sanders had something of a Russell-like intimidation on rival forwards. Sanders became a vital member of the squad as the "second season"—the NBA playoffs—approached.

"I'm better in the playoffs because they're shorter and because they mean more," Russell once said, realizing that a 60–20 won-lost record in the regular season meant nothing to sports historians if you couldn't win the four games that counted in a seven-game playoff.

"He used to throw up all the time before a game or at halftime—a tremendous sound, almost as loud as his laugh," John Havlicek recalled recently. "It was a welcome sound, too, because it meant he was keyed up for the game. Around the locker room, we'd grin and say, 'Man, we're going to be all right tonight.'"

The one player who most seemed to ignite the com-

Elgin Baylor, leading scorer in the playoff, floats in for a layup

"Elgin was unbelievable." RED AUERBACH

petitive spirit in Russell was Wilt Chamberlain, the giant "Big Dipper," as he called himself, towering several inches above seven feet. Their rivalry became one of the most celebrated in professional sports, as they filled roles created as much by their actions as by fans and media. Russell was the intense, committed psychic warrior and winner. Chamberlain was the stiff locker-room lord and loser, who coveted love and respect but could not bring himself to bend for such values.

Wilt had enjoyed his best pro season in 1962, as he followed coach Frank McGuire's instructions to assault the basket every chance he got. He led the league in scoring with a phenomenal 50.8-point average that included 100 points in one game against the New York Knicks in Hershey, Pennsylvania. (Both marks are still NBA records.) Wilt was on the floor for all but eight of the 3,890 minutes the Warriors played in the regular season. He was a Colossus. And in the Eastern Division finals, he and Russell neutralized each other enough to send the playoffs into a seventh game, at Boston. And that game was still tied, with two seconds left, when Sam Jones took a jump shot.

"Sam's shot was from about twenty feet, dead center," Jim Loscutoff related years later. "But it seemed like someone, maybe the good Lord, grabbed the ball and guided it into the basket."

The Warriors still had time to try a desperation pass from midcourt to the basket, with the hope that Chamberlain could grab the rebound and stuff it. The total reliance on Chamberlain was the difference between the Warriors and the Celtics. Boston could win if Russell batted down balls, rebounded, and intimidated, but Philadelphia needed Wilt to score, score, score. With two seconds left, the 13,909 fans in Boston Garden knew exactly where the ball would go.

Tom Gola passed the ball toward the basket, hoping for a favorable carom off the backboard. The ball bounced, but the two giants, Chamberlain and Russell, were scrambling for possession when the final horn sounded.

The Celtics again were home free, blessed by the luck that some people associated with their green uniforms.

Now it was time to meet the Lakers, who had won the Western Division title by eleven games and eliminated Detroit in a six-game playoff. While the Warriors had stressed an offense geared to a single big man, Los Angeles posed different problems: no two players

could chuck any better than Elgin Baylor and Jerry West.

At six feet, five inches and 225 pounds, Baylor had brought a new style to NBA cornermen with his uncommon quickness and body control. He immobilized defenders with an assortment of head fakes, a strangely effective nervous twitch, and a teasing high dribble. He could stop on a dime for a twenty-foot jump shot or yo-yo a dribble into second gear and maneuver through and around for inside shots.

"There was really no way to stop Elgin Baylor," said Jim Loscutoff, who had guarded him through the years. "You just hoped you could keep him under control."

aylor had been called back into the Army Reserves at Fort Lewis, Washington, during the regular season and had played only 48 of the 80 games. But he had averaged a spectacular 38.2 points, second only to Chamberlain, and the Lakers had carefully saved military leave time for Baylor to use during the playoffs.

"The fact that he hadn't played the full season, with all the trouble and aches, probably left him stronger physically than the others in the playoffs," coach Fred Schaus recalled. "And unlike some players, Elgin never lost his touch."

Another Laker with a golden touch was West, whose finesse and scoring ability had helped take him and Schaus from West Virginia University to pro basketball. If Baylor was the new breed of forward, West, at six feet three inches and 175 pounds, became the stereotype for the wiry, jump-shooting guard who could score from as far away as twenty-five feet.

Cynics who had watched West in college and with the victorious United States Olympic team in 1960 had scoffed at his ability to absorb the physical punishment and brutal travel associated with the pros. But West refused to accept such skepticism and averaged 30.8 points during the regular season. During Baylor's absence for Army duties, West had assumed command of the batallion.

The Lakers' weakness was at center. For years in Minneapolis, before the club went west, George Mikan had been their giant, the most potent force in the early years of the NBA. The Lakers had tried a number of players at the position after Mikan's departure, but none had worked out. With the emergence of Baylor and West, L.A.'s attitude shifted from concern to resignation: hell, we've got to live with it, let's do the best we can with what we've got.

The Lakers shifted to Los Angeles for the 1961 season but were eliminated by St. Louis in the Western Division finals. Now in 1962, for the first time, a truly national playoff had evolved, another indication of the growth and expansion that had changed the face of professional sports in the late fifties and early sixties.

The 1962 playoff dramatized the jet age in professional basketball, just as the installation of the twenty-four-second clock in 1954 had radically changed the philosophy and style of the game. In earlier years, playoff games usually involved limited travel between cities east of the Mississippi: Philadelphia–Fort Wayne, Boston–St. Louis, Boston–Minneapolis. This one would have two games in Boston, two in L.A., then back and forth, game by game.

The series began routinely in the old Boston Garden. With six players in double figures and a typical 35–22 spurt in the third quarter, the Celtics won, 122–108. Boston fans seemed almost blasé after the tumult of the seven-game confrontation with Wilt. A crowd of only 7,467 showed up at the Garden, perhaps remembering how the Celtics had drubbed the Minneapolis Lakers in the 1959 finals. In the minds of Celtic fans, the West-Coast Lakers, even with Baylor and West, were not the Warriors or the Hawks. Not yet, anyway.

As usual, the Celtics looked like they had just left a street fight. Frank Ramsey, who had suffered a severe muscle pull in the Warrior series, was taped like a mummy and seemed to hobble—except when he had the ball or when Russell was firing a pass for the fast break. Tommy Heinsohn, who had gained an assortment of nicknames all related to his shooting habits ("Gunner" and "Ack-Ack," to name two), also seemed weak from a series of virus infections late in the season. And in the opener, K. C. Jones collided with the Lakers' Jim Krebs and paid the price for the mismatch—a broken nose.

Any indication that the Lakers would be awed or intimidated by their East-Coast rivals—as they had been three years earlier—ended the next day when they won, 129–122. A 43-point second quarter carried L.A. to a 73–59 halftime lead. At one point in the third quarter, the Celtics trailed, 90–66. West and Baylor combined for 76 points and the Lakers added 37 of 42 foul shots, much to the dismay of Auerbach and startled Boston fans.

The Lakers—or, more specifically, West—stole the third game from the Celtics before a record crowd of 15,180 at the Los Angeles Sports Arena. The Baylor–West combo pumped in 77 of the points. But it was a steal by West of an inbounds pass from Cousy with three seconds left that settled the closely contested game. West had tied the game seconds earlier on two foul shots. He picked off Cousy's pass at midcourt, drove toward the basket with Cousy in frantic pursuit, and made the shot as the final buzzer sounded, in the tradition of a Hollywood hero.

Auerbach, who had been badgering the referees, particularly on fouls, stormed off the court. He did not believe that West could have completed the steal and gotten off the shot in under three seconds. His protests were in vain, and the Celtics trailed in a championship series for the first time since 1958.

"Russell was at his best in situations like this," Carl Braun recalled. "He took it upon himself to get psyched up."

Russell made the first field goal and free throw to start the fourth game in L.A., and the Celtics never trailed en route to a 115–103 victory. But when the series shifted east, the ubiquitous Baylor stunned a capacity crowd at Boston Garden with perhaps the finest single performance in NBA playoff history. Hounded by three players, the former Seattle University All-America fired shots from everywhere, scored 61 points, and almost single-handedly put the Lakers in a position to wrap up the series in the sixth game at Los Angeles. Baylor's assault shattered the air of supremacy that had hovered over the Celtics. If he could be that effective on the road, how could he be harnessed at home? Had Baylor found the solution to beating Boston by ignoring Russell and firing over him?

For the first half of Game Six, the Lakers seemed poised for the kill. West, the country boy from Cabin Creek, West Virginia, who had captivated the L.A. crowds, was breaking away for long jump shots that seemed to glide through the net without the formality of touching the rim. Baylor—his nervous neck muscles jerking and twitching as he gained position and unsettled the de-

"I thought it was going in." FRANK SELVY

fenders—was continuing his assault on frustrated Celtic forwards, teasing Russell to switch on baseline drives and then slipping slick bounce passes or lobs underneath to Krebs or Rudy LaRusso, the underrated six-foot, seven-inch forward.

With the Lakers in front 65–57 at halftime, the Celtics at last seemed ready to be had.

"What made playing Boston so tough," Frank Selvy, a Laker guard, recalled years later, "was that you never knew who could hurt you. With the Warriors, it was Chamberlain. We had Elgin and Jerry. But the Celtics had five or six guys who could get so hot on offense that they could turn on the whole team."

No one on the Celtics can recall whether the sounds of Russell's halftime nausea stirred the club in the second half of the sixth game. But Sam Jones's shooting was a definite influence. At six feet, four inches, the soft-spoken Jones had been culled from the small-college ranks of North Carolina A. & T. by Auerbach in 1958—a "sleeper," in the lexicon of pro scouts. His early years were spent on the bench, in a secondary role behind Cousy and Sharman. But Sharman's departure before this 1961–62 season, for a coaching job in a rival league, had opened a job in the backcourt. Auerbach found that both Jones boys complemented the thirty-three-year-old Cousy, who was to retire a year later. Sam was silky and smooth and seemed to use a backboard for scientific confirmation of his shooting eye. K.C., shorter by several inches, was the tenacious defensive tiger, who relished stealing passes and hawking hot-shooting guards into losing their touch.

Auerbach knew when they belonged together. In the final sixteen seconds of the Celtics–Warriors final, with the score deadlocked, the five Celtic players on the court had been Russell, Cousy, the Jones boys, and Heinsohn.

In the first six minutes of the second half against the Lakers, Auerbach again went to his shooters. Sam showed his touch with five field goals that triggered a 34–16 Celtic spread. To the dismay of Doris Day and friends at courtside, the Celtics won, 119–105. The series headed east again for one final shoot-out.

Much has been said over the years about a so-called "home-court advantage" in basketball. The theory is that a team, on its home court, is familiar with such nuances as the tightness of the rim, the lighting facilities, and the composition of the court. In high school

and college competition, where facilities traditionally were small and cramped, the overhanging balconies, soft wooden backboards, and crowded courtside seats became the accomplices of successful home teams.

At Boston Garden, the checkerboard pattern of flooring was cited by some players as a nuisance element instituted by Auerbach to break a dribbler's concentration. On other courts around the league, soft spots on portable floors could make a ball lose its bounce and lead to a turnover unless the player was aware of their presence. Positioning of scoreboards also affected a player's flow, particularly in the closing seconds of a twelve-minute period.

Physical layouts were only one factor behind the home-court theory, however. Psychologically, many players performed differently on the road, before hostile audiences, than they did before the friendly chants of a home crowd. Unlike baseball teams, which traveled to a city for a two or three-day stay, pro basketball teams had to perform on a succession of one-night stands. As travel became longer and more hectic, using planes instead of trains, players saw themselves as airport minstrels grabbing sleep on jet planes they distrusted or in hotel lobbies that looked the same in each city. Players began road trips with their minds telling their bodies they were tired before the first shot.

The home court for a seventh game of an NBA playoff was determined on the basis of the regular-season record, one of the few incentives for a club with a playoff berth already locked up. In 1957 and 1960, as in 1962, the Celtics had finished with the best record in the league, which entitled them to play the seventh game against the Lakers at Boston Garden.

History was with the Celtics in the 1962 final. In the six previous NBA championship finals that had gone to a seventh game, the home team had won each time. On two occasions, 1957 and 1960, the Celtics had been involved, once in a 125–123 double-overtime classic with the Hawks in '57.

Both coaches approached the game in character. Auerbach stuck in a few needles about the officiating, pointed to foul-shooting statistics from the second and third games, and wondered privately if the referees would protect Baylor and West. Schaus tried to think positively: the Lakers led in games, 2–1, at Boston Garden in the series, so why not again?

The first quarter began with the two teams trading

light jabs, like fighters feeling their way before unloading the heavy guns. The score was tied eight times, including 22–22 at the close of the period. In contrast to other games in the series, the pressure of the seventh game seemed to stiffen the movements and shooting habits of such marksmen as Baylor and Sam Jones. Baylor missed his first six shots, and Jones, who had carried the Celtics in L.A., made only one of his first ten in the opening half.

"I told Elgin not to worry, to do what he had always been doing," Fred Schaus recalled. Execution was a trademark Schaus stressed in drills, and the Lakers often spent hours running patterns until it seemed they could do them blindfolded.

"I don't want my players to run patterns blindfolded," Schaus had snapped when asked why he employed such rigid training tactics. "I want them to run patterns right."

At halftime the Celtics led, 53–47. But with a twenty-four-second clock mandating frequent shots, and with the explosive potential of West and Baylor—who had followed Schaus's advice and rammed in eight of his last twelve—a sense of uncertainty still pervaded Boston Garden. In the Celtics' dressing room, Auerbach tried to calm his players. Ramsey walked over to Sam Jones, whose confidence seemed shattered.

"Loosen up, man," Ramsey said. "It's just another ball game."

"If a guy like that could speak so relaxed," Sam Jones later related, "I knew I could relax, too."

The Celtics came out swinging in the second half and extended their lead to 68–59 in the third quarter. But in a forty-one-second span shortly before the close of the period, West turned a Laker fast break into a three-point play, and Baylor rammed in a pair of jump shots to move L.A. in front, 74–73. The period ended with the score tied at 75–75. The Celtics were reeling. Heinsohn, weakened from the flu, had lost his shooting eye, and no Auerbach diatribes could restore it. Cousy, normally imperturbable under pressure, showed no touch at all, missing ten of thirteen field goals and eight of ten foul shots. Loscutoff spent most of the second half trying to avoid fouling up or fouling out in pursuit of Baylor.

"Hot Rod" Hundley waves vainly as Sam Jones goes in for a shot

The one player who seemed oblivious to pressure was Russell, who had pulled down 19 rebounds in one quarter and played with unsurpassed passion.

With slightly more than four minutes left, the Celtics were ahead, 94–91. But the job of defending against Baylor had produced too many personal fouls. First Sanders, then Loscutoff went to the bench with the ultimate sixth foul. And then Heinsohn fouled out, too, leaving no more experienced forwards to play alongside Ramsey. Auerbach scanned his bench for somebody to guard Baylor and chose Carl Braun, the slender retread from the Knickerbockers. Baylor already had poured through thirteen field goals and 38 points against Boston's best frontmen. Now he was matched against Braun, who was six feet, five inches but basically lacked the strength and muscle to jockey with Baylor.

The pace quickened in the closing minutes, with Russell still the fulcrum in the seesaw, controlling the boards, turning rebounds into baskets, and converting crucial free throws that the Lakers had gambled he would miss. Even when he was called for charging, nullifying a basket with three minutes left, it was for being too aggressive.

Bob Cousy goes into high gear and flashes past West on his way to basket. Overleaf: Bill Russell clears a Laker shot with fantastic leap

With sixty-five seconds left and the Celtics leading by 100–96, the home team seemed on the verge of clinching a crown after all. The Lakers' LaRusso was charged with an offensive foul. But the free throw was missed, and Selvy grabbed a loose ball, drove the length of the floor, and scored to make it 100–98. Forty seconds left. Could the Celtics hold the lead and run down the clock?

"I think the guys might have been a little uptight then," Heinsohn later noted. Confirming this, West intercepted a Cousy pass, and the turnover resulted in another Selvy basket off his own rebound. Eighteen seconds and the score was tied!

The Celtics again worked the ball upcourt before Ramsey gambled on a driving hook shot. It missed, no foul was called for contact on the shot, and LaRusso grabbed the rebound.

Schaus immediately signaled for a time-out from the bench and instinctively shot his eyes to the scoreboard clock overhead. Five seconds left. Time for one more play.

"The thing that I remember most about that situation," Schaus said, after having left the NBA for a head-coaching position at Purdue University, "was that we did have the ball late, with the score tied. We did have the opportunity to win the game on the last shot, which is not something you took for granted against a club like the Celtics. And we did get off a good shot."

Both benches plotted strategies for the closing seconds. Auerbach decided to switch Russell onto Baylor, gambling that the Lakers would look to him for the shot. Braun had played Baylor tough in the closing minutes, shutting him out of field goals and limiting him to only one intentional foul shot. But with a championship on the line, the ultimate one-on-one challenge had to be Russell on Baylor.

Schaus made a key substitution, inserting Rod Hundley, nicknamed "Hod Rod" because of his showmanship and ball-handling abilities. The Laker coach outlined tactics: the first option was to look for Baylor, the second was to set a pick or screen, if possible, for West. If that failed, go for the next best shooter, Selvy.

Selvy took the ball from the referee for the inbounds pass, with Cousy hawking him near the sideline. Hundley, who was to receive the inbounds pass, spotted Russell taking up his position beside Baylor. Option One was out, he decided.

The next five seconds became a frantic blur. With Russell on Baylor and the Celtics sagging on West, Hundley, at the top of the foul circle, saw his options fading until he suddenly spotted Selvy along the left end line. He was open. Yes, open. Cousy had been faked on the inbounds pass and then picked off by Baylor. Russell, refusing to bite and leave Baylor, had not switched men. Selvy was free for the shot.

"I was trying to put as much pressure on my man at midcourt as I could," Cousy recalled. "I was jumping up trying to deflect the inbounds pass. I deflected one, but they got it out again. This time, Selvy timed it so that I was up in the air when he made the pass."

Selvy, considered one of the best pure marksmen in the NBA, had not enjoyed a good shooting game, missing seven of his nine field-goal attempts. But this time he was not being pressured. "I've got to figure Selvy made that shot nine out of ten times he took it," Jim Loscutoff recalled. Selvy shot the ball. Depending on who you talk to, the distance of the shot ranged from eight feet (newsmen) to fifteen feet (Loscutoff and Cousy) to twenty feet (Selvy).

"I thought it was going in," Fred Schaus said. So did Elgin Baylor, who had broken for the basket behind Russell as the ball hit the near rim.

"I pulled my hand away," Baylor told Schaus afterward, realizing that he could have tapped in the rebound. "I pulled it away because I thought it was going in."

But the ball did not go in. It skidded along the ring of the basket, which is a teasing five-eighths of an inch in diameter, hit the other rim and fell into Russell's giant paws, just as the buzzer went off. The title would be decided in overtime.

"I often thought if they were to win, that was the year and that was the play," Cousy recalled.

The Celtics were no strangers to overtime periods in playoffs. Their dynasty had begun with the drama of the double-overtime victory over the Hawks in the seventh game of the 1957 final.

"There is something strange about overtime games," Tom Heinsohn recently remarked, and his view is shared by many professional athletes who must pump themselves up again for an extended showdown. "The overtime often has no relationship to what took place during regulation time."

How true? One of the Celtic heroes in the 1962 final

would be a benchwarmer, Gene Guarilia, who was pressed into emergency duty to guard Baylor in the overtime, after Ramsey became the fourth Boston player to foul out. Guarilia had almost no playoff experience. But he knew that Baylor, even if tiring, would be pressing just as hard in overtime.

The Lakers could not buy a basket in the first four minutes of the overtime. They led only once, 102–100, on two foul shots by Baylor.

Russell was everywhere. He scored the first Boston basket on a feed from Guarilia off a fast break, dunking the ball almost defiantly for the psychic shock it could have on the Lakers. He converted one of two foul shots, then another with two minutes left, after Baylor fouled out trying to muscle around Russell for a rebound.

The Celtic crowd gave Baylor a prolonged standing ovation, worthy of a champion, as he took his seat on the Laker bench after having scored 41 points and grabbed 22 rebounds.

But it was Russell's statistics that glowed as brightly as the 110–107 final score, after the irrepressible Cousy dribbled out the last twenty seconds to protect the lead. The Big Man scored 30 points, his high for the series, and collected an astounding 40 rebounds, which equaled his playoff record. He also made fourteen of seventeen foul shots.

"The thing I remember most about the game getting over was ducking under the scorer's table to protect myself," Cousy said. "The fans poured on the court as if they had been keeping everything inside of them for too long."

The Celtics reached their dressing room, their crown shaky but intact, and gave Auerbach a mighty shove into the shower. Clothes, cigar, and all.

Russell was exhausted, mentally and physically. He and Jerry West, who had finished with 35 points, were the only two who had played every moment of the fifty-three minutes. The sweat dripped off Russell's pencil-thin moustache like water from a rainpipe, and he seemed almost too tired to talk.

"Look at that kid, go write him up," Russell said, pointing to Gene Guarilia, who had shut off Baylor from the floor during the overtime. "Imagine asking a kid who's been on the bench to come in and play a man like Baylor."

This was another one of Russell's laws: never take all the credit yourself for a team victory.

Slick pass from Cousy to K. C. Jones leads to a Celtic basket in the third game

Jerry West hits two foul shots before stealing Celtic pass and sinking basket to win game

The Shot

Frank Selvy never thought the shot was that easy. "If I had been the first guy they were looking for on the play, I would have had an easy lay-up," he said "But I was surprised I even had the ball."

Selvy's last-second miss in the seventh game of the 1962 National Basketball Association final-round playoff between the Los Angeles Lakers and Boston Celtics has gone down as one of the memorable moments in professional basketball.

> ## "I think the team was a little tight because we thought we had had a chance to win . . . I would trade all my points for that one last basket."
>
> FRANK SELVY

"It was a classic second-guess situation," Carl Braun observed. "Most good shooters would rather take a full shot in a situation like that. If it's not a lay-up or a jump shot at the foul line, it can be a son of a bitch. Selvy got struck in no-man's-land."

Few players arrived in the NBA with as strong a set of shooting credentials as Selvy. At Furman University in Greenville, South Carolina, Selvy had led all major-college scorers during the 1953–54 season with a record 41.7-point average. He scored 100 points in a game against Newberry College.

Selvy carried his shooting eye into the NBA but was forced to interrupt his pro career for military service.

"Laying off for three years does a lot to you," he said, echoing the feeling of many who believed that Selvy's amazing shooting touch was never the same after his service tour. "I probably ended up being a better all-around player when I got out and joined the Lakers, but I have no regrets,"

Selvy did regret missing the shot that would have interrupted the Celtics' long reign as champions.

"I remember I thought the shot was good," said the six-foot two-inch guard, who returned to his home state after his playing days. "It hit the front rim, then the back, and seemed to dip. But all the time, I thought it was good."

Selvy disputes the notion that he was close enough for an automatic basket.

"It was a fairly tough shot," he said. "I was almost on the baseline, so far in that I couldn't bank it. I wasn't really expecting the ball either, and there was no time left to make a good shot. It was a good play. We got a shot off. We possibly could have gotten a better one, if Jerry West had thrown in and Rod [Hundley] could have hit him. But I still thought it would go in."

In fifth game, Heinsohn is called for pushing with two seconds left, Lakers ahead by 118–117

The Sub

His four minutes of playing time in the final game would go down as the high point in Gene Guarilia's professional basketball career.

"I remember when Red Auerbach walked down the bench looking for someone to guard Baylor, after Ramsey fouled out in the overtime," Guarilia recalled recently. "He pointed to me and said, 'All I'm telling you is hold him and grab him, but don't give him any three-point plays or cheap fouls. When we get the ball, just hustle your ass downcourt.'"

At six feet, six inches, Guarilia had been selected by Auerbach in the college player draft before the 1959–60 season. There was an interesting tie-in. Guarilia had attended George Washington University; so had Auerbach, many years earlier. But old college ties didn't get Guarilia into many games. In 1961–62, his best season, Guarilia played in only forty-six games and hit for an average of 3.5 points.

Yet, during the overtime period against the Lakers, Guarilia emerged as a hero in stopping Baylor, whose hard-driving play had caused four Celtic players to foul out.

"I knew Elgin liked the low hole because he would wheel across to the front of the basket," Guarilia recalled. "When he tried to do that, I would get in front of him." Baylor tried several shots during the Lakers' cold spell in the overtime and missed. Each time, Guarilia was on him.

"I have long arms and Baylor wasn't getting off his feet that well because he was tired," Guarilia said. "Each time he shot, I managed to tip the ball. I knew I did; I could feel my hand getting a piece of the ball."

Friends always wondered why Guarilia never scored in the overtime, but it didn't bother him. "I never scored that much," he said. Which was true. In parts of four seasons, he scored all of 387 points in 119 brief appearances.

Was he rewarded for his heroics the following season? "Yeah, I got a raise," he said. "But not much."

Guarilia left pro basketball one year after his moment of glory to become a coach at Pittston Area High, near his hometown of Duryea, Pennsylvania, where he lives today.

"I remember saying to Satch after the game I thought he'd done a terrific job defensively, despite the fact that Elgin scored 61. I felt he was under extreme defensive pressure most of the night."

BOB COUSY

249

Baylor sinks two free throws on Heinsohn foul, scoring record 61 points in Lakers 120–117 win

Selvy hits two quick baskets in closing seconds of regulation time to tie score in seventh game

Lucky Carl

It wasn't that Carl Braun felt uncomfortable on the Boston bench. It was just that his whole playing career had been spent with the New York Knicks, trying to beat the Celtics.

Now, like a drowning man pulled from the water, Braun had been rescued from the Knicks in the twilight of his career and rewarded with an NBA championship. In Boston.

"We wanted to win this one for Carl," Red Auerbach said after the seventh game. "And Carl helped win one for us."

The rise of the Celtics to championship greatness in 1957 coincided with an equally faltering turnabout in the fortunes of the Knicks, who managed to escape the Eastern Division cellar only once before Braun, a player-coach out of work, was blessed with the move to Boston.

"I went up there with the idea of replacing Bill Sharman," he said. "But they already had K.C. Jones, Sam, and Cooz. If I had known I was going to sit most of the year, I never would have gone, but I didn't gripe about it."

Even today, looking back on his experience in the 1962 Lakers playoff, Braun never had the feeling that he earned the coveted championship ring. "If a two-and-one-half-minute effort, or however long I was in there, was worth the bucks they were paying me—and I was only making like $10,000 a year or something around that figure—I was stealing the money. I felt I should have contributed more."

"I think we always had a psychological edge on the Lakers. We always felt that we could beat them."

RED AUERBACH

With forty seconds left to decide the championship, Celtics and Lakers are tied, 100–100

Selvy misses game-winning shot just before buzzer, and the game goes into overtime period

"We had no special strategy against the Celtics . . . Take our shots . . . Just try to keep Russell off of the offensive boards . . . Just try to stop their fast break."

ELGIN BAYLOR

What Braun remembered most about trying to stop Elgin Baylor, the great Laker forward, was the physical mismatch involved.

"I had ripped up my ankle during the Philadelphia series, and I couldn't run," he said. "I was limping, but I still had to play him. All I could do was hold him and try to keep him from getting the ball. I couldn't stop him if he decided to drive on me."

Braun saw the Lakers' offense as somewhat self-defeating, with so much emphasis on Baylor and Jerry West.

"They'd clear a side and let Baylor and West go one-on-one with people," he said. "I always felt that hurt them. It never let them use guys like Rudy LaRusso, who was a helluva player. I never had a feeling they had a team in their offense."

Russell scores a basket in overtime period on pass from Cousy to put Celtics ahead

Cousy puts on a show of fancy dribbling in final seconds as Celtics protect their lead

Bill Russell in 1966, when he took over from Red Auerbach

On Top

The term "dynasty" has been flaunted so often in sports as to make every two-time winner seem about as perpetual as the Bourbons of France. In the case of the Boston Celtics, however, the word "dynasty" may be appropriate.

After one victory and one near-miss from 1959 through 1966, the Celtics won eight consecutive playoffs in the National Basketball Association. These were not fluke titles. In all but one season, 1966, Boston also finished with the best regular-season record of any club.

Before the Celtics defeated the Los Angeles Lakers in the 1962 seventh-game overtime thriller, they also beat the St. Louis Hawks and the San Francisco Warriors. The streak ended when the Celtics were defeated by the Philadelphia Warriors in five games during the Eastern Division finals in 1967, as the Warriors and Wilt Chamberlain headed for their world title.

Bill Russell replaced Red Auerbach as coach in the 1966–67 season. Still the star center, he helped regain the throne for the Celtics in 1968 and again in 1969 to complete one of the most awesome eras of dominance in professional sports: eleven titles in thirteen seasons.

"Rudy LaRusso was in my opinion one of the most underrated players who ever played in the league."

TOMMY HEINSOHN

Red Auerbach hugs Bob Cousy after Celtics beat Lakers again in 1963

This book was prepared and produced
for Mobil Oil Corporation
and McGraw-Hill Book Company
by BMG Productions, Incorporated

Executive Editor: Bernard Garfinkel
Design and Layout: Irwin Glusker and Associates
Ulrich Ruchti
Editorial Associate: Beverly Reingold
Photo Research: Russell Burrows
Barbara Baker